# DISORDERS IN HIGHER EDUCATION

The American Assembly, *Columbia University*

# DISORDERS
# IN HIGHER EDUCATION

Prentice-Hall, Inc., *Englewood Cliffs, New Jersey*

A SPECTRUM BOOK

Library of Congress Cataloging in Publication Data
Main entry under title:

Disorders in higher education.

(A Spectrum Book)
Papers prepared for the 56th American Assembly at
Arden House, Harriman, N. Y., Mar. 29-April 1, 1979.
Includes index.
1. Education, Higher—United States—Congresses.
2. Universities and colleges—United States—Con-
gresses. 3. Higher education and state—United
States—Congresses. I. American Assembly.
LB2301.D57      378.73      79-9350
ISBN 0-13-216440-X
ISBN 0-13-216432-9 pbk.

Editorial/production supervision by Betty Neville
Cover design by 20/20 Services Inc.
Manufacturing buyer: Cathie Lenard

Excerpts from the letter on page 51 are used by permission of the Senior Vice President, University of Wisconsin System.

The excerpt from "Unions and Academia: A Bargaining Frontier" on page 95 is used
by permission of the *AFL-CIO American Federationist,* the official monthly magazine
of the AFL-CIO.

The excerpts on page 180 are reprinted with permission from the November 1977
issue of the *Yale Alumni Magazine and Journal;* copyright by Yale Alumni Publications, Inc.

PRENTICE-HALL INTERNATIONAL, INC. (*London*)
PRENTICE-HALL OF AUSTRALIA PTY. LIMITED (*Sydney*)
PRENTICE-HALL OF CANADA, LTD. (*Toronto*)
PRENTICE-HALL OF INDIA PRIVATE LIMITED (*New Delhi*)
PRENTICE-HALL OF JAPAN, INC. (*Tokyo*)
PRENTICE-HALL OF SOUTHEAST ASIA PTE. LTD. (*Singapore*)
WHITEHALL BOOKS LIMITED (*Wellington, New Zealand*)

# Table of Contents

# Preface

The final report of the sixty-six Americans who comprised The American Assembly on *The Integrity of Higher Education,* at Arden House, Harriman, New York, in April 1979, opened with these words:

*American higher education has long and effectively served the nation . . . but public confidence in it has been eroded in recent years. Consensus on what constitutes legitimate higher education has been reduced, and expectations of it—and claims for it—have not been fulfilled. Financial resources and enrollments will not grow appreciably and, in fact, probably will decline.*

These conditions, the participants stated, make it imperative that we take steps now to address the most serious disorders afflicting the moral and intellectual integrity of our colleges and universities. Failing to do so will only worsen the current malaise. As one university president points out on these pages, we can no longer take for granted that each university and college in this country stands for the highest levels of integrity. Faced, therefore, with shrinking enrollments and even the threat of further government regulation, our institutions of higher education will do well to rid themselves of unbecoming conduct—before, he might have added, it is done for them.

And so this book, when it was designed by Messrs. Frederick deW. Bolman and Clarence C. Walton as background reading for the Arden House Assembly, was meant to be addressed not only to colleges and universities—their presidents, deans, professors, students, and trustees— but also to those who have ever walked in the academy, so to speak, or who have been touched one way or another by its works—which means most of us.

The American Assembly, a national public affairs forum, does not take an official position on anything it publishes. And whatever one may think of the opinions herein, it should be made plain that the authors are speaking for themselves and not for The American Assembly or for The Ford Foundation, Exxon Education Foundation, IBM and AT&T

corporations, all of whom contributed generous support toward the underwriting of this project.

Clifford C. Nelson
*President*
The American Assembly

*Frederick deW. Bolman*

# 1

# Not in Our Stars

> *The fault, dear Brutus, is not in our stars,*
> *But in ourselves, that we are underlings.*
> —Julius Caesar

Has demoralization beset our universities and colleges today? To ask that question is to ask if there is fault. If so, to question further—may fault be in ourselves?—may be one way to renaissance.

It is crucial in any age to ask how we are faring with institutions vital to our life and well-being. We have developed critical abilities within our social structures to change our ways; let us remind ourselves how this happened in our universities not long ago; and recall, too, that in our society the most poignant renewal comes when the reformers are the performers.

The modern university as now important in society is only some 100 years old—younger than this republic. For centuries people had gathered together to learn, first in Europe and then in many small centers or col-

FREDERICK DEWOLFE BOLMAN, *former president of Franklin and Marshall College, was executive director of The Exxon Education Foundation in 1970–77. Dr. Bolman, who holds degrees in philosophy and mathematics, has written numerous studies in higher education, including* How College Presidents are Chosen, *and has been consultant on education to a number of institutions, public and private. He is a member of The Society for Values in Higher Education. Dr. Bolman has been a visiting professor of philosophy at Columbia and Princeton Universities and serves on the board of directors of several education foundations and associations.*

leges in America; but, in one century, higher learning in Europe and America moved from that of Aristotle to that of the atomic bomb. It was a century which eclipsed the growth of knowledge of more than 2,000 years. This youth of the modern university must be borne in mind to assess its integrity today, because during its genesis certain values were perceived, which gave the university its present meaning and mission.

Until well into the last century, university and collegiate learning was humanistic and classical, based on rules we may call theological scholasticism. To some extent this permeated learning for the professions as well. Basically, that learning—and hence, university work of various kinds—meant three things. First, there was the need to analyze, extend, and apply inherited wisdom. Second, there was the need to define what areas of life were proper for reason and what must be left to faith. Finally, the uses or methods of reasoning were defined in ways of long-inherited logic—circumscribed systems often defining the nature of truths to be found.

There was research and experimentation from the twelfth century on, as C. H. Haskins and others discovered. Also, mathematics was developing to the point when in the late seventeenth century Leibnitz and Newton, knowing the limits of geometry, devised the calculus. Much of these developments took place outside the universities and had little impact on them at the time.

But experimental science in all its growing vigor, begun outside the university, won a place in the citadel of learning just over a century ago. In short order, an intellectual revolution took place. All branches of learning—including that for the professions—were altered. The university became a new entity in life, very much unlike its antecedents.

"Scholasticism" was replaced in centers of learning by perspectives strongly influenced by the development of experimental science. For one thing, interest in the present and future displaced that in the past. In all areas, doors were opened to search for new theory and new practice. For another, new concepts of objectivity were embraced—many stemming from laboratory work. Learning became more open; scholars wanted to share findings and learn from one another in quite a new way. Finally, the very uses and methods of reasoning underwent change, thanks in large measure to the growth of experimental science. No one again could rule for a university which was the correct interpretation of Aristotle. Mathematics and its applications, experimental science, and all other learning were, at least in principle, free to pursue truth regardless of consequences.

As the nineteenth century wore on, the modern university embraced three targets: training, research, and public service. Training meant education for almost any career requiring "higher learning"—whatever that meant to a particular faculty. Research and apprenticeship in research became the higher reach of the university and, with it, the desire to share through publication, leading ultimately to the university presses. Public service meant the application of learning to any and all of life's problems, from an immediate community to agriculture and pharmacy, and to the public, through university extensions. All of this was a tall order of accomplishment, and it took place in decades. The university reformed itself, because it perceived new realities.

In the development of the modern university, we see that new measures of the institution evolved. While differently applied in Western countries, these measures appear to be: *cohesion of purpose, social benefit*, and *public recognition*. In a sense, these were measures of the medieval and renaissance centers of learning, but all of the significances of those terms were quite radically changed in the late nineteenth and early twentieth centuries. Let us be clear, there was no "dark ages," least of all for the soil on which the university evolved. We have much to revere in our differing origins at Bologna, Paris, and Oxford, to name but a few. But new issues arose reforming the university and, therefore, the measures of it. Let us briefly look at them today.

### Cohesion of Purpose

The modern university developed its cohesion of purpose through a new allegiance to the acquisition of knowledge and to a new openness to those able to follow. Brought about by the scientific revolution, it was meritocratic in a careful sense. The western model had various roots in France, Germany, England, and the United States. A foreign commentator recently emphasized this renewal of purpose in the past century.

> . . . the idea of what constituted higher education was common to all the systems. It was that education at this level had to be based on specialized science and scholarship and that it had to be linked to research, at least to the extent that professors were expected to be qualified and successful researchers. . . . In principle all the reformed systems of higher education were perfectly meritocratic and pragmatic. (Joseph Ben-David)

Much of what follows is based upon recognition—and acceptance—of this allegiance.

But the university, and so the college, in the United States had a different development from the European and English models. Colonialism, ever-expanding frontiers of many sorts, a federated republic, land size, economic growth problems—all had a hand in a unique development of the university. It is true, in 1636 Harvard College began to provide domestic classical learning to potential leaders, including the clergy, in our society. English general education and its notion of *in loco parentis* became the model, modified somewhat by the Scottish universities which were nonresidential, had lay boards, granted degrees without further authority, and helped new learning to spread. But our universities were not born until 1875 when The Johns Hopkins University was founded purely as specialized graduate faculty, following the German model. These two strong traditions, from England and Germany, powerfully influenced all colleges and universities in this country. Then other things happened to make us yet more unlike our mentors from abroad. Coherence of purpose became different, sometimes more difficult.

A vogue-ish word was coined, the *multiversity*, and it clearly was stamped "made in the U.S." The word came after the facts. While originating amid state-wide public systems such as those in California, it was applied easily to private centers such as Antioch College in Ohio. In special ways we have experienced geographic and intellectual diaspora.

But the roots for all that lie further back in the past. Pluralism of means and ends has been the American way in higher education from the onset. In colonial days it was not in the English tradition to organize and centralize colleges and universities. When our Constitution was drawn, such matters were left, when thought about, to the states. We had no national focus or centralized control as evolved in Europe and later, in a different way, in England. We left ourselves free to build the best— perhaps, therefore, the worst—colleges and universities in the western world. By 1850 England had five universities, the United States, nearly 800 colleges. We had room to experiment and let the devil take the hindmost, which he often did. Our prestigious universities have offered courses and programs in "the dynamics of cushioned packaging" requiring advanced calculus (one Ivy League course ended with the "bounce test")—but they, and they alone, spearheaded the Manhattan Project and developed the atom bomb.

But cohesion of purpose is not hard to define for the American university if we stand by the criteria of acquisition of knowledge through specialization, research, and dissemination. Naturally, this leaves out any moral perspective, and it was partly here that the criteria for cohesion were challenged in the late 1960s. A new advocacy of irrationalism broke out on illustrious campuses, not just among students, but among faculty as well. Daniel Yankelovich sought to chart this: to place sensory experience ahead of conceptual knowledge, to celebrate all the unknown, to devalue detachment and objectivity, to arrive at truth by direct experience, participation, and involvement.

While no part of the university proper, yet a blatant query as to the meaning of cohesion of purpose, student-sponsored "colleges" arose from Stanford to Dartmouth. One course attended by students and, perhaps, some faculty bore the beckoning title of "Candle Power." The multiversity seemed to have run riot, but that form of ambiguity petered out. Yet, irrationalism has left wounds. A kind of relativism permeated the campus leading to solipsism in some scholarly fields.

Equally enduring and difficult for the problem of cohesion of purpose of the university has been the development of educational systems in the public or state systems of higher education. Demographic expansion, legislative demands for accountability, and increasing demands for degree and other credentials for upward mobility have helped form such state public systems by whatever devices and stratification of levels. Not all is bad; but much may be getting worse under these circumstances. Learned voices from within such systems refer to growth in intellectual mediocrity, inflexibility of many sorts, confusion of mission, and Balkanization of systems by special interest lobby groups working on state legislatures. State educational systems tend to become another branch of government.

Further, two or more public systems within a state may tangle in near-to-death battle, as in New York or, differently, in California. The cohesion of purpose of the university cannot even make the agenda in the power struggle. Winners walk away, but with an unknown prize.

New issues of survival have been forced on our universities—or has survival been misunderstood? The question here is one about values obscured by what Alfred North Whitehead in another connection called "the goading urgency of contingent circumstance." In a bizarre sense, America has made of its universities and colleges a dinosaur. When dinosaurs could not get food, they died—but they then left room for other forms of life. Is that our fate?

We face the problem of enrollment, and all budgets are, as the phrase goes, "enrollment driven," since income from tuition or state support, now most of university income, is weighted by students. In fact, we have a market economy in higher education. Our institutions were not prepared—did not prepare themselves—for this fact. Few university economists in the 1940s or 1950s spoke to their presidents or legislators about economic dinosaurs or marketing, yet birthrate tables were in almost daily print. A man on the moon and other matters became more important for almost all resources.

Hence, the enormous growth in enrollment, personnel, and plant for American higher education in the 1960s was seen as benign. When open admissions broke out in the East and South (in the Midwest it was not new), this was accepted and taken into account—if the bills were paid. But when, in the early to mid-1970s, economic recession and leveling-to-decreasing enrollment were known, a new scream for students came from every campus in America, each wanting quality it had gotten before and all knowing they must compete in new ways. State and federal governments were egged on to greater support in various forms for students, partly, it must be said, to help our universities and colleges to survive. Foreign students who could pay or be paid were attracted; new programs, many vocational, were offered; and the phrase "a learning society" was dusted off to attract a new age group for continuing education.

Thrust for survival is not the worst of motives. But, on the brink, few have collected their wits to say poignantly and meaningfully what survival and life may be about. One sign of ambiguity appeared in our universities in the 1960s. Amid the student riots, demands for black studies, and campus violence and death over the war in Vietnam, there arose demands for student participation in university governance. Faculty and administrators alike on campus after campus quickly confused democratic values and rational authority. Over these issues many university presidents lost their heads—figuratively if not literally. With them stood a confused faculty. Someone once mumbled that it was like asking passengers on all incoming flights to vote on who should be in the control tower when each plane landed.

The university and college in the United States today have little perception of cohesion of purpose. Irrationalism, educational systems, pragmatism limited to institutional survival have eroded our sense of mission in any coherent form. The federal government cannot be blamed. Our umbrella in Washington—the American Council on Education—has seldom been able to lead us to a grand design for higher learning. Meanwhile, industry and labor are building their own colleges, some degree-granting. Some forms of proprietary postsecondary education have gotten new life.

On the first measure of the modern university, cohesion of purpose, let us rate ourselves low. But, let us realize that, for quite different reasons, though due to some of the same social forces, our western colleague universities are in similar straits. After 100 years, the university in the western world is at bay, which is understandable given all that has happened from the reign of Aristotle to the reign of the atom bomb. We are quite lucky. We know we can do better, and we also have the ability to discover how.

### Social Benefit

A scond measure of the university today is that of social benefit. Here we must view those external pressures brought to bear on an institution and assess how that institution reacts to such pressures. Whitehead once said that knowledge keeps no better than fish. The modern university struggled to become an asylum for almost any point of view; it has never conceived itself as an ivory tower apart from the world.

While in Europe each national government gradually came to pay and supervise most institutions of higher education, our federal government had no authority to play any such role. Shortly after the American Revolution, states took initiatives to provide public funds to establish their own colleges and universities. Then a U.S. representative from Vermont, Justin Morrill, after a five-year struggle, pushed through Congress what became known as the Morrill Act of 1862—grants of federal land to states, benefits from which were to be used for higher education in agriculture and the mechanical arts. Consequences were not always happy, but Morrill, by then a senator, pushed through another Act of 1890 providing annual federal funds to the land-grant institutions and stimulating state legislatures to do the same.

The public clearly wanted to benefit from higher education, and clearly it did. Scientific agriculture revolutionized this nation and made possible the ground for another revolution—the development of the world's leading industrial economy.

But social benefits of the university were as clearly seen by some in private institutions. While still a professor of jurisprudence and political economy in 1896, Woodrow Wilson wrote an essay on "Princeton in the Nation's Service." It is worth pausing for.

Of course, when all is said and done, it is not learning, but the spirit of service, that will give a college place in the public annals of the nation. It is indispensable, it seems to me, if it is to do its right service, that the air of affairs should be admitted to all its classrooms. I do not mean the air of party politics, but the air of the world's transactions, the consciousness of the solidarity of the race, the sense of the duty of man toward man, of the presence of men in every problem, of the significance of truth for guidance as well as for knowledge, of the potency of ideas, of the promise and the hope that shine in the face of all knowledge. There is laid upon us the compulsion of the national life.

Collegiate action has tried to follow this rhetoric in the United States. Most visible, but not quite in keeping with Wilson's values and hopes, have been university knowledge and service in time of war. From Oak Ridge, the Manhattan Project, Los Alamos, and many other centers fed by university researchers, came the atomic bomb and, of course, atomic energy.

But more peaceful service has been rendered the nation by the university. The history of the improvement of medical education—and that for other professions from architecture to zoological garden development —has been written largely at the American university. And other occupations needing advanced knowledge and research have been served. Columbia became a university in 1880 with its first graduate faculty in the School of Political Science. Business programs and then graduate schools for teaching and research were admitted to and nurtured by the university. Labor studies programs in the dozens for labor leadership (not to be confused with industrial relations programs, which serve primarily management) have entered our colleges and universities which award associate, baccalaureate, and some doctoral degrees in the field.

Extensively the American college and university have indeed been "in the nation's service." The issue always remains regarding quality of education and research, but we have learned to live with our changing brand of pluralism and sometimes have skills for betterment.

But the college and university in America as the symbol, if not always the substance, of individual upward mobility, led to pressure problems not always skillfully met. Our nation as melting pot has been more pot than it has melted. Sizeable, if minority, groups have immigrated—by force and voluntarily—which have not had opportunities for higher education equal to the first and many other immigrants. Conscience, but more forcefully and extensively, the federal government, stepped in to redress inequity in the future.

The university was challenged, if not ordered, to perform a new service often called "open admission." Some midwestern states had long insisted that entry to their public higher education required only high school graduation. Sometimes summer sessions were used to delete the unable. But, in other parts of the country, colleges and universities—excepting our community colleges which, from inception, had required only a high school diploma—had to make major adjustments. Because of neglect prior to college age, many minority students were ill-equipped for higher education. Remedial work on entry to college was developed, sometimes at the expense of maintaining quality in other collegiate tasks.

Success in serving individuals has been reported—for example, City University of New York. Serious questions, at the least, have been raised as to whether such entry policies truly benefit a minority group as such. American jargon, second to none, quickly referred to the new admissions as a "revolving door"—many admitted, many flunked out.

Our minority brothers took quick note of this and came forward with a new demand: proportional output from colleges and universities. This issue surfaced, among other places, at a memorable meeting of educators in a major foundation office nearly a decade ago, at which some blacks and whites on each side of the issue left, literally, in tears. The argument by proponents of proportional output had been that remedial studies on entry should guarantee success in graduation and that, in any case, requirements for the latter—for all degrees—should be changed to accommodate the concept of proportional output. The cry of opponents was that all this would kill the social benefits of the university.

While our citadel of learning has not resolved that problem, another was forming which may one day have a happier outcome. We here refer to the growing plight of the liberal arts in America. However the substance under that rubric has changed—physics entered one Ivy League undergraduate college by the term "natural philosophy"—the newer demand has been for more "career" (vocational) training. While college catalogues had long formed, as one wag used to say, "the greatest fiction library in the world," there was much more than lip service to a cluster of ideas as to what a liberal arts education was and what it accomplished. That cluster has all but disappeared, and many curriculum revisions seem more contorted than a pretzel. Has the ideal of developing the best in human character vanished? Add to this trends toward degree credit for experience and universities without walls (i.e., without prescriptions other than individual ones), and one wonders whether our willingness to be "in the nation's service" has not outstripped our ability to serve.

Another area of the modern university conceived from its infancy as of social benefit has been research. Our award of faculty status called "publish or perish" stems from the nineteenth century German notion that the advance of knowledge must be made public. Our heritage here is mixed. John Cardinal Newman in 1873 viewed research as anathema. But Americans abroad for their education were more influenced by the Germans than the English. Laboratory research, the first to enter the German university, was in pharmacy, shortly after 1820.

About a century ago there were no laboratories, or even libraries to speak of, in American colleges. The classroom provided for America's version of *explication de texte*. Occasionally students were sneaked beyond university walls to observe a private laboratory; books other than prescribed texts were few and kept, with little regard, literally in university closets, for idle students to try to enter. One hundred years ago our colleges and universities were not in shape to advance knowledge.

But, changes came rapidly and, again, this country's involvement in war provided incentive and substance, at least in some areas. World War I and World War II saw the, by then, already developing libraries and laboratories greatly fortified and expanded. Libraries were cheaper to acquire and maintain than laboratories with their increasing costs of instrumentation and maintenance. Government had to invest fast and heavily. The initiation of an individual income tax helped. By the time the Russians lofted the first man-made satellite, our nation was prepared to invest and to do so yet more heavily. Competition with Russia for defense and space exploits led to what some have called "government science." Much of it was based in universities. Programs of categorical grants for research, often determined by peer groups, became an important part of the university's social benefit, first in the sciences and, to some degree, in the social sciences.

With so large a proportion of university research paid for by the federal government—in one of our foremost institutions, over 80 percent of all research funds come from the federal government—no wonder that an economic recession beginning in the mid-1970s, entailing federal budget cutbacks, seems a threat to universities. Some assessment, based on government and related data, claims the story is not critically adverse. Some others claim that concern for the next generation of research is being blunted.

Meanwhile, our governments, state and federal, are disdaining unfettered advance of knowledge through research. A senator makes much public noise over what he dubs his "Golden Fleece" awards and holds up to public ridicule selected topics of research, e.g., why convicts want to get out of jail or why certain animals and man clench their teeth when threatened. At a recent meeting of scientists and educators, one spokesman took heart that Howard Jarvis (promoter of Proposition 13 limiting taxes in California) was not around in the Spanish court in 1492 to scotch the "impractical-sounding voyages of Columbus."

Acceptance of research into the university a century ago recreated college and university life and work; yet now the concept of social benefit may be so used against the university as to destroy research. The imposition of review boards and federal audit powers may unduly inhibit research involving human subjects.

The voice of university integrity has been heard from. For example, when the government grants research funds, outcomes of which must be "classified" and kept secret, scholars and institutions rebel. They see a distortion of social benefit. Or, when a foundation wished to pour millions of dollars into a university to establish a center for urban studies when our cities were on fire, one university felt it could not in conscience respond.

While the issue of support of the hard and soft sciences in the university has not yet been resolved, a patent neglect is much of what we call the humanities. Albeit with our pluralism of types and programs of institutions, we surely are heading toward greater government support and, hence, direction of higher learning—a course no one knows how to change. With our national government "endowments" for the arts and humanities have come problems for the advance of knowledge in those areas outside, as well as inside, the university. Are these funds for popularizing and massively "consuming" extant or specially created items of public appeal, or are they for creative advance in the arts and humanities? As a people, we are not sure of an answer. We think we know what truth is about in the sciences, but the pursuit of truth, goodness, and beauty in all ways was better understood by some ancient Greeks than by most Americans.

One great difficulty is that the university has given up the task of distinguishing the good of the people from the will of the people— important to democracy, as Rousseau pointed out long ago. "Futurism," a new mode of soothsaying with the aid of computers, is inside and outside the university. It is concerned more with material protection in days ahead than the catholic appraisal of the quality of our lives.

Social benefit as a measure of the university is difficult to assay, but is as important as cohesion of purpose. Historians may have to say of us at this hour that both society and its universities have not clarified the issues sufficiently to take intelligent, collective action. Again, the American dilemma in this regard is only slightly different from the situation in other western countries.

## Public Recognition

Let us turn to a third measure of the modern university which comes close on the heels of that of social benefit—public recognition. By this term, we mean the formal character of the interaction between an institution and supportive external power. Such power may be constructive or destructive of the other measures of the university—cohesion of purpose and social benefit. And this power may provide material sustenance as well as granting privileges and permission for certain modes of institutional operation.

From their earliest days, universities in various ways had been dependent upon "emperors, popes, and kings" for permission to operate. Religious orders could and did stimulate and define acceptable teaching. Students, in some instances, held power over their teachers. Henry VIII extracted from the English universities a favorable judgment about his divorce, and then ruled the universities with heavy hand. In some cases, institutional freedom and privileges had seemed nearly absolute; Sir Maurice Powicke says of the medieval universities that they were "intensely self-conscious and self-important." Such autonomy, however, was gradually curtailed throughout history. In some cases, loss of institutional freedom meant loss of academic freedom for teachers.

Of course, the issue always is' the specific character of institutional freedom needed by the university to perform its function in and for society. In the early days of the thirteenth century, when faculty at the University of Paris felt their function threatened by civil authorities, they closed the university and migrated elsewhere. In 1231 and later, papal bulls had to define the rights of faculty and scholars.

Despite early Protestant turmoil in the American colonies, which affected our colleges and sometimes curtailed their autonomy, the history of England and the United States in higher education was different from similar growth on the European continent, in large part because colleges and universities, privately begun and supported, long remained so. Often no less hemmed in by such nongovernmental power, growing diversity of support in America provided diversity of autonomy among colleges. Even for a single institution, the waves of Protestant belief changed the nature of autonomy for that college from time to time. With our first public institution, the University of Georgia chartered in 1785, the drive —but not always the achievement—was for sectarian freedom. The American university has known diversity, but seldom lack of constraint from outside. The early power of charter by the Crown in England was replaced by that of state legislatures or their appointees. (The University of the State of New York, or Regents, dates back to 1784-87.)

In subsequent history to the present time, increase in public funding has been accompanied by increase in public control in both England and America, although in each in quite different ways. In this country, initially federal bounty—long before 1862 four million acres of federal land for endowment—went through the states. In colonial days, Harvard, William and Mary, Yale, and others received state grants or rights, e.g., in the first case, fares from a ferry and then a bridge across the Charles River. Federal subsidy directly to institutions began with World War I; in 1918 over 140,000 students were federally sponsored at over 500 institutions. World War II saw a massive increase in direct federal subvention for students and research. Since then, the needs of national defense and national scientific and technological prowess continued the federal flow of dollars to private and public colleges and universities.

Throughout the entire history of the university, the nature of public recognition—the character of interaction with external power—has changed for the university as times and circumstances have dictated. We may be sure that public recognition will continue to change. In our western democracies, such change in large part hinges on the change or the prevailing drift of public opinion. In this country, we have witnessed successive decline in the prestige of the church, then government, and now higher education.

For the past quarter century or so, all of education in America has gradually come under public scrutiny, criticism, and censure. Early in that time, elementary and secondary education began to receive attention and rebuke for what was considered its lack of performance. In the past decade, not just students but the public has been increasingly critical of the universities. One can say that public malaise since our involvement in Vietnam and the economic recession has simply crept over into the university, and the public is thus chastising its own image. But

critics claim that the overall quality of college and university faculty
has gone down. Faculty morale has deteriorated so that few want to
teach and, when they must, for few hours a week to spare time for individual prowess and rewards in research and outside consultation. Student morale may be at an all-time low; most students seem not to want
to learn, but simply to possess a degree. Then the press heralds symbols
of intellectual dishonesty, such as an artificial prehistoric man, a
trumped-up IQ curve, externally-applied dye on animals used in cancer
research.

If priests and politicians have lost their charisma, so have professors.
Federal and state governments have little option, at least with this third
leadership group, but to act in constraining, if highly irritating, ways.
While national histories are different, of interest in the English-speaking
world is the difference between the *Report of the Committee Appointed
by the Prime Minister under the Chairmanship of Lord Robbins,
1961-63,* in England and views reflected a decade later in documents of
the privately-sponsored Carnegie Commission on Higher Education in
the United States. Critics contend that the former defends institutional
autonomy against public encroachment, the latter defends planning and
coordination in response to public demands.

Martin Trow sees in many countries—including ours—"the struggle to
contain diversity" which results in government control of standards,
costs, functions, and forms. Some sensitive critics voice despair and ruin
should education in America be elevated to a cabinet post in our government, for that could lead to the worst experiences in Europe, an all-
controlling national ministry of education. Burton Clark pleads that
"planning and autonomous action are both needed as mechanisms of
differentiation, coordination, and change."

Our colleges and universities are struggling with this third measure
of the university, public recognition, the interaction between an institution and supportive external power. But it is fair to question whether
this struggle is not more marked by discontent and exasperation over
details than by a clear and philosophical perception of the ever-changing
nature and measures of the university in days ahead. Indeed, our very
diversity of opinion in this respect may be our downfall in the face of
superior force. Further, it is not reasonable to invite rape and then complain that it has happened; on our campuses the more general idea of
the university in western society has not been explored, even though
a quarter of a century ago all the cues and signals and stimuli were

present for that action. When the privately-supported Commission on the Financing of Higher Education, under the direction of John D. Millett, began its research in 1949, it foresaw economic and institutional consequences of an increasing and then a declining collegiate enrollment amid inflationary costs. No collective and cohesive vision has issued then or since. No one outside the university has power for that kind of vision.

Regretfully, we must concede that, as to the third measure of the university—public recognition—our citadels of learning are both distraught and, in thought, disorganized. The public in this present context, more university-educated than ever before, is given no vision to which to respond.

In a day when the three measures of the university we have suggested and reviewed—cohesion of purpose, social benefit, and public recognition —show our travail and uncertainty, it may not be entirely quixotic to ask this question: have we outlived the need for the university? Little is permanent in life, and conscious redirection may provide greater permanence for greater values.

Many will treat the question as a travesty of inherent values. But, let us face other possibilities in order to secure our answers. We could return to separate professional schools—an old path in this young nation and older still in England and the Continent. We could develop new forms of apprenticeship for other vocations and trades, as there are some signs we are already doing. We could let all research flee from the university to government, industry, and other appreciative groups, again, as is in part already happening. We could leave general education (the liberal arts) to our junior and community colleges or offer such programs in our secondary schools, as in Europe. Continuing education could readily be carried on by professional associations, industry, labor, government, the high schools, and community colleges.

In any case, we may in fact be dismantling our universities. Is that because we lack in the university that consensus for direction and governance so that what Edward Shils described as "The Hole in the Centre" has become what physicists call a "black hole" where all light disappears? Is the fault not in our stars—but in ourselves?

Unlike our government, our university has no Declaration of Independence and no Constitution. Perhaps the academy must always ride loosely in the saddle. Yet historic growth now requires new vision for the university. While he addressed the people and their government, let Walter Lippmann speak as if for academic ears to hear about their enterprise today.

The particular projects we debate so angrily are not so important, the fate of the nation does not hang on any of them. But upon the power of the people to remain united for purposes which they respect, upon their capacity to have faith in themselves and in their objectives, much depends. It is not the facts of the crisis which we have to fear. They can be endured and dealt with. It is demoralization alone that is dangerous.

Richard E. Anderson

# 2

# The Money Crunch:

## A Financial Analysis

### Introduction

The cause of every problem is not always an economic one. Problems occur for a variety of reasons. The resolution of problems, however, is invariably constrained by economic considerations. If unlimited resources were available, most problems could be resolved, disguised, or buried. When resources are limited, as they almost always are, we are forced to make choices. When resources are severely limited, we must make choices which are unpleasant and often compromising. It is this third condition, of severely limited resources and painful choices, which has come to characterize the decision-making environment of American colleges and universities during the past few years. Any consideration of the educational integrity of these institutions, therefore, cannot be divorced from its financial context.

Since institutions of higher learning are like living organisms, it is virtually impossible to dissect one part without adequate comprehension of its impact on other parts. More specifically, it is difficult to address higher education's economic problems without awareness that reactions

RICHARD E. ANDERSON *is a professor and coordinator of Joint Programs in Higher Education Finance at Teachers College, Columbia University. Author of* Strategic Policy Changes at Private Colleges, *Dr. Anderson has written widely on fiscal matters in higher education in the United States.*

to the financial crunch, including proposed resolutions of that problem, have impact on faculty quality, course programs, public image, and the like. Nonetheless, focus on the economic side yields illuminating results. To further the analysis, I propose to deal, in some detail, with these four items:

1. an examination of the higher education marketplace, with emphasis on the product and the determination of its value;
2. a review of the recent financial history and the primary causes of economic difficulty;
3. a review and critique of the responses—and their implications—to the economic problems; and
4. a set of recommendations which flows logically from the analysis.

THE HIGHER EDUCATION MARKET

There are certain special features of the higher education process and the market in which it is bought and sold. An understanding of these special features is important in order to understand the effects of a general financial crisis upon the system as a whole and upon its subsegments.

One of the most significant features of higher education is the complex nature of the production functions. The products are classified under the general headings of instruction, scholarship, and community service. These are produced by creating a pleasant environment, by offering lifetime employment to the majority of the senior professional staff, and by requiring students to select, in a generally haphazard fashion, from the educational offerings. In truth, we haven't the foggiest notion of how we produce what we do.

The higher education processes are similar to electronic "black boxes" —energy goes in and special effects are produced but no one except the designer understands how or why. In higher education not even the "experts" fully understand the inner workings. Additionally, most of higher education products are *joint products*; that is, they result from the efforts of several faculty and departments. In engineering terms, this is the equivalent of a number of black boxes wired in parallel. Consider some of the goals of a liberal education: communication skills, understanding the culture, and critical thinking. None of these is the sole responsibility of any one faculty member or department. From a management point of view, this presents almost insuperable difficulties. It is impossible to hold anyone, except the academic dean or the president, responsible if results are inadequate.

The dean and the president need not be overly concerned about their jobs, however, because it is so extraordinarily difficult to measure student achievement, scholarship, or community service and, thus, to determine if results are truly "inadequate." This condition describes the second special feature of higher education—inability to gauge outputs accurately. When the United States Steel Corporation produces iron and steel, it is relatively easy to measure output and evaluate management efficiency relative to other steel companies, or even relative to other substitute materials. In the automobile industry the measurement issue is more complex but still manageable.

Institutional researchers at colleges and universities, however, have only the vaguest notions about measuring and evaluating output. They cannot count missing rivets nor gauge acceleration nor review the "failure rate" of graduates' first 20,000 miles. Researchers are trying to evaluate the product, but they generally must rely on the crudest empirical measures—cost per credit, cost per degree, or dollar return on dollar investment. There are efforts underway to measure the improvement in critical thinking and in moral development, but these efforts are woefully inadequate and not widespread at the present time. Moreover, even if reliable and comprehensive measures could be developed, how would they be equated with costs? What is the worth of a social critic? Is it greater or less than that of a scientist? A businessman? The determination is, of course, impossible to make.

This discussion is not intended to imply that higher education is the only industry with severe measurement problems. Most professional service industries have similar problems. A major difference, however, is that there is typically more reliance on a competitive market for the delivery of services. In law and medicine, for example, the state establishes minimum competency and standards, but the consumer chooses the provider. In medicine, low-income individuals are also provided with vouchers to ensure greater access. Higher education has an unusual mix of public and private institutions. (This public/private division also obtains in hospital care. Both public and private hospitals, however, charge full cost for services and are reimbursed by third party payers.) For the production of research, this distinction is less significant with most large-scale research efforts supported by the government or foundations. For the provision of community services and degree-credit instruction, this public/private distinction is quite significant. Public institutions receive 75 percent of their funds *for instruction* from public sources. Tuition and fees account for only 17 percent. At private institutions tuition and fees account for 60 percent of instructional revenues while direct government aid is only 5 percent. This discussion oversimplifies the patterns of support of higher education, but the point is that there is this fundamental dichotomy in higher education: one sector relies heavily on public support and the other on tuition and fees. This distinction, of course, has important implications during a period of financial crisis.

In addition to the public/private distinction, there is a reasonably rigid status hierarchy in American higher education. National research universities and selective liberal arts colleges are at the top of this hierarchy. Two-year colleges are at the base and regional four-year institutions in the middle. A major cause for this institutional ranking is the salience of the credentialing function in higher education. Simply put, a college degree is testimony to a student's fundamental abilities as much as it represents any increments of skills and knowledge. Therefore, when "selling" higher education it is as important *who* buys as *how many* buy. The relative prestige of institutions determines, to a large degree, the value of the credential and, hence, the perceived value of the education. Institutions which are closer to the top of the hierarchy have considerably more flexibility in changing mission and maintaining or expanding enrollments than those at the bottom.

FINANCIAL BACKGROUND: THE PRIMARY CAUSES OF DIFFICULTY

By almost any standard the recent growth in American higher education has been phenomenal. In 1960 there were 2,000 degree-granting colleges and universities. In 1976 there were 3,000. Enrollment grew from under four million students in 1960 to over eleven million in 1975. Since 1975, however, total enrollment has stabilized, with both modest increases and decreases being registered in succeeding years. Of real significance is the fact that the *rate* of enrollment of eighteen-year-olds has declined. Total enrollment has been maintained by virtue of *larger* high school graduating classes and by institutions reaching "new" students. The changing patterns of student enrollment were unforeseen just a decade ago. For example, enrollment projections made in 1968 by the National Center for Education Statistics (NCES) were 8 percent below actual enrollments. Examining the components of that projection is instructive. *Women* accounted for 49 percent of actual enrollments in 1977 instead of the 44 percent projected. Forty percent of the students were *part-time* in 1977 compared with the NCES expectation of 27 percent. *Nondegree credit* enrollments accounted for 13 percent of the actual total in the latter year instead of the 11 percent projected. These data suggest that women, part-time, and nondegree credit students have been largely responsible for maintaining enrollments in the late 1970s.

These special groups are, however, unlikely to have as significant an impact in the 1980s. First, women have essentially achieved educational parity with men. Further enrollment gains from their increased participation is doubtful. Second, most of the current part-time students are below age thirty-five. Many of these individuals are trying to "catch up" in education with their cohort. In the future, a larger percentage of young adults will already have attended college and the pool of potential undergraduate students will be smaller. (Of course, the applicant pool for graduate schools may be enlarged.) Finally, the actual size of the young adult cohort will shrink as the baby boom ages.

An additional deviation from the enrollment projection of 1968 is that 78 percent of the actual 1977 enrollments were in public colleges and universities. NCES forecast that only 69 percent would be enrolled in the public sector. This difference indicates an acceleration of the shift toward public higher education.

When discussing income and expenditures, one is tempted to lay out a bedazzling array of tables and charts. I will defer and instead summarize only the most significant trends—keeping statistics to a minimum. From the patchwork of revenue data the four most important areas for discussion are the trends in government aid, tuition and fees, gifts and endowments, and auxiliary income. Government support for higher education has increased rapidly in the past few decades. In 1950 approximately one-third of higher education revenues came from local, state, and federal governments. In 1976 the fraction was one-half. A large part of this increase reflects the ascendancy of public over private higher education. With a larger percentage of students enrolled in publicly supported higher education, the relative public support of higher education increases accordingly. But public support of private institutions also increased during this period—from 11 to 21 percent of total current fund income. Moreover, these data understate collegiate sector's increased dependence on government assistance because they represent only "institutional revenue"—that is, government money paid *directly* to higher education institutions *in support of current operations.* During this time period there has been a large increase in other forms of public support,

including student loan subsidies, aid for construction, and state scholarship programs.

A significant attribute of public, particularly federal, support is its
relative instability. The federal share of institutional revenue rose from
9 percent in 1950 to 21 percent in 1965. By 1974 it had declined to 16
percent, reflecting a loss of federal interest in university-based research.
This squiggle in public priorities created severe hardships on many
campuses. A large number of faculty that were supported by research
money, were shifted to general institutional budget lines; others were
dismissed. In addition, state legislatures are beginning to take a longer
and more critical look at their higher education expenditures as taxpayers are becoming generally restive. The amount of public support
available for higher education in the future is indeed a cloudy issue.

The relative contribution of tuition and fees to institutional income
has increased gradually but steadily. At private institutions the contribution of tuition and fees to total current revenue has risen from 33 to
36 percent between 1960 and 1977. At public colleges the increase has
been from 10 to 13 percent. The percentages, however, belie the importance of tuition for the support of education. Much of the public support is for the research and community service components of higher
education. The Carnegie Commission has estimated that tuition and
related fees account for 60 percent and 17 percent of revenues *for instruction* at private and public institutions, respectively. These are, of
course, average figures. Many institutions rely even more heavily on
tuition. Moreover, virtually all public colleges and universities are dependent on enrollment to justify public support. This dependence is
either directly through formula funding mechanisms or indirectly by
way of generating political support. This heavy reliance on student related revenue is creating tremendous competitive pressures to maintain
enrollments.

The significance of gift or endowment income varies very widely
across the range of institutions. For most public colleges and many private ones these sources are of relatively slight importance. For many
institutions, however, gift and endowment income has provided the
margin of survival. Indeed, there has been great pressure to maximize
income from these sources. But this pressure can create problems for the
future. Many institutions, for example, are expending all current gifts.
Others are defining endowment income in an incontinent manner. That
is, their definition of income may result in spending 6 or 7 percent of

principal while inflation remains within a seemingly intractable 6 to 9 percent range. To maintain purchasing power of an endowment, total return, plus additions, must equal or exceed the sum of spending and inflation. Invariably this is not the case, and future generations of college students will have to make up the difference. It is not surprising that the relative support from endowment income has been declining. It fell from 7.4 percent of total current income at private institutions in 1960 to 4.7 percent in 1975. In addition, public colleges and universities are competing more aggressively than in the past for "their share" of private gift income. When there are legal constraints on fund raising by public institutions, it is becoming increasingly common to circumvent the controls and establish nonprofit foundations whose sole purpose is to raise money for a state college or university. Although the increased interest of public college officials in private gifts is understandable, officials at many private institutions tend to regard this as an "invasion of turf." The acrimony between the sectors is likely to grow as the search for private funding intensifies.

The primary components of auxiliary income are receipts from housing and boarding students. This revenue declined from 17 percent of total current income in 1960 to 12 percent in 1974. This drop is indicative of the transformation of American higher education from a residential to a part-time educational experience. This trend is not likely to abate; and, beyond the educational significance, it means that auxiliary operation can absorb less total overhead.

The most significant aspect affecting costs in higher education is inflation. Inflation impacts colleges and universities with particular severity because of the nature of the products—instruction, research, and public service. All three require heavy investments in highly skilled manpower, and, in spite of the promise of technology, it has not proven cost-effective in delivering higher education's products. Computers have greatly expanded the *form* of instruction, particularly technical education, and expanded the *scope* of research, but this technology has not reduced costs. As wages rise, many industries replace labor with capital equipment. In higher education this transformation is difficult to achieve. As a result, costs in higher education, like in other service industries, tend to rise faster than the rate of inflation. The Carnegie Commission suggests that because of this colleges would do well to hold cost increases to about *2 percent above the rise in the consumer price index.* Although this may reflect an overly narrow or pessimistic view of the long-term role of technology in education, it is not unrealistic in the short term.

Keeping inflation in mind, we can review the expenditure trends in American higher education. Not unexpectedly, these trends parallel those occurring in revenue. Most striking are the declines in research and auxiliary operations. A review of other institutional accounts suggests relative stability. These data, however, are often aggregated at a level which is too large to be meaningful. For example, "student services" expenditures have shown no significant increase or decrease in the last ten years in spite of the conventional wisdom that this is a particularly vulnerable area during times of fiscal restraint. The reason is that the "student services" account includes admissions, an area that has received considerably more resources as institutions seek to maintain enrollments. Similarly, the account labeled "maintenance and plant operations" has been relatively stable, with expenditures at about 9 percent of current operations; since, however, this account includes the highly inflationary fuel expenditures, it follows that stability in the entire account indirectly confirms reports of decreased maintenance expenditures. In addition, a better measure of maintenance effort is the ratio of dollars expended per dollar of plant. In a study of private liberal arts colleges I found that this statistic declined from 4.3 percent to 3.4 percent over a span of ten years. Depreciation is a related cost which is totally ignored. There are several reasons for excluding depreciation from college and university accounting, and this is not the place to review that debate. We can conclude, however, that the omission of adequate depreciation from the present surplus and deficit figures results in a significant underestimation of the consumption of capital. This is particularly important for private colleges which have no direct access to public funds for the renewal and replacement of the plant. To speak, therefore, of deferred maintenance is to admit to a major, albeit commonly concealed, problem.

Institutional student aid expenditures have also remained relatively stable, although there has been a noticeable shift from strictly need-based aid to aid based on both need and merit. This has occurred as growing numbers of institutions look at their aid as an instrument for recruiting. The result, in effect, is a decrease in actual student aid and an increase in what might be more properly termed "tuition discounts."

A great deal of attention has been focused on the decline in *instructional* expenditures relative to other costs. Data on private colleges (from Bowen and Minter's *Independent Higher Education*) illustrate that, with doctoral universities excepted, the percent of revenues directed to instruction is falling at about a half a percentage point a year. Doctoral universities run counter to this trend because of the rapid decline in research spending. This decline effectively raises the relative expenditures in areas other than research. The reason for this pattern of declining instructional expenditures is not, in my opinion, an overt neglect of the academic program but that the market for faculty is sufficiently weak that institutions have been able to keep raises in faculty salaries below the rate of inflation. Of course, the long-term effects of this salary deprivation on the quality of instruction, research, and public service must be considered. One can surmise that it will ultimately have negative consequences.

RESPONSES

The affluence of higher education in the 1960s has ironically become a major source of its financial distress in the 1970s. In the early 1960s the United States placed enormous faith in education to resolve, in relatively short order, internal and external threats to the nation. Each year of his Presidency, John F. Kennedy delivered a message to Congress explicitly on the state of education. The first sentence of the first message expressed his expectation for America's schools and colleges:

> Our progress as a nation can be no swifter than our progress in education. Our requirements for world leadership, our hopes for economic growth, and the demands of citizenship itself in an era such as this all require the maximum development of every young American's capacity. . . . Our twin goals must be: A new standard of excellence in education—and the availability of such excellence to all who are willing and able to pursue it.

President Kennedy and, later, President Johnson went on to spearhead legislation which provided well for all levels of education. Higher education was supported with grants for construction, student aid, equipment, the improvement of libraries, and a number of other special activities. State and local governments quickly joined in the expansion of American higher education.

It is difficult to quarrel with President Kennedy's goals, but, in retrospect, we know that excellence and equity are not easily achieved. At that time colleges and universities welcomed public assistance and became willing partners in promising an excellent education; more than that, they implicitly promised upward socioeconomic mobility to all who would spend four years. The promise was built more on hope than fact. These were the halcyon years for higher education when it grew prodigiously. Enrollments, faculty, and degrees granted all doubled in the years following Kennedy's first message on education. These gains were not simply numerical achievements. By the end of the decade, America had the scientific knowledge and technical infrastructure to put men on the moon—an achievement truly symbolic of the advance in science and technology. Lower-income students were attending college in record numbers. Students from all income levels were active in politics, the civil rights movement, and opposition to the Vietnam War.

In many ways higher education became a victim of its own success. It helped create and demonstrate this country's technical superiority over the Soviet Union. Public interest, subsequently, turned elsewhere. Moreover, the disruptive nature of social change further inhibited public support for colleges and universities where social criticism tends to originate.

The real source of higher education's financial problems, however, did not result from its successes but from its failure—simply stated, it failed to deliver upward socioeconomic mobility on the scale promised. In retrospect this failure was inevitable. There was not enough room in the upper socioeconomic strata for all who wished residence. Consider the following: 1) Socioeconomic achievement for an individual is largely determined relative to the income and status of others, not by absolute income or purchasing power. The value of higher education, particularly to lower- and lower-middle-income families, is as a vehicle for socioeconomic advancement. 2) Although higher education is one route for socioeconomic advancement, it is not the only one. Some of the limited room at the top will be taken not by those who attend college but who excel in running a business or union, or who have special talents in sports, entertainment, or the arts. Some will reach the top by way of marriage. 3) In 1969, 44 percent of all male eighteen- and nineteen-year-olds entered college, and it may be presumed that most viewed higher education as a means to a professional or managerial career. As a rough index of opportunities, in 1975 professional and managerial jobs accounted for about 25 percent of the work force; clearly many collegians could not be accommodated. Since the young are not totally unaware of the job market, the predictable result occurred. By 1973 the rate of college attendance for eighteen- and nineteen-year-old males declined to 33 percent and a decline in the rate of female attendance followed shortly thereafter. This discussion oversimplifies the causes. The end of the draft and problems with financing an education undoubtedly contributed to this decline. But these were incidental to the impact created from the imbalance in supply and demand—a point well documented in Richard B. Freeman's *The Over-Educated American*.

These declining attendance rates precipitated the financial crisis now besetting American colleges and universities. It is important to note that the cause was *not* a decline in the number of traditional age college students. That is a problem for the 1980s. The problem of the 1970s results from disillusionment with the social and economic value of a college degree. The declining rate of attendance, begun in the 1970s, will be compounded by a decline in the *absolute number* of eighteen- and nineteen-years-olds in the 1980s. Between 1977 and 1986, the number of high school graduates will fall by about 18 percent—a very precipitous decline by demographic standards.

Because the array of data and statistics can become confusing, it is appropriate to summarize the more significant points. The production functions of higher education are complex and the products difficult to measure. There is an important distinction between the funding of public and private higher education, the public sector receiving most of its support from government and the private sector primarily dependent upon tuition. Moreover, there is a fairly rigid institutional hierarchy. Those institutions at the top of the hierarchy have considerably more flexibility than those at the bottom.

The past decades have been ones of rapid growth in enrollment and public funding. Recently both have leveled off. Enrollments have been maintained only by seeking and admitting "new students." Although higher education has become heavily reliant on government support, future prospects for such aid are unclear. Both endowment and auxiliary income have fallen in relative terms, and this trend is likely to continue.

The labor intensive nature of higher education makes it difficult to substitute less expensive capital for labor. Thus, inflation hits colleges and universities with particular severity. Colleges have been meeting this crisis by deferring maintenance, reducing student and other services, and by holding faculty salary increases below the wage increases received by other professionals. In addition, the nature of tenure creates special problems for administrators trying to deal with these financial problems.

The most severe problem facing higher education, however, is the prospect of declining enrollments. Directly and indirectly, enrollments generate the largest share of resources for higher education. To maintain enrollments, colleges and universities have been actively building new clientele. It is unclear whether this new clientele will enroll in sufficient numbers in the future to maintain institutional resources. Regardless of the success of this strategy, it is indisputable that colleges and universities are competing for students in a manner that would have been unthinkable just a few years ago. The nature of the financial problems has made the struggle for students, public support, and gift income crucial for those institutions wishing to maintain positions for their staff or even to remain solvent. The best description for higher education in the 1980s is *critical competition*.

### Implications

Colleges and universities have responded to the mounting financial problems in a variety of ways. These adjustments have included a search outward for more funds for their current endeavors, a restructuring of operations to improve efficiency, and a review of products to determine a better fit with market demand. All of these efforts have advantages, but all have deleterious effects as well. Using the prior analysis of the special features of the higher education process and market, specific examples for each of these general responses are considered.

THE SEARCH FOR MORE FUNDS

The search for new sources of revenue has, quite naturally, concentrated heavily on governments. The Carnegie Commission, in *The More Effective Use of Resources* (1972), suggested that the federal government will need to fill the resource gap for at least a few years. Unfortunately, Washington has not responded as hoped; the harsh fact is that since the publication of that book, the federal government has significantly *reduced* research expenditures. This reduction has become responsible for many of the financial problems at research-oriented institutions. Yet the federal lode is perceived by educators as being so large that they continue to hope to mine it successfully. In the early 1970s, for example, higher education associations in Washington lobbied unsuccessfully for direct institutional grants; later in the decade, some of these associations encouraged Congress to provide tax credits for tuition payments. This was cut off by a determined administration at the last moment. Individually, institutions are scurrying for federal research and development funds, and many maintain Washington offices to facilitate the quest. Colleges and universities are also intensifying efforts to solicit foundation money to support their instructional, research, and public service programs. In addition, they are approaching businesses and looking for a fit between the needs of industry and the training and research capabilities of higher education.

In some ways there has been a *fundamental change* in position. Instead of seeking support for their ongoing activities, institutions now approach governments, foundations, and businesses to inquire how they may serve the needs of these external organizations. To the degree that this has occurred, these efforts could be considered in this chapter's section "Looking at the Marketplace." However, the efforts have concentrated largely on seeking resources for their present operations and, thus, will be considered in this section.

Why colleges and universities pursue these new sources of support is easy to explain: they have slack capacity in their organization. Teachers or researchers are generally underutilized. New funds allow colleges and universities to continue their present scale of operation—reducing or eliminating the needs for special economies. Without such funds salaries would be depressed even further or layoffs would occur. Layoffs would primarily affect the most junior faculty because of the restrictions of the tenure system. These younger colleagues are often considered the most energetic and innovative members of the community. Moreover, a large-scale reduction in junior faculty could create a gap in scholarship when the senior faculty retire.

In truth, the disruptive effects of major efforts for institutional economy are unknown because we know so little about the production of learning and scholarship. The special ambience, often considered necessary for effective learning and scholarship, could be destroyed if new funds were unavailable. On the other hand, because we have such limited understanding of how colleges and universities actually work and, further, because of the existence of multiple products, there is a temptation to use available faculty in any endeavor for which funding is available. Liberal arts and community colleges are seeking research, development, and demonstration support as enrollments sag and their teachers remain underutilized. Presuming that these faculty were hired for their teaching ability or for scholarship in their respective disciplines, one may legitimately question how well they can carry out research or demonstration projects not consistently related to their own abilities. Similarly, as research universities become more dependent on tuition revenues, researchers are likely to find themselves in the classroom more often than in the laboratory. The forced fit between present faculty and the availability of funds is partially a result of the tenure system. Colleges have made a commitment to protect the jobs of their senior staff. This compact was made in good faith because of the belief that productive scholarship requires some form of economic security. Whether this assertion is true—or a piece of academic fiction—is impossible to determine because we know so little about the processes of scholarship or about measuring scholastic achievement.

The measurement problems also have implications for the redistribution of existing funds. For example: public two-year colleges have claimed that they do not receive a fair share of state support. The state subsidy per two-year college student is invariably lower than the subsidy for each four-year student. Two-year colleges make the argument that their students come from less advantaged backgrounds and need greater support. Four-year colleges counter that the training they provide is more advanced and, hence, more costly, and therefore they deserve more financial support. *In fact, both assertions are unsupported by any substantial empirical evidence!* We do not know how to measure how much learning is occurring. Thus, any change in funding mode by state legislators is made at the margin, or, more likely, funds are distributed on the basis of political rather than analytical arguments.

This measurement difficulty also pertains to the distribution of state and federal funds to private higher education. Perhaps more important to the private sector are the implications of too heavy a reliance on the public treasury. It is uncertain *how much* and *what form* of public support represent a threat to independence. But this support does represent a potential problem. In New York, a state which provides considerable aid to private colleges, there are only three accredited colleges which still retain openly religious orientations. All others have succumbed to the lure of direct state assistance and declared themselves "secular." Another state which provides significant support for its private colleges required a religious institution to open a presidential search beyond the membership of the supporting church. The order came from the state's Equal Opportunity Commission and the alternative was a loss of state support. Both Brigham Young University in Utah and Hillsdale College in Michigan have run afoul of federal equal opportunity regulations. The levers exercised on these institutions were, again, financial ones. Some authorities have argued that academic freedom is best protected when colleges are not overly dependent on any one source of income. They define the income sources as the federal government, the state government, philanthropy, and tuition and conclude that if colleges and universities are overly dependent on tuition, independent scholarship will be threatened. I suggest that tuition is not nearly as monolithic as the other sources because each student is an independent actor; his decisions are not inextricably tied to decisions of other students. Using this analysis, I see considerably less threat to academic freedom if students, rather than governments, are the ultimate decision-makers.

In addition to placing private institutions under greater control by public agencies, the competition for public funds is increasing the animosity between the sectors. Public institutions tend to view the state treasury from a proprietal prospective—as their exclusive source. They argue that because they are *public* institutions the state has an obligation to ensure their fiscal well-being before supporting private institutions. In truth the state's primary obligation is to ensure that *high quality* education, regardless of its source, is available and accessible. They do not, in my view, have an obligation to maintain jobs in the public sector. Viewing increased competition for funds from the other side of the coin, many private college administrators are distressed when public institutions solicit private donations. Except where this is prohibited by law, there is no reason to believe that private gifts should be solely directed to private institutions.

The competition for dollars is not only between public and private institutions but also between two-year and four-year colleges and between liberal arts colleges and research universities. To the extent that funds are distributed according to the status hierarchy of institutions rather than institutional needs and capabilities, acrimony in higher education will grow.

To conclude: virtually all colleges and universities are seeking new sources of support for operations. Many have full-time lobbyists in Washington and in state capitals, and nearly all have full-time fund raisers. Unfortunately, the outside sources of support are not growing. Some have indeed shrunk, and it appears that they will continue to do so. To the extent that the hunger for funds becomes a public squabble between the sectors and/or between levels of institutions, disillusionment with higher education will build and funds may become even more difficult to obtain.

SEARCH FOR EFFICIENCY

With sufficient new funds unavailable, colleges have sought to use their present resources more effectively. Accordingly, there has been a rapid increase of interest in and implementation of management information systems, cost/benefit studies, and management-by-objective. Although the concepts are unassailable, their actual utility in higher education is open to considerable question. One reason is the aforementioned *joint-product nature* of higher education. The essence of the new management techniques is the linking of resources to outputs. But when outputs are highly interrelated, as they are in higher education, then these techniques may be suggestive, at best, and diversionary or dysfunctional at worst. Consider computer planning models; virtually all are "student driven." That is, the number of students passing through the system determines what the resource allocations should be. None of these models takes into account the research and scholarly efforts of faculty—the activities which typically govern promotion and the awarding of tenure. If tenure is awarded on the basis of scholarly publications and other professional activities (standards set largely outside the institution), how can college administrators expect to gain much insight from a model which centers on managing student credit hours as a means to improve productivity?

Almost all of the analytic management tools used to improve the efficiency of colleges and universities require measures of output. In higher education we must be content with output proxies. We cannot measure the cost of education; rather we measure the cost per degree or cost per credit hour or cost per full-time equivalent student. Ultimately we must rely on subjective measures of how much students learn. *If we consider the cost per student or similar measures to be reasonable guides for action,* administrators or legislators can increase efficiency by either increasing enrollments or reducing faculty or both. Of course, any changes of this nature, if made mindlessly, could have deleterious educational consequences. Unfortunately these temptations are not hypothetical.

This discussion may seem unfair, but consider the following. If educational reforms were simply improvements in the product, one would expect that the distribution of the costs of these reforms would range from positive to negative. That is, some improvements would make the product more expensive and others less expensive. In the auto industry, for example, fiberglass bodies made some cars less costly and automatic transmissions made them more expensive. In higher education, virtually every innovation (e.g., the external degree, credit by examination, credit for life experience, the elimination of language and science requirements, and the elimination of residency requirements for graduate degrees) has made obtaining a degree less expensive for the consumer in terms of dollars, time, or effort.

The foregoing comments should not be considered an attack on educational reform generally or on any one of the specific innovations listed above. But it is safe to generalize that the changes, on balance, will bring a diminution in the efforts to obtain a degree and probably a decrement of learning as well. If this seems overly critical, one need only consider the prestigious professional schools which are currently overwhelmed with applicants. Virtually none openly embraces these "reforms"! Generally, one can receive advanced placement through examination, but not credit; and institutions with which I am familiar are reducing the amount of transfer credit they will accept. The point is this: we should look hard at the changes in the delivery of education. Certainly we can improve the efficiency of the system. *But although many, if not most, of the recent changes have lowered the cost of a degree, their effect on efficiency is questionable.*

The radical distinction in funding public and private higher education makes the measurement of efficiency particularly troublesome. In the public sector many of the critical decisions with regard to the appropriate level of efficiency are made by the state legislators. Because they are distant from the educational process and involved with a variety of other budgetary and legislative problems, they tend to rely on mechanistic funding formulas. In fact, they have little good information to judge efficiency except from the pressure they receive from the electorate. Accordingly, the success of a school's football team is as likely as other factors to affect its annual appropriation. If administrators of public institutions are constrained in their quest for efficiency by legislators in the state capital, it is also highly unlikely that their institution will cease to exist. Because of their state subsidies, each has a limited local monopoly which ensures at least a minimum number of students. Although both sectors seek to be efficient, the private sector endures the

burden that regardless of how efficient it becomes, it must charge a price
several times higher than that charged by public institutions for a
basically similar product.

## LOOKING AT THE MARKETPLACE

When enrollments or research funding decline, a common response is
to "look at the market." Administrators ask: "What is wanted? How
can we provide it?" This reaction is reasonable and has several beneficial
effects. Primarily, it prevents an industry from becoming complacent or
stagnant. A common diagnosis of how railroads ended up in severe financial trouble is that they considered themselves in the railroad, not the
transportation business. As a consequence, they failed to shift resources
into trucking or air transportation. Colleges and universities may be a
little late, but no one will accuse them of ignoring other possible markets.
Here again let us recall the special nature of the learning industry: we
know very little about how learning and scholarship occur. Yet, faced
with declining enrollments, many institutions are incorporating new
programs and embracing new missions with relative nonchalance. The
new functions are typically attached to, rather than replacing, previous
programs and missions. Thus, liberal arts colleges are adding business
and other vocationally oriented areas of study. Women's colleges are admitting men, and men's colleges are admitting women. Religious institutions are becoming secular. Secular colleges are adding "values" programs. And all, as Blaug and Mace point out, consider adult education
to be the "new Jerusalem."

We know very little about the effects of these changes because our
measurement tools are very crude. Bowen and Minter claim that private
colleges are doing relatively well because, among other reasons, they are
increasing the number of programs they offer. I would argue that program proliferation and mission change are often signs of financial weakness and, in some cases, of actual panic. I say this on the basis of my
study of religious and single-sex colleges which had become secular
and/or coeducational. Comparing institutions which changed their mission with those that did not, I discovered that the major difference between the groups was that the changing institutions were in considerably
greater financial difficulty prior to change than those institutions which
did not change. Because I was concerned with more than just the financial effects of change, I chose colleges for the study that had previously
used the College and University Environment Scales published by the

Educational Testing Service. By readministering these scales at all colleges in the study, I could gauge the "environmental impact" of the changes. Indeed, I found that the schools which broadened their missions enrolled more students and were able to moderate their financial liabilities. However, at most of those "change" colleges there was a very noticeable deterioration in campus morale, in sense of community, in campus propriety, and, to some extent, in the quality of the student-faculty relationships. The deteriorations were not present or were of considerably smaller magnitude at the colleges which did not change. It is surprising that efforts to gauge the environments of colleges and universities are rather infrequent. College personnel are quick to claim that campuses are "special places" but apparently reluctant to document that statement.

Measuring the effect of colleges on students is particularly difficult. Alexander Astin, who has probably done as much investigation in this area as any researcher, is also concerned about the changes which are sweeping American higher education. In *Four Critical Years* he states that recent trends are essentially paradoxical: they lead to less student growth and achievement rather than more. These trends are occurring, he believes, because of the "centrality of money in policy making." Unfortunately, as the financial crisis becomes more serious, money will be unlikely to show any movement to the periphery. The challenge for higher education is to change the system so that the fiscal pressures are fairly balanced by educational concerns.

The dual system of public and private colleges and the hierarchical nature of higher education have effects on the strategy of turning to the marketplace. Economic theory states that firms competing for customers in an open market will create pressures for efficiency such that only those that deliver the highest quality product at the lowest price will survive. Those firms which are inefficient or cannot judge what consumers desire will be unable to attract a sufficient number of customers to survive. The metaphor used is one of an "invisible hand" which guides the production of goods and services. I argued above that with government heavily subsidizing one sector, the quest for efficiency is distorted. Administrators at public colleges are making decisions based on funding formulas and on the potential political ramifications. Unable to artificially depress costs, private colleges are placed in a disadvantageous position vis à vis public colleges. Students may prefer a single-sex college or a liberal arts college; however, if the cost of attendance at a public college is several thousand dollars less each year, many students will find that although the private education is worth more, it is not worth *that much* more. The hierarchical nature of higher education also obstructs the operation of the free market which, in theory, requires ease of entry by producers. If we view higher education as a series of markets, rather than one market, it is clear that the most prestigious institutions are relatively free to enter new areas of competition while the least prestigious are quite constrained. Although Harvard, for example, can attract funds for remedial education, a nearby community college will find it impossible to fund a program in theoretical physics. This problem is particularly severe in the competition for students. The more prestigious schools, whose degrees are considered better credentials, are able to maintain enrollments by admitting students who otherwise would have attended schools with lesser reputations. At the bottom of the pile are private two-year colleges. They are expensive relative to public institutions; they lack prestige; they are, not unsurprisingly, the institutions most likely to have closed during recent years.

This review of financial trends in higher education during the 1960s and the early 1970s underscores a variety of significant points. The more salient are these:

1. Resources are increasingly inadequate in the face of escalating and hard-to-control expenses.
2. Costs are increasing because, in an era of inflation and rapidly rising wages, colleges and universities find it difficult to replace labor with less expensive machines. Tenure, of course, exacerbates the inflexibility of many institutions.
3. Another reason for the recent decline in resources is a shift in federal priority away from university-based research.
4. The major cause of financial problems, however, was that higher education, as it expanded from a basically elitist to an open access orientation, made an implicit promise of upward mobility to the "new students." Higher education no longer served as "gate keeper" to the upper socioeconomic reaches and, thus, these "new students" were destined to be disappointed.
5. As this occurred, many potential students stopped coming (attendance rate for eighteen- and nineteen-year-old males fell from 44 percent to 33 percent in four years). This decline was temporarily offset by the inflow of older students, more females, and more part-time students.
6. The attendance patterns of older students now seem to be leveling off and the participation *rate* of women has declined.
7. In the 1980s higher education will experience an 18 percent decline in the number of eighteen- to twenty-year-olds.
8. With limited resources, declining enrollments, and rising costs, higher edu-

cation has entered an era of *critical competition,* where some institutions will not survive and others will be greatly changed.

## Recommendations

### INSTITUTIONAL REFORMS

The fundamental failure of higher education in the 1960s and 1970s was, as noted, its failure to deliver upward socioeconomic mobility on the scale promised. Because of this failure, its credibility has worn thin. A primary challenge facing institutions of higher education in the 1980s is to prevent further erosion of their credibility. This can only be done if, when institutions seek new efficiencies, they maintain or improve the quality of their present products. When they seek new funds and new students, colleges and universities must be prepared to deliver a product equal to the expectations of the funding organizations and of the "new students." The difficulties are enormous. Tenure greatly inhibits flexibility. Institutional management must deal with this problem creatively.

Presidents and staffs can become so overwhelmed with budgetary issues that concerns over institutional ambience and reputation for excellence are ignored or given only perfunctory acknowledgement. If there is an overriding lesson in the current travail, it is this: declining enrollments and the financial consequences thereof are symptoms, not causes. Students do not choose an institution because enrollments have risen; often the enrollees are blissfully unaware of enrollment patterns. But they do have perceptions of the value of the educational experience. Because of this, college and university officials must be concerned with a healthy social and learning environment, with an image that mirrors reality. This requires special efforts to measure and evaluate the graduate who is then their product. Similarly, when new programs are added—in adult education, career education, or values clarification—academic administrators and faculty should be as explicit as possible with respect to their expectations from these programs. Then they should build measures to evaluate the output—measures that go beyond the number of bodies enrolled. Simple expediency will not work.

### PUBLIC POLICY RESPONSE

With resources becoming increasingly scarce in the 1980s, public policy makers have a duty to allocate public support for higher education to the most efficient institutions and to insure that funds are rationed in such a manner as to assist students most in need. That is, public funds should not replace private funds, but augment total available support. Unfortunately, these objectives are not well served by current methods of financing. This accusation does not apply to the federal government. The thrust of new federal aid for higher education has been to assist low-income individuals—those who probably would not enroll in higher education without such assistance. The individuals choose the institutions which meet their needs. Because the recipients are poor, federal funds are unlikely to replace personal resources.

Federal assistance, however, is relatively modest when compared to state support of higher education which accounts for two-thirds of all public support of higher education and is overwhelmingly directed toward public institutions. State funds are rationed to public institutions on the basis of rigid formulas and/or political considerations. I submit that the production of education and scholarship are such complex and enigmatic processes that formulas and politics are unreliable criteria with which to gauge and reward institutional efficiency. Moreover, the current system of finance excludes over half of the institutions from this benefit—that is, private institutions which fulfill a necessary social purpose. It should be underscored that state support of private institutions represents only about 2 or 3 percent of total state spending on higher education.

In addition, the policy of direct state aid to institutions replaces available private resources because, under current methods of finance, many students from middle-income, upper-middle-income, and wealthy families (who would have enrolled and paid full tuition) receive a state subsidy only by attending a public institution. Thus, total available support for higher education is reduced.

A voucher system, in which state money would be directed to low-income and lower-middle-income students, instead of institutions, would have many advantages over the present system. The most efficient and attractive institutions would enroll more students; government officials would not need to be intimately concerned with such matters as student-faculty ratios or tenure policies; institutions which creatively managed their instructional program and tenure process would be successful, and those which did not would lose students. Wealthier students would pay their own way, and (to the extent that they currently attend public institutions) total support for higher education would grow.

There are criticisms of a voucher system. One is that conditions for perfect competition do not exist in higher education. But this is true of almost any sector of the economy. The response here as in other sectors must be to try to increase competition. Only for the so-called natural monopolies—and higher education is not such a creature—has the thrust been toward regulation rather than competition.

Concern is voiced that students have inadequate information on which to base institutional selection. A reasonable reaction is to improve information. Information about *increments* in learning are particularly needed to dismantle the hierarchical nature of colleges and universities.

Some critics of vouchers fear the "tyranny" of the marketplace, which is to say that institutions will provide any education students want. It is, however, hard to imagine greater institutional sensitivity to market behavior than at present. If this were a real concern, states could provide direct support for certain courses or programs. If, for example, vocational studies are viewed as having less public benefit than liberal arts, it would be possible for the legislature to directly subsidize liberal arts education. Under the present system we subsidize business students in the public sector, but not liberal arts students in the private sector. *If critics of the voucher system are seriously concerned about student choice of study, one would think they would advocate public support of areas of study, and not types of colleges.*

Another concern is the prospect of large-scale student "emancipation" from parental support. A possible solution is to award vouchers to parents to support their children's education. For those students who are truly emancipated and do not qualify, student loan programs should be expanded. (Ideally the repayment schedule for these loans would be based on future income.)

Let me summarize by restating my two major recommendations:

1. As institutions seek new markets and new efficiencies, they should pay careful attention to institutional environment and to the quality of their products—seeking always to understand better what they produce and how to measure these products.

2. To facilitate and reward institutional efficiency and responsiveness, we should totally revise our public system of finance. Since state legislators should not—and cannot—determine *institutional* efficiency and desirability, they should concentrate on the *student* by directing state funds to lower income students and by improving the information base upon which students base college selection.

*Carl Kaysen*

# 3

# The Growing Power
# of Government

## *Introduction*

In recent years, relations between governments—both federal and state—and higher education have been deeply troubled. From the academic side, there has been a well-articulated and widely heard stream of complaints, much of it directed at "overregulation" and "government interference." From the side of government, those responsible for enforcing the laws and applying the regulations have often expressed their disappointment—usually less publicly—at the failures of the academy to obey the rules and have found its complaints self-serving. Fifteen to twenty years ago, all this was unheard. In the eyes of higher education Washington was then a munificent patron. Support for scientific research was growing rapidly; a drive to encourage and assist new "centers of excellence" through institutional grants and student fellowships led to new or enlarged graduate programs in a broad spectrum of fields; and

---

CARL KAYSEN, *David W. Skinner Professor of Political Economy at M.I.T., is on leave to serve as vice chairman and director of research of The Sloan Commission of Government and Higher Education. Before joining M.I.T., Dr. Kaysen was director of the Institute for Advanced Study, Princeton, New Jersey, from 1966 to 1976. He has written a number of books on the problems of higher education, including* The Higher Learning, the Universities and the Public.

grants and loan guarantees were made available for the construction of dormitories and, later, academic buildings.

In the same period, public institutions' experience with their state governments was, in general, equally agreeable. Existing institutions were expanding in size, scope, and program level. New institutions and branch campuses of established ones were being created in large numbers. Growth engendered a buoyant and optimistic atmosphere, in which the notes of "master-planning" and "coordination" rang with quite different overtones in both campus and capitol than they do today.

Four developments over the past fifteen years are chiefly responsible for this change. They are: first and most obviously, the growth of federal regulation applicable to and applied to colleges and universities; second, shifts in the magnitude and character of federal funding for higher education; third, the end of the enrollment boom; and, finally, the worsening cost situation of the institutions. The first and second of these developments bear directly on relations between government and the academy; the last two, only indirectly. Yet these may well be more important in explaining the intensity of academic reactions to what governments are doing.

The unfavorable demographic and economic contexts affect all of higher education. Fifteen years ago, colleges and universities were at the peak of their steady postwar growth. In the period 1950–65, enrollments grew at an average annual rate of over 9 percent: nearly 400,000 students were added each year. This growth derived from a combination of the increasing size of the eighteen-year-old age cohort and a sustained increase in the fraction of the college age population enrolling.

The number of eighteen-year-olds has reached a peak and will begin to decline almost steadily for fifteen years to a level only 75 percent of its peak value. The size of the cohort of eighteen- to twenty-four-year-olds, which covers most of the population in higher education, begins to shrink two years later, but lasts as long and goes about as deep. Further, the current ratios of high-school graduates to eighteen-year-olds and first-time enrollments in higher education to high school graduates are both high by historical standards: 75 percent and 62 percent respectively. The former ratio increased fairly steadily from 56 percent in 1950 to about 75 percent in 1966 and has fluctuated within a small compass since. The latter has moved fairly steadily from 43 percent in 1950 to 62 percent in 1970 and, again, shown only small fluctuations since. Whether there is enough possibility for future growth in either or both of these ratios to counter the unfavorable demographic prospect remains to be seen, but the recent record provides little basis to expect it. Unlike the underlying demography, however, both high school completion rates and, to an even greater extent, college enrollment rates can be influenced by public policy.

The unfavorable cost situation of higher education, especially (but not only) of its private sector, has deeper roots. In the first place, there is a sense in which colleges and universities are always operating at the margin and under great pressure to spend all the money they can get and a little more. As nonprofit institutions, they do not aim at always achieving a surplus of revenues over costs but, at best, a balance. Publicly supported institutions usually present their budgets and receive their support in a way which achieves just this result. Then, each institution has a large inventory of desirable activities to undertake that will improve the quality of its performance: increasing the range and variety of course offerings, reducing class size, expanding the library, adding new laboratory space and equipment, raising faculty salaries, etc. There are always enough urgent items in the inventory to consume any emerging surplus.

Secondly, the nature of higher education is such that there is a tendency for its costs to grow more rapidly than its revenues at constant price levels. Colleges and universities operate on what is essentially a handicraft technology, with high utilization of costly skilled labor and little or no opportunity to benefit either from scale economies (above a rather small size) or technological advance. Indeed, some very important resources, such as libraries, seem to suffer from significant technical diseconomies of scale. Yet large and growing, and thus more costly, libraries are essential for research and advanced training in many disciplines. Compensation for both faculty and staff employees is broadly determined by competitive forces, both within and outside the academy. The rise of incomes in the whole economy reflects technological progress and other sources of increasing productivity per man. Many forces press academe to increase its pay scales in a roughly parallel way. Thus it experiences a long-run upward trend in unit costs.

The two decades of rapid expansion in the whole system added a further impulse to higher costs. Increased enrollments demanded more teachers, and supply expanded slowly and with a lag. Competition for faculty, especially for leading men with established reputations and promising younger men, was keen. It had a special edge in the sciences, where rivalry between public universities with more recently established and newly expanded research programs and the private universities which had dominated the much smaller research scene before World War II was fueled with federal money. The result was a rapid increase in academic salaries, both absolutely and relative to other occupations. It was not confined to natural scientists, though greatest for them. Considerations of equity within institutions helped faculty in the humanities and some of the social sciences to achieve larger gains than rising demand alone might have produced. Extension of the coverage of minimum wage laws, social security, unemployment insurance, increasing unionization, as well as the general forces of economic growth led to increases in the costs of administrative, clerical, maintenance, and housekeeping staff as well.

Until well past the middle of the 1960s, increasing enrollments and the continued growth in federal support of research generally contributed enough on the revenue side to cover these increasing costs. In the late sixties, the situation began to change. The growth of federal research support in real terms ceased. Private institutions began to feel the pressure to raise tuitions. As inflation generated by the Vietnam War gathered momentum, these pressures increased, and tuitions started to climb. The further inflation triggered by the Arab oil embargo and the subsequent escalation of oil prices in 1973 accelerated the process. In the period 1966–67 through 1976–77 average tuition at all private four-year institutions rose by an average of more than 9 percent per year, compared to a 6 percent average annual increase in the Consumer Price Index (CPI). Increases in tuition and fees at public institutions began only much later; up to 1974 they were below the rate of increase in the CPI.

The continuing inflation had similarly unfavorable effects on publicly supported institutions, though it took somewhat different forms. More intense demands on state budgets, reflecting both an expansion of services (including higher education) and rapidly rising employment costs in the public service, left governors and legislatures less willing to provide large annual increases in the budgets for higher education. The slowing of enrollment growth and the prospect of future decline added to this reluctance to fund increased budgets. The same pressures led to some rises in tuition and wider differentials for out-of-state tuitions over those for state residents.

The underlying demographic forces hold no cheerier prospect for the public than for the private institutions. The falling off of the cohorts of college age is paralleled by a rise in those at older ages. Their demands for public services center on health care and welfare services of various kinds, rather than education. With fewer children and, soon, grand-children for whom higher education is an important public good, the political weight of the older cohort will be shifted to support increases in the services they require for themselves. Governors and legislatures can be expected to respond, and the relative weight that higher educa-tion can claim in total state expenditures will diminish.

These unfavorable circumstances, and the prospect that they will per-sist and even worsen, form the context in which the increase in the extent and scope of government regulation and the shifts in the character of federal support have been experienced.

Government regulation of higher education can be divided into three categories:

1. rules and standards generally applicable to all organized activity in society (with or without an associated receipt of government funds),
2. rules affecting activities specific to higher education, and
3. rules related to financial accountability in connection with support for ac-tivities specific to academic institutions (such as student aid and research support).

Examples of the first category are provided by legislation governing various aspects of employer-employee relations such as the Fair Labor Standards (Wages-and-Hours) Act, the Occupational Health and Safety Act, and the Employee Retirement Income Security Act. Likewise, Title VI of the Civil Rights Act, which enjoins discrimination on the grounds of race, color, national origin, or religion, protects anyone entitled to participate in, or participating in, any program or activity receiving federal financial assistance. Executive Orders 11246 and 11375, pro-hibiting discrimination in employment on any of the same grounds and prescribing affirmative action by employers to achieve nondiscrimi-nation, apply to all organizations holding federal contracts of $10,000 or more.

These laws and regulations and others of similarly broad scope serve social purposes that have commanded the degree of acceptance necessary for the enactment of legislation in a democratic and pluralist society. Colleges and universities are not alone in finding them burdensome and costly. Yet legislatures which have approved them have made the cal-culation, implicitly if not explicitly, that the social benefits justify their costs.

Examples of the second category include the Family Education Rights and Privacy Act (Buckley Amendment) and Department of Health, Education, and Welfare (DHEW) regulations governing the use of human subjects and the care of animals used in research. An example of a different kind of regulation in the second category is the Health Professions Educational Assistance Act (1976) which, among other things, requires that medical schools seek to alter the distribution of medical students among areas of specialization as a condition of receiving federal capitation funds. Unlike other examples cited, this reaches directly and deeply into the heart of educational enterprise.

The nature of the third type of regulation is almost self-evident: rules prescribing the purposes for which, and terms on which, federal grants, loans, and contracts are available and persons or organizations entitled to receive them; reporting and auditing requirements placed on the recipients; and the like.

The number of regulations of all three types has grown rapidly since the mid-sixties, with the greatest growth in the first and second categories. The third has also grown, as new student aid programs have been legislated, with their corresponding eligibility requirements, application procedures, and reporting rules. Rules governing research grants have changed relatively little, but their burdensomeness appears to have increased with the slackening of growth in research support.

Most of the laws and regulations that have stimulated the anxious concern of academe so far have fallen into the first and third categories. Those in the second category are relatively few; and almost all are concerned with medical schools, their associated hospitals, and biomedical research, rather than higher education generally. The Buckley Amendment is exceptional in this respect.

The greatest volume of complaint appears to arise in response to the first category of regulation, which is the one that does not focus specifically on higher education. There are several reasons for this. The rules connected with the receipt of federal funds (in the form of research support or student aid) impose administrative burdens and costs of the same sort—and frequently of greater magnitude—as do those of the first category. They also give rise to similar dissatisfactions: unnecessary red tape, duplicative or irrelevant paperwork, and incompetent government administration. However, they accompany tangible benefits of great value to the institutions; almost no institution gives up the benefits to avoid the costs, although everyone has the choice. No direct tangible institutional benefits correspond to the costs and burdens of compliance with regulations of the first category; hence, the complaints are, so to speak, free. Many administrators and professors who express strong support for the goals of these enactments and regulations nonetheless view the whole process of regulation in this area as a transaction in which "they" impose costs on "us" in pursuit of "their" social goals. The further possibility must be allowed that, for some, complaints about the burdens of compliance and the incompetence of administration are means of expressing disapproval of the social goals that inform the regulations.

It is difficult to estimate the cost burdens that the regulatory process imposes on academic institutions. The Sloan Foundation sponsored self-surveys of a sample of twenty-one institutions drawn from all parts of the higher education spectrum in the summer of 1977. These suggest a representative figure for compliance cost of, at most, something like 2 percent added to the operation budget through increases in clerical and administrative staffs. This number, while it clearly varies widely for specific institutions, is on the average neither overwhelming nor insignificant. The figure alone cannot answer several fundamental questions. Do the results justify the costs? Could equally good results be achieved more economically? Who should bear the cost? And, of course, such an estimate does not, because it cannot, assign a dollar value to the effects of changes in regulation on the way institutions operate. This is widely experienced as an increase in formality and bureaucracy at the cost of ease, informality, and collegiality. The cost estimate also does not cover the diversion of time and energy of senior administrators and faculty members to the problems of compliance, finite resources which might otherwise be spent on more centrally educational problems.

At the extreme, regulation is seen as threatening to impair the capacity of academic institutions to perform their functions effectively by transferring crucial decisions on who should teach, who should be taught, and even what should be taught from the academic community that is competent to make them to governmental bureaucracies that are not. Thus the regulations simply subvert the academic enterprise and destroy its capacity to function effectively.

The significance of the burden of regulation must be seen in terms of the context within which colleges and universities experience it—specifically, the unfavorable economic and demographic prospect facing higher education. This has certainly made both the dollar costs of compliance and the less tangible organizational and psychological costs of coping with new, externally-imposed demands more of a burden. The dean who would find it irritating in any case to appear in a proceeding to answer an allegation of sex discrimination will find it doubly so if he is preoccupied with trying to justify the budget for the maintenance of his present faculty, 80 percent of whom have tenure, when the enrollment in his program has already begun to fall.

An equally important aspect of this context is the large and still increasing role of the federal government as patron of higher education. One of the most widely applicable sanctions for the violation of the various laws and regulations prescribing nondiscrimination in its many aspects is denying federal funds to offending institutions. While this action—though it has been often threatened—has not yet been applied, the prospect is frightening, and few institutions could survive it.

In 1977, the dollar value of all kinds of federal support for colleges and universities amounted to between an eighth and a sixth of their aggregate current fund revenues. The corresponding share for the states —the major supporters of the public institutions—was about one-third.

Federal expenditures for the support of academic science in that year were $3.8 billion. This was 75 percent of all expenditures for scientific research at universities and colleges, and nearly 9 percent of their total current fund expenditures in that year. Expenditures for student aid by the Office of Education, the Social Security Administration, and the Veterans Administration totaled nearly $7 billion. Most of this money goes to students, not institutions. A substantial part, but not all of it, returns to institutions as tuition, fees, room, and board. Aggregate current fund revenues from tuition, fees, room, and board in 1977 was $14 billion for all of higher education. Assuming that only 50 percent of the federal student aid returned to the institutions and the remainder went to nonacademic providers of subsistence and other needs, such as books and transportation, this means that 25 percent of tuition, fees, room, and board was financed from Washington. Furthermore, nearly 40 percent of all enrolled students received some form of federally-financed aid, and, for some large fraction of these, aid was crucial to the decision to attend. State appropriations for most public institutions depend chiefly on formulas geared to enrollment. Thus, federal aid that enables students to attend them has a multiplier effect for public institutions by attracting corresponding state funds.

The relative dollar weights of student aid and research support in federal programs have shifted greatly in the last fifteen years. The present two-to-one ratio in favor of student aid was just the reverse fifteen years ago. Student aid programs are relatively new and are still growing rapidly in dollar volume, while the growth of research support in real terms has almost ceased. Thus the shift in relative importance will continue.

As far as public policy goes, the shift is the result of the addition of new programs with new purposes rather than a conscious devaluation of the support of research. The central thrust of the student aid programs has been egalitarian: to provide financial assistance to enable young men and women from low-income families who might not otherwise do so to go to college. The chief criterion for eligibility is financial need. By contrast, programs of research support are basically meritocratic, even elitist, in orientation. The central criterion for support is relative scientific merit, judged competitively. But the change has not resulted from one set of values replacing the other, but rather from the legislative recognition of a new public purpose, added to the quite different public purposes served by funding academic science.

The two programs have quite different clienteles. Student aid programs involve almost every college and university in the nation, and nearly all have benefited from them. Most of the support of science goes to only a relatively few institutions—about 100 universities among the 3,000-odd universities and colleges. Yet this number includes most of the leading institutions in every dimension: general prestige and breadth of reputation, quality and quantity of professional as well as graduate and undergraduate education. (Only a much smaller number of liberal arts colleges share to any extent the same national prestige.) The cessation of growth in research support has had its major impact on these universities. The growth in student aid has not provided them equivalent compensation, since many of them are consistently overapplied at the undergraduate level and in the professional schools as well. Thus the shift in federal programs has had a largely negative effect on academe's most visible and audible segment.

An examination of the relations of government and higher education must recognize the fundamental lack of unity in government programs, whether of regulation or support. There is no single federal policy toward higher education. Federal support comes from a congeries of programs, each with its own history, purpose, clientele, and political base. Equally, regulation is the product of diverse processes, involving various sets of actors with different ends in view. Much of it, as already observed, had its chief targets and goals elsewhere and was applied to higher education incidentally or as an afterthought.

In general, those who regulate higher education at the federal level have little or no connection with those who provide support, and the latter are themselves widely dispersed. The intimate connection that exists among research, scholarship, and education is recognized by some of the agencies providing an important part of research funding, but less so by those concerned with student aid. The committee organization through which Congress functions tends to separate these activities from one another. No single federal agency now has cognizance of or responsibility for the whole of higher education. The creation of a Department of Education at the cabinet level, as now proposed, will not change the situation. In particular, no one is concerned with the total effect of the wide range of federal activities on the functioning of the academic enterprise as a whole.

### The Role of the States

Historically the states have been primarily involved in education, and despite the recent sharp increases in federal involvement, the states remain on the same level of importance as the federal government. They still are the major providers of public money and, increasingly, regulators, though in a significantly different mode. At the state level the major issues are explicitly ones of governance rather than regulation. These arise directly in the context of the provision of support, and thus the two concerns are united by their very nature. The states, of course, have always had the power to prescribe the mode of governance of the public colleges and universities. Since education is a state and not a federal function, the federal government has never had any broad corresponding power. Thus an examination of the impact of state policies starts with a fundamentally different formal framework than that appropriate to the federal level. Until recently, states have followed the models of the private sector and chosen to organize colleges and universities as autonomous institutions under their own boards of trustees. Board members were in some cases appointed, in some cases elected, and there was often a group of state officials who were trustees ex officio. In a number of states, the autonomous structure was given constitutional status.

Despite their formal autonomy, the history of public institutions is replete with instances of legislative or gubernatorial interference in faculty appointments and the substance of instruction, but these are now increasingly rare. The typical "normal" operation is one in which almost all academic decisions are made by the institutions, subject to the budget and appropriation powers of governor and legislature. Exceptional decisions, major new ventures, or unusual expenditures were subject to approval at the capitol; everyday operations were not. (Admissions criteria were an exception to this rule; they were often prescribed by legislation.)

While the varying arrangements of the fifty states are difficult to describe in general terms, the new institutions, such as the comprehensive colleges and community colleges, have typically been endowed with much less autonomy at birth. In many states there is a single governing board for all institutions of one type, often headed by a strong executive, and the individual institutions are left with little independence vis-à-vis the "system."

In the past decade or so, however, the states have increased the extent of centralized control over higher education within their boundaries, taking on more of the administrative functions that were formerly exercised by individual public institutions and in some cases taking tentative steps to extend their jurisdiction to private institutions as well. This trend is likely to continue. The next ten or fifteen years will be a period of declining enrollments and, in all likelihood, tight state budgets. The executive and legislative branches of state governments, as they are forced to respond to growing demands on limited state resources from other sectors of their economies, will increasingly seek to control expenditures for higher education. These efforts to control costs will be perceived by public and private institutions as attempts to control the institutions themselves.

It is, of course, difficult to talk of the varying experiences of fifty states except in highly abstract terms. A few examples can lend the weight of specificity to these generalizations. In California, both executive and legislative budget offices through "letters of intent" add restrictions or prescriptions on expenditures that are not contained in the Budgets passed by the legislature. In recent years these have become increasingly detailed, especially in respect to the California State Colleges and Universities (CSCU) System, and control such matters as how faculty members' time shall be allocated among various activities and what relative weights they should have.

Financial reporting can also become an instrument of control, simply by the growth in detail that must be reported. In Washington, one community college was required to report fifteen times on certain personnel transactions in the 1973-75 biennium, seventy-five times during

1975-77 biennium, and—it is estimated—will need to produce 300 reports in the current biennium. During this whole period, the level of activity at the institution was roughly constant.

In Wisconsin, the vice president of the University System expressed his concerns about this problem in a letter to the state auditor in July, 1976:

> One of the general concerns I have . . . is the increasing and apparent need [by numerous state and] federal agencies to have more and more information on the way in which universities are managed, on their goals and objectives, and on performance evaluations and monitoring; all of this superimposed on similar demands made on this institution by the Board of Regents and Central Administration. My concern is with the escalating workload put upon the campuses by our collective efforts, all undertaken in the name of accountability. As the UW System seeks to evaluate its academic management efforts over the next two years, it will be our intent to try to reduce the impact we have had on increasing this workload by streamlining our procedures, delegating responsibility, and perhaps eliminating some steps. If we are successful in this effort, we will reduce the workload, reduce the need for increasing administrative budgets at the expense of instruction or instructional support budgets, and permit the institutions and the faculty to direct more of their energies and resources to fulfilling the purposes of instruction, research and public service for which they were created.
>
> The basic question is, "When do we reach the point of diminishing returns when the human and fiscal costs of increasingly rigorous and formal processes of monitoring and evaluation exceed the value of any changes or corrections resulting from such processes?" I have an ever increasing feeling that we have reached and perhaps gone past this point of diminishing returns and that we need to give greater emphasis to the concept of delegation . . . unless this dismal prospect of consuming vast quantities of time and resources, the latter of which is becoming an endangered species, in watching and monitoring each other and with our productivity measures being the number of audits, surveys, and reviews we complete and the number and size of the reports that ensue.
>
> All of us need to be worrying about the increasing fiscal and human costs associated with these activities and the increasing possibility that our zeal for accountability may serve to strangle institutional initiative, inventiveness and innovation which in the past have been the hallmarks of great educational institutions and systems.

Earlier, in 1975, an attempt by the Legislative Audit Bureau, a staff arm of the Wisconsin legislature, to do a program audit at the University's Madison campus was successfully repulsed by the Board of Regents of the UW System. Instead, the Legislative Audit Bureau was confined to an examination of Madison's and the System's procedures for program evaluation.

The Nebraska legislature created a Postsecondary Education Advisory Committee in 1977, made up of members of its Budget and Education Committees. Through this Committee, the legislature itself acts as the overall governing board for public higher education in the state.

The most important issue of governance, then, is the tension between institutional autonomy and centralized control. Attempts by state legislatures and executive agencies to control costs—for example, efforts to avoid what is seen as wasteful duplication of programs or to increase teaching loads or student-faculty ratios—will be regarded as infringements on academic freedom and institutional autonomy. Perhaps the best way to frame this issue is: can an agreement be reached that specifies those issues to which the state government has a reasonable and legitimate responsibility for oversight and those to which, for the good of both actors, state government must have a "hands off" policy?

In part this is a matter of organization, and a strong coordinating board or statewide governing board can act as an intermediary which stands between the elected politicians and their staffs—who are ultimately responsible for how public money is spent—on the one hand, and the academic institutions on the other, representing each to the other. But organization alone is not sufficient, as the contrasting examples of Wisconsin and California show. In addition, the actors must have the desire and capacity to use the organizational design in accordance to its purposes, rather than seeking to circumvent it.

A second broad issue of great importance is how state support should be allocated among competing sectors of public higher education within a state during a period of fiscal stringency and retrenchment. Cutbacks in funding can be distributed more or less equally among the institutions with the highest academic standards or the greatest popularity, at the expense of the weaker units within the system. Of particular interest is whether "flagship" institutions will be able to maintain their fiscal and qualitative dominance, and to what extent competition for students and funds between state college and community college systems will weaken both, as the mission of each comes to resemble that of the other more closely.

This question again turns on issues of government organization. Today most public institutions receive the bulk of their funds on the basis of formulas geared to enrollment. Under conditions of expansion, these formulas served well. In the period of contraction now beginning, they threaten to spread fiscal malnutrition more or less uniformly, with negative effects on the quality of all institutions, both directly, and through the incentive to compete for students by lowering standards. Alternative funding mechanisms that provided a substantial part of the budget of each institution in a way that did not fluctuate with enrollment would diminish these negative effects. However, they would be defensible only if there were an organization (in each state) that had the power both to monitor quality standards and recommend shutting institutions down on rational criteria, when sustained declines in enrollment indicated the need to do so.

### Federal Regulations in General

At the federal level, the very pervasiveness of legislative enactments and administrative rules makes the subject of regulation a difficult one to grasp. At one level of analysis each regulatory rule could be systematically tested against such criteria as:

1. Does it serve a socially desirable end?
2. Are the means actually effective in achieving the end?
3. Are the costs of administration, enforcement, compliance as low as possible and reasonable in relation to the value of the ends?
4. Is the distribution of benefits and burdens fair?

The information requirements for such an analysis are enormous and do not seem achievable in any finite time.

It is some help to follow the tripartite classification of regulation introduced earlier. Regulations of the third type, governing the receipt and disbursement of federal moneys, are part of the programs of research support and student aid to which they apply. Most of the regulations of the second type are specific to medical education and biomedical research. Thus, regulations of the first class, applicable broadly to organized activity in our society, are the kind that are most appropriate to discuss in general terms.

Initially, regulatory policies in this category developed within the context of business organizations. The regulations governing the employee-employer relationship (wages, hours, pensions, safety) are good examples of such policies. The initial antibias policies were developed similarly within a business context. The forerunner of the present Executive

Order 11246, barring racial discrimination by governmental contractors, was aimed primarily at employment practices in the construction industry.

Two major changes in governmental policy account for the increasing regulation of the academic enterprise in the past fifteen years. One is the *extension* of regulations applicable to business organizations to academic institutions not previously covered. The second is the growth of new regulation governing activities associated with the receipt of federal funds that from the outset did not *exempt* academic institutions. The record, therefore, shows a deliberate governmental policy to regulate all organizations, academic or otherwise, alike.

Two broad policy questions can be raised about all these regulations. First, are there good and persuasive reasons for exempting colleges and universities from their reach? Second, if there are not, are the procedures of enforcement applicable to the business sector equally appropriate when extended to colleges and universities? Both questions assume the validity of the regulatory purposes for the larger society, not because they cannot be questioned—since there are those who do—but because that appears to be an issue which our political processes have settled.

For the purpose of these questions, it is helpful further to subdivide the first of the three classes of regulation, again in three. The first subdivision comprises the complex of laws and regulation defining and prohibiting discrimination, insofar as they apply to faculty, senior administrators, and students, but not clerical, technical, and maintenance staffs. The second includes the obligations on employers to bargain in good faith about terms and conditions of employment with properly elected representatives of their employees, again only so far as it applies to faculty and senior administrative employees. The third subclass includes all other regulatory legislation and rules which apply broadly to organized activity on a large scale. Its major exemplars are other laws and regulations applying to the employment relation, including the Social Security Act, the Fair Labor Standards Act, the Occupational Health and Safety Act, the Employees Retirement and Income Security Act, and laws and regulations designed to protect the environment in respect to air and water pollution and the like.

The regulatory policies represented in this third subclass share some common characteristics. They generally relate to the health, safety, or welfare of individuals, particularly employees, but also other persons associated (however tangentially) with the academic community. They are applicable to all organizations and thereby affect their operating costs but do not affect the structure and functions of colleges and universities in an important way. The problems associated with increased cost burdens are not negligible in the resource-scarce world of higher education. However, regulations which primarily affect costs pose very different problems for analysis and policy than those touching structure and function. The only plausible grounds that can be advanced for treating higher education differently in respect to this kind of regulation is that the cost burdens they impose cannot be sustained. But if this argument is plausible, it is only barely so and falls short of carrying conviction. This is so for two reasons. First, the costs involved are modest; including Social Security taxes—the largest item in the bill—they might amount to a 5 percent element in the average institution's operating budget. Second, recalling the underlying assumption that these measures are here to stay for the rest of society, it is neither free nor fair to insist that academic institutions be exempted from these costs. It is not free because of the costs in the quality of the staff, especially nonacademic staff, such an exemption would produce; it is not fair because it would require that academe's lowest paid employees absorb the costs by foregoing the benefits of regulations, rather than passing the costs on to be shared among faculty, senior administrators, students and their parents, and the taxpayers of the fifty states. Finally, it is almost certainly politically impossible.

In contrast to regulations which primarily affect costs, those in the first and second subclasses impinge directly on two of the central processes peculiar to higher education by constraining the selection of faculty or students. Both antidiscrimination policies and collective bargaining create similar tensions within the academic system. Both are seen as threatening the basic structure. The characteristic organizational model for the university or college is that of a guild of scholars who collectively choose and train their own members and who choose from among those who wish to become students. They also decide what is to be taught and how it is to be taught. This organizational model has evolved to provide the sustaining environment for the intellectual activity that is the heart of higher learning. Not every college or university is fully patterned on the model, but it remains the paradigm for academic institutions in general.

While the academic world is broadly sympathetic to the policy goals served by this class of regulation, it is also generally fearful that the methods now used to achieve these goals, especially those defined as affirmative action, are threatening the historic foundations of academic organization. Particularly, the central concept of collegial decision by academic peers is perceived to be threatened by regulations affecting employment borrowed from union/industry experience and regulations affecting educational processes borrowed from public school desegregation cases.

It has been observed that disagreement concerning the proper means to achieve ends may mask disagreement concerning the ends themselves. It may be equally fair to observe that such disagreement in this case is an echo of a more basic American dilemma. The tension between the academic concept of choice by collegial decision of the qualified and the populist concept of representative entitlement is an expression of a deeper duality in American values—traditional individualism versus a new egalitarianism. In the current controversy surrounding the regulation of higher education, the basic dilemmas arising from these dual values are thrown into sharp focus.

The policy goals of nondiscrimination and equal opportunity served by these regulations have great social importance, as evidenced by their repeated ratification in new legislation by Congress and the continued reinforcement of their purposes by the courts. Exemptions from them for the academic sector, on whatever grounds, present a question of the greatest difficulty. This is even more clear when the function of higher education in providing an indispensible channel of access to high status and high income occupations is considered. Further, total exemption would be unwise, as well as unlikely. Statutory enactments and judicial rulings have, in fact, caused academics, as well as the rest of society, to broaden the outlook of their collective decision-making process.

If exemption is ruled out, is it possible to adapt the regulatory processes more closely to the characteristic features of academe? The agencies that enforce the policies now ignore or discount the differences between academic and business organizations. Can these differences be respected within the regulatory process and still achieve the statutory ends? How? Some possibilities are sketched below.

With respect to higher education, should there be unification and consolidation of the laws and regulations concerning nondiscrimination and equal opportunity? At present there are at least a dozen relevant statutes and executive orders, and their responsibility for enforcement is divided among a half-dozen different agencies and bureaus. There are two aspects to this issue. The first is whether the standards—the content —of the nondiscrimination mandates should be made uniform; the second, whether the enforcement responsibility for such unified or separate standards should itself be consolidated. To what extent would such unification and consolidation promote the desired differentiation between the regulation of business and higher education? Would the desired differentiation be promoted through the development of a corps of administrators with continuing and exclusive responsibility for the enforcement of such regulatory policies within institutions of higher education? Would such a corps better reconcile the goals of academe and the goals of regulation?

Beyond unification of standards and consolidation of enforcement responsibility, what measures can be devised to make academic institutions more responsive to public goals as expressed in statutes and legal rulings and yet preserve the collegial concepts of the present structure? Presently the enforcement initiative lies primarily with government agencies. The academic community is involved in the process only in a defensive, reactive manner. What methods other than more regulatory involvement can be developed to give the academic community more responsibility for itself?

Academic self-evaluation in light of publicly enunciated goals might be one step in this direction. Every academic institution might be obliged to publish an annual self-assessment of its performance over the whole range of nondiscrimination goals. Then the initial burden of assessing and evaluating the impact of its decisions would lie with the academic community itself. Disclosure by means of such an annual report would force institutional self-analysis as well as public accountability. Such a process does not avoid regulation, but it might give more "credit" for honest effort and self-evaluation than the present regulatory mode and in the end pay more respect to the present structure and function of academic organizations.

Disclosure and self-assessment alone would not be sufficient. Self-assessment should be combined with the creation of grievance and mediation machinery, to provide a means for the informal and nonadversarial resolution of specific complaints with respect to these policies. Useful mediation machinery requires the existence of some organization(s) to which both aggrieved individuals or groups and colleges and universities could and would turn when internal grievance procedures failed to provide satisfactory resolution of complaints.

Another aspect of regulation deserving attention is the appropriateness of the sanctions available to the enforcement agencies. Many of the laws relating to nondiscrimination link the statutory command to the receipt of federal funds. The penalty for noncompliance—as defined by the enforcement agency—then becomes the cut-off of federal funds, a drastic sanction indeed. Its all-or-nothing quality limits its usefulness; both the enforcement agency and the institution see it as somewhat unreal. Though a cut-off of federal funds has been threatened a number of times, to date it has never been carried out. Some degree of flexibility and choice in possible remedies appears necessary to make the sanctions more useful in achieving the policy goals of the statutes.

None of this, of course, would change the present legal protections accorded individual rights. The legal command will still be required, both to settle those disputes which remain unsolved by the steps sketched above and to provide an incentive for the institutions to maintain their own initiative in a committed and effective way. What the new procedures would do is to defer the call on the formal legal machinery to a later rather than an earlier stage in the process of dispute resolutions, with the aim of developing institutional initiative as a substitute for administrative regulatory direction.

With these changes, the administration of the nondiscrimination statutes and regulations in higher education would in some respects come to resemble more closely that common in regulated industries, where such agencies as the SEC and FCC are expected to develop both an intimate knowledge of the industries they regulate and some concern for the impact of regulation on the performance of the industry. The single-purpose, single-goal agencies now responsible for enforcement, such as the Office for Civil Rights in DHEW, lack both the specialized knowledge and the concern. However, the emphasis on institutional initiative and the creation of a series of informal steps in dispute resolution before the application of formal, legally binding proceedings are not typical in the federally regulated sectors of industry.

The successful operation of such negotiating and mediating procedures would also involve a change in the role of the courts as regulatory agencies. Because aggrieved individuals, especially in situations involving allegations of forbidden discrimination on grounds of race, sex, and —more recently—age, and handicap, seek direct redress in the courts, rather than relying on the agencies of the executive branch to vindicate their rights, the courts have become major actors in the educational scene. Such was the *Bakke* case, the longest-lived and most extensive litigation in which higher education was involved since *Adams* v. *Califano* (the case brought in 1970 by the NAACP against the Secretary of DHEW to force the Secretary to enforce Title VI in six state systems of higher education). The formality of court procedures, their expense, the inevitable intensification of conflictual elements that the adversary process entails, all warrant the search for ways to diminish the role of the courts.

The strategy of such a change must focus on postponement, on making litigation the last rather than the first step in the process of dispute settlement, since the constitutional role of the courts as ultimate arbiters of the legal rights of individuals remains. Here again, analogy of the traditional forms of industrial regulation may be opposite. Appeals to the courts in those areas can take place only after administrative remedies have been exhausted. In the context of higher education, these administrative remedies would have to be understood as giving a central place to the informal procedures already discussed.

The second subclass of regulations, that concerning the obligations of colleges and universities to bargain collectively with their faculties, remains. At the moment, experience with faculty unionism is still brief. Most of it has occurred in public institutions, under state statutes defining the collective bargaining rights of public employees. At present, about 600 campuses—about 20 percent of the total number—have collective bargaining agreements; 87 percent of these are public institutions. The legal status of faculty unions in private institutions is now in doubt, since the Court of Appeals for the Second Circuit decided in 1978 (*Yeshiva* v. *National Labor Relations Board* [*NLRB*]) that the faculty of Yeshiva University were supervisors and managers, exempt from the National Labor Relations Act's command to allow union organization of employees and oblige the employer—the university—to bargain with the union that succeeds in a representative election. (At this writing, that decision has been accepted for review by the Supreme Court.)

Depending on how faculty unions actually behave, the argument can be made for assimilating this set of questions to either the first subclass of regulations, and allowing the same rules and procedures to apply to higher education as to employer-employee relations in other kinds of organizations, or the third, and seeking either exemption or special procedures.

This issue turns on whether unionization is or is not compatible with the pattern of collegial government by a guild of masters, described above as the essential model for the core of the college and university. This cannot be settled by abstract argument, and experience, so far, is too brief to provide an answer. An optimistic view of the outcome is more appropriate to the private than the public sector of higher education. In the latter, continuing rapid growth of union organization seems likely. Where it occurs, unionization will reinforce the tendency toward centralization of decision-making at the highest levels of state government. Faculty unions like those of other public employees, will more and more seek governors and legislators as their bargaining partners, rather than campus administrators or boards of regents.

### Medical Education

The government's involvement with medical education and the medical schools themselves goes much deeper than it does with the rest of higher education for two reasons. First, there is an intimate association of medical education with the provision of medical care in hospitals affiliated with—and frequently owned and operated by—the medical schools. Thus the schools, and their parental universities, have a role as a major provider of an essential service to the general public: hospital care for acute and complex illnesses, which has no parallel in other parts of the university. Then the costs of medical education are high, and the federal government covers a large share of the costs, directly and indirectly. Direct support comes in the form of capitation, student aid, and various training grants. Indirect support comes through research money and also Medicare and Medicaid reimbursement for hospital care. Even more important, manpower planning and manpower direction play an increasing role in federal policy to an extent not found in other areas of higher education. This, in turn, reflects the increasing concern of the federal government with the quantity, quality, and distribution of health care. Finally, further extension of federal responsibility for the availability and cost of medical care is almost certain to occur in the near future, although what form it will take remains to be seen. This, in turn, can lead to more far-reaching efforts at federal manpower planning in medicine and more involvement in medical education.

Four sets of issues are the loci of strain in government medical school relations: the cost and financing of medical education, access to medical schools, the supply of physicians, and their distribution among specialties. All are interlocked.

The first set of issues concerns the relation of the costs of education to those of research and patient care. At present, it is difficult to separate these costs, yet there is continuing pressure from both the states and the federal government to do so, for both governments believe that such a segregation might help reduce patient care costs. Increasingly detailed scrutiny of expenditures of federal research funds is having the same effect. To the extent that these efforts are successful, the place of research grant and patient care dollars will have to be filled either by higher tuitions or increased direct federal and state support for medical education.

This raises the question of who should pay the costs of medical education. A situation in which places in medical school are severely rationed, incomes of physicians are high, and the cost of education heavily subsidized from public funds seems paradoxical. Should the students pay the full costs of their education, with the aid of loans and income-contingent repayment schemes? Or should tuitions be kept low and repayments take the form of national service for a certain period following completion of training? If this scheme is used, should tuitions and federal contributions be more nearly uniform for all medical schools, instead of the wide variations in private, federal, and state support now shown?

These questions in turn lead to the issues revolving around access and supply. The high ratio of qualified candidates for admission to places in North American medical schools will continue to generate public pressures on the admissions process. Since candidates over thirty are almost never accepted, age discrimination will probably surface as an issue. Americans who fail to get places here will train abroad in increasing numbers in schools of questionable quality. This raises questions of equity, since Americans who train abroad receive no public subsidy. Further, the effect of retaining strict controls on domestic medical school admissions is to increase the number of physicians trained outside the standards of the American medical profession.

How should the number of new entrants into medicine be determined? It is now the product of a combination of controls: those exercised by the Association of American Medical Colleges on the number of places in accredited medical schools and those exercised by the agencies of federal government on the terms by which funds for medical education are provided. Over the past fifteen years, federal pressure and money have led to an increase in the annual supply of new physicians by nearly 50 percent. The consensus of the profession, the medical schools, and federal officials concerned with health care seems to be that the supply is now ample and may even prove excessive in the near future. This conclusion rests heavily on the view that a further increase in physician supply will raise the aggregate costs of medical care, as well as require costly new investments to provide for training still more physicians.

Closely linked to the aggregate supply issue is that of the distribution of physicians by specialty and location of practice. It is widely agreed, even by those who believe aggregate supply is sufficient, that medical schools and teaching hospitals have been turning out too many specialists and too few primary care physicians. Recent federal legislation has aimed at correcting this imbalance, and primary care is receiving new emphasis in medical school curricula. Similar questions arise about the geographic concentrations of physicians in suburban and upper-income areas, so that both rural and low-income urban residents have little access to medical care.

A central theme in all these related questions is the role of the federal government as manpower planner in medicine. That role is now large, and the present direction of policy is certain to increase it. The consequence will be increasing federal intervention into more and more aspects of medical education. The broad question is thus whether there is an alternative direction of more reliance on the market in regard to numbers and in self-financing and loans with regard to cost that would promise less government involvement.

### Research Support

The federal government is the main patron of academic science. Federal grants and contracts for scientific and technical research in academic institutions (including university-managed federal research centers) account for nearly one-third of all federal funds for higher education. The federal agencies that provide this support do not, by and large, conceive of it as part of a broader higher education policy. Rather, they regard the support of academic research as the chief instrument for providing an essential public good: the maintenance of a healthy research establishment that produces a broad stream of contributions to the growth of scientific and technical knowledge. Over the past three decades this federal-academic partnership for the performance of research has been enormously successful, both in advancing the United States to a position of unquestioned world leadership in basic science and in generating scientific and technical knowledge that can be applied to improve the nation's health, prosperity, and military security.

In spending public money to support academic science, the federal government has a clear responsibility for certain kinds of oversight and regulation:

1. to determine how much public funds are expended in support of academic research, and to what broad policy goals the nation's research effort is directed;
2. to ensure that the recipients are held accountable to the public for the proper use of those funds; and
3. to ensure that federally sponsored research activities do not pose threats to the public safety and welfare.

At the same time, it is widely agreed that scientific research is most productive and advances most rapidly when technical judgments as to the values, methods, and risks of research—that is, judgments that determine which particular research projects should receive support, and how each project should conduct its research—are left largely in the hands of the scientific community. Moreover, federal regulations place burdens on those who comply with them by diverting their resources from the activity that is regulated to the process of compliance. Both of these factors place limits on the extent to which the federal government should regulate academic research—limits which it has overstepped in recent years.

One finds examples of excessive federal oversight and regulation generating problems in every aspect of the research relationship, beginning with the process by which research proposals are submitted and reviewed. In recent years, the burden on investigators of preparing and submitting research proposals has increased substantially. This is partly the result of changes in funding patterns: over the past ten years, as funding agencies have decreased both the dollar amount (in real dollars) and the duration of awards, investigators have found it necessary to submit proposals more frequently and also to submit multiple proposals for a single project. But much of the burden is the result of agency requirements for extremely lengthy, detailed, and specific proposals which investigators claim add little or nothing to the quality of the proposal, its prospects for success, or the ability of peer reviewers or agency program officers to evaluate it.

The peer review process itself is coming under increasing scrutiny. The General Accounting Office (GAO) recently recommended that the National Science Foundation set up detailed procedures to govern the ways in which its program officers reach decisions, including how they make use of peer reviews. GAO's view is that only by establishing such procedures and subjecting them to outside audit can the fairness of the peer review process be guaranteed. The practical result of such rigid procedures would be to substitute the judgments of government officials and auditors for those of the scientific peers.

Another aspect of overregulation is an increase in the extent of financial oversight—an insistence on documenting in great detail how every dollar that supports research is spent, an unwillingness to reimburse those costs which the federal auditors believe are documented with insufficient precision or which they believe do not relate closely enough to the actual conduct of research, and a desire to standardize both federal oversight and university accounting practices.

Academic administrators must recognize, for their part, that some degree of financial oversight is entirely appropriate and inevitable. In the past they have enjoyed relatively lax enforcement of regulations governing the handling of federal research funds. Some universities still do not have accounting control systems which are adequate to ensure that research dollars are actually used for the purposes intended by the funding agencies. At least a few universities have had a casual attitude toward charges against grants, which could result in small expenses which had no relation to research inadvertently being charged to research grants.

However, this does not excuse the excesses of federal financial oversight, exemplified by the regulations governing effort reporting. These regulations require all personnel involved in a federally sponsored research project to document the amount of effort which they contribute to that project. That investigators should be required to adhere to some standard of minimum effort is reasonable and proper, but the Office of Management and Budget and the federal audit agencies, in enforcing and monitoring these regulations, have required an unrealistic level of detail and precision. They fail to give sufficient recognition to the fact that an investigator's work on a particular research project is not perfectly separable from his work on other projects, his teaching, or his work on faculty committees. To a large extent these are joint products, and auditors cannot, in principle, distinguish with perfect precision between those hours of effort that are allocable to research and those that are not. Furthermore, federal auditors and regulators fail to recognize that the investigator's scientific curiosity and his desire to establish his reputation among his peers provide a far more powerful incentive for him to devote adequate effort to his research (and, in general, is more effective at ensuring that he uses the research funds at his disposal wisely and properly) than any form of financial oversight. The best, and perhaps the only effective control over the investigator's level of effort and his use of federal funds is that any failure to devote adequate effort to a project or any misuse of federal research funds, will be reflected in the quality of the research produced and will weigh against him in the peer review of his subsequent proposals.

Finally, federal officials fail to give sufficient weight to the cost of financial oversight, both in terms of the dollar cost of compliance and of the loss in research productivity that occurs when investigators are distracted by oversight requirements. Given the strong controls exerted by the peer pressures inherent in the research enterprise, there is a heavy burden of proof on federal regulators to demonstrate that additional government controls are worth the costs that they impose.

A different set of issues is involved in efforts to regulate the substance of research. One such issue is exemplified by the regulation of recombinant DNA research. The basis for regulation is traditional, and eminently reasonable: public health and safety. The problems arise from conflicts in judgment over what risks are and from higher level conflicts over whose opinions and judgments deserve credit in weighing those risks. In this case, the consensus of the relevant scientific community was followed, and the adoption of wider and more stringent regulations was forestalled.

A more difficult set of problems is posed by the complex of regulations involving experimentation with human subjects. Here there are genuine conflicts of value involved, as well as problems of judging risks in the light of uncertain value. How the importance of the knowledge that investigators wish to gain and the privacy and personal welfare that potential subjects wish to preserve can be balanced is not an issue for scientists alone to resolve. The regulations that the Department of HEW has proposed to deal with human subjects, which would require that experimentation on human subjects be reviewed by Institutional Review Boards composed partly of nonscientists, provide a reasonable mechanism for deciding this kind of issue. However, the regulations are so broadly worded as to require oversight of investigations, such as social science interviews and sample surveys, that clearly pose no risk to human subjects. Furthermore, the regulations set forth procedures for detailed HEW auditing and oversight of this review process. This oversight, like the financial oversight discussed previously, is unlikely to improve the protection provided to human subjects by any significant amount, while it is more likely to increase significantly the financial burden of regulation and its intrusiveness into the research process.

Another body of regulations governs the use of hazardous substances in the research laboratory. Such regulations can be imposed without unreasonably constraining academic research, as evidenced by the wide acceptance of federal standards on the handling of radioactive substances. However, some of the more recently developed regulations, such as those proposed by the Occupational Safety and Health Administration (OSHA) to cover the use of hazardous substances and potential carcinogens, do raise a problem. The OSHA rules were written primarily to deal with the use of hazardous substances in industrial processes, which typically use many fewer different substances in vastly greater quantities than are encountered in a scientific laboratory. These rules need to be reexamined before they can reasonably be extended to govern the use of research quantities of potentially harmful substances.

### Student Aid

The largest part of federal support for higher education comes in the form of student aid. The several programs provide money for eligible students enrolled in eligible programs in eligible institutions. Somehow these layers of eligibility must be defined and monitored. The natural consequence is thus a large grant of regulatory authority to the Office of Education.

So far, this regulatory authority has been relatively little exercised. Following the enactment of the Education Amendments of 1972, the main effort of the administrators has been to "get money out." By 1976 this general spirit had created predictable problems, and a central ingredient of the Education Amendments of 1976 was to refine the monitoring of the system. Perhaps most significantly, the commissioner's authority both to admit institutions to and exclude them from the programs was extended. Substantially misrepresenting "the nature of its educational program, its financial charges, or the employability of its graduates" were activities intended to invite exclusion.

One story—admittedly extreme but nevertheless true—gives the flavor of what is at issue from the viewpoint of the guardians of the public purse. There exists a private liberal arts college, duly accredited by one of the major regional accrediting commissions, which has, among its offerings, an off-campus program in a home for the elderly. The program involved "read-aloud" sessions twice a week, and for participating in this program the elderly students receive twelve credits per semester and are thus "full-time." Having social security benefits as their only source of income, the students qualify for maximum federal and state grants totalling $2,900 per student per year. When, in the course of their work, state auditors raised questions about the program, the accrediting association and the relevant association of private colleges responded with accusations of bureaucratic meddling in the academic process. The program continues.

Regulations to implement the 1976 legislation were published during the summer of 1978. Among others, they included—either in final form or as suggestions—the following:

1. institutional exclusion if the dropout rate exceeds 33 percent during the year,
2. institutional exclusion if more than 50 percent of the students had federally guaranteed loans,
3. institutions required to keep detailed admissions records on all students,
4. institutions required to publish employment rates of their graduates,
5. institutions required to keep Basic Equal Opportunity Grant (BEOG) and campus-based funds in separate bank accounts,
6. institutions required to bond or guarantee 10 percent of the federal funds which they disburse, and
7. students required to maintain satisfactory progress as a condition to retaining federal aid.

None of these seems, in itself, outrageous. The second, aimed at degree-factories and proprietary vocational schools established in response to the availability of federal money, may seem inappropriate to honorable institutions; the fourth is difficult for the traditional liberal arts college or undergraduate college of a university, a large fraction of whose graduates go on to professional education at another institution. The third, fifth, sixth, and seventh represent what any well-managed institution would itself prescribe.

Given the heterogeneity of eligible institutions—the whole spectrum of the "collegiate sector" from community colleges to research universities, plus vocational and technical schools, both nonprofit and proprietary—it is hardly surprising that a set of regulations designed to cover them all and guard against potential abuse will appear unnecessarily intrusive to some. Yet, it is unrealistic to expect that public money should be provided without some safeguard against fraud and abuse, all the more so in the era of Proposition 13.

A final example of the need for regulation in the context of student aid is provided by the problem of default in the National Direct Student Loan Program (NDSL). Initially supported by annual federal appropriations, the program was intended eventually to become self-supporting as a revolving fund. In the mature phase HEW loans were to be roughly balanced by repayments. This goal has not yet come close to being achieved because, although some institutions have a commendable record on collections, the record in the aggregate is dismal. For the most part, institutions have simply assumed that Congress would continue to appropriate what the students failed to repay, a political calculation which has turned out—unfortunately, in some ways—to have been absolutely correct. More recently the mood is changing, and there are calls for accountability. The colleges are beginning to take their role in collection more seriously. Unfortunately, they are doing so only in the context of external discipline.

The responsibility for this situation is not entirely the institutions'; the Congress must share the blame. It is hardly surprising that universities and colleges are not particularly effective collectors of student loans, once the borrowers have left the campus. Congress certainly can be blamed for having assigned the task to the institutions; but they need not have accepted it. External pressures in the shape of the Secretary of Health, Education, and Welfare, and dramatic exposes on television have led to some improvements. A longer-term solution, however, is more likely to come from giving the responsibility to a more suitable set of agents.

*Lloyd H. Elliott*

# 4

# The University
# and Special Interest Groups

Groups with special interests have long influenced what is taught in the university. During the colonial period our institutions of higher learning were persuaded by the special interest groups whom they served —clergy, teachers, and public servants—to build a curriculum which would serve the interests of potential practitioners in those fields. That such "fields" were very broad academically seemed only to give the colleges more flexibility, and certainly not to separate the campuses from these "special interests."

Since those beginnings special interests have expanded to include business, labor, government, professions, subprofessions, public interests, technical, vocational, and an inexhaustible array of groups within our society. The constant pressures, influences, and demands of these groups offer both strengths and weaknesses to the university. Even the most rational responses of higher education to these many pressures may frequently serve, even with the best of intentions, to erode the autonomy of the university. Since the special interests represent the reality of the

LLOYD H. ELLIOTT *is president of* The George Washington University. *Formerly president of the University of Maine, Dr. Elliott has been a professor of educational administration. He is an officer of numerous academic associations and director of several major corporations. Dr. Elliott is also author (or coauthor) of some thirty-five articles and papers in the field of education.*

world today, the university must be a part of that world while, at the same time, remaining at arms length in order to serve better the very world which sustains it.

This chapter will be concerned primarily with four types of externalities. These include:

1. *Institutional Accreditation,* or the process whereby the *overall* quality of an institution is determined and which has been carried out with generally benign effects by the university community itself for the benefit of its members;
2. *Specialized Accreditation,* which is concerned with the quality of a *particular program* such as law and medicine and which has been carried out— often with mixed results—by the universities and the professions themselves;
3. *The Relationship of Business, Industry, and Labor to the University* and, as far as labor is concerned, with the significant manifestation of its interest through faculty unionization; and
4. *The Role of Foundations in Higher Education* and the power they can exercise for both good and mischievous ends.

Before moving directly into the analysis, a few caveats should be noted. Exposing some of the dangers which flow from the accreditation process might lead the unwary to conclude that federal or state regulation is the best answer. Such an inference is precisely contrary to what is in mind. Rather, it is the relationship of the academic to the federal government that has become increasingly uneasy; the academicians' encounters with officials from the U.S. Office of Education, the Veteran's Administration the Affirmative Action agencies, the Federal Trade Commission, and others have deepened the conviction that, for all its weaknesses, voluntary accreditation is to be preferred over the coercive power of government. There is irony in the situation. The professoriate has been in the forefront of the movements toward government control of business and union activities. Only now is it learning the practical meaning of such controls—and what it learns it does not like.

A second caveat is to be borne in mind when pressures from business, labor, and foundations are viewed. Each represents a legitimate and necessary institution in our society. Since trained manpower is absolutely essential for a complex industrialized society, it follows naturally that such institutions will seek to influence the one that is primarily responsible for producing the human products required. If the academic community sometimes feels it is being seduced from its lofty goals by these outside forces, it must only be recalled that as the song has it—it takes two to tango. Institutions are bought only when there is a willingness to sell, and the integrity of a university must shine most clearly when the outsider's price is high and its purpose low.

## Institutional Accreditation

### BEGINNINGS AND DEVELOPMENTS

Accreditation of universities had its informal beginning in the exchanges of correspondence among the first colleges and universities; formal accreditation came in the late nineteenth century and full development by the end of the first quarter of the twentieth. It was made necessary by the growth and expansion of higher education which required institutions to serve students and professors who moved from one part of the country to another or who found it necessary—during the course of the years of formal education—to move up the educational ladder: from grammar to secondary school, from secondary school to college, and from college to university. As one institution "recognized" students and/or teachers from another school or campus, the concept of "accrediting" was born. When a college president or a professor wrote to admit or to invite a new student or colleague to join a given institution, recognition was extended to the institution, as well as to the invited individual. If that person performed at the level expected by the one who initiated the invitation, other professors were called to follow.

As secondary schools and colleges sprang up, it became increasingly difficult to keep abreast of developments in their various programs and in the quality of instruction; further, as more and more students enrolled at all educational levels, the administration of individual entrance examinations or the personal interview became increasingly burdensome. Geography was another factor which had to be considered. Students could not travel half-way across the continent, with the time and expense required in those days, without some assurance that admission would be accorded them upon arrival on the chosen campus. It became clear that means must be found to assess the student's educational achievement that would be acceptable to a university in another part of the country. In this context were the regional associations born. If the institution was accredited, prospective students and faculty, as well as other universities, knew that a certain quality had been achieved.

ROLE OF REGIONAL AGENCIES

For many years the entire country has been divided and served by regional accrediting associations. It was 1913 when the first listing of "accredited" colleges and universities appeared—the work of the newly created North Central Association of Colleges and Secondary Schools. Geographically, this regional group consisted of the upper mid-continent states from Ohio to the Rocky Mountains. Membership has always been, and continues to remain, voluntary. Membership has, however, come to be an important asset to the institution and therefore is vigorously pursued: accreditation opens doors to students and graduates for transfer, for further study, for licensure. The regional associations employ professional staff; with necessary funds coming from the member institutions, and have governing boards which, in recent years, have added public members to those who come from the schools and colleges. Sometimes accused of being self-serving, the associations have nonetheless worked effectively to strengthen America's educational institutions.

The chief role of the regional associations is the assessment of the *overall quality* of the school or college. Such assessment is carried out by a visiting team of volunteers who are experienced in similar educational institutions. The important work, therefore, is done voluntarily by colleagues within the same profession; during the visit accreditors often talk to trustees and administrators, faculty and students, staff and alumni; they check financial records and grading practices; they visit libraries and laboratories. By the end of a visitation a sophisticated team knows the basic strengths and weaknesses of an institution. Over the years untold services have been freely given by thousands of volunteers who serve on the visiting committees to institutions already accredited and assess the adequacy of newly established institutions.

Procedures for institutional accreditation are extensive. The lengthy self-study that is usually required includes reports on the training and experience of faculty, the level and achievement of admitted students, extensive information on curriculum, and a clear statement of requirements for graduation. In addition, the institution is usually required to set forth its own acknowledged objectives, outline the ways by which such objectives will be achieved, and present evidence of successes and failures. Needless to say, each institution is required to set forth its current resources—libraries, laboratories, classrooms, and related facilities—as well as operating funds and prospective income. Costs for a review of an accredited institution or of the application of a new institution are borne by the institution itself.

In more recent years regional associations—now six in number and covering all states and territories of the country—are examining in greater detail the claims which an institution may make through publications and advertising on behalf of its programs. As institutions have become increasingly competitive in recruitment of students, the associations have assumed greater responsibility as protectors of the public interest and have increasingly attempted to influence institutions on the nature and extent of such advertising. It is fair to say that governing boards have, in many cases, become far more alert to—and more active in—all the activities of the institution as a result of discussions with visiting accrediting teams and through reviews of written reports.

VOLUNTARISM, ACCOUNTABILITY, AND THE PUBLIC INTEREST

Since volunteers, coming preponderantly from the institutions themselves, have conducted the work of institutional accreditation, it is understandable that the accusation would be leveled that the entire process is one of "self-service." The task facing a visiting committee, the group formally charged with renewing or withdrawing accreditation, is a difficult and far-reaching responsibility. To illustrate: all worthy educational institutions attempt to strengthen the students' interests in things intellectual, to enhance knowledge and skills, and to foster behavioral goals which are morally and ethically sound. Establishing definitive evidence for the achievement of these and related objectives is often difficult, if not impossible. The most important decisions inevitably carry subjective judgments, opinions, and impressions as well as being shaped by volumes of objective data. An inquisitive, skeptical public may reasonably ask: what guarantees are provided to protect students from being shortchanged in the academic activities which they will pursue?

Because of the nebulous, subjective, and even temperamental evidence on which the university will be judged, it would seem that institutional autonomy and increasing accountability are on a collision course. Much of the university's work, perhaps its most vital, must be accepted on faith and less on a hard-nosed judgment of its balance sheet. That faith will inevitably be built upon reputation, but reputation rests on opinion, attitude, rumor, and myriad other subjective measures. The university must respond through greater accountability to the changing times, and voluntarism can produce the necessary manpower required to assure increased accountability—provided institutional accreditation does not become the province of government.

All of this suggests that facts, objective data, and quantitative matters are necessary to the accrediting process; in practice, however, it is in the process of *judging* such data that the power over the university is to be found. If the critical judgments are made by informed, sensitive, and authoritative peers from other campuses, complemented by interested and concerned representatives of the broader public, the concept of voluntary accreditation can offer results which are positive for all constituencies. Volunteer evaluators, as visiting teams are constituted, have rendered vital guidance over the years, and their efforts have resulted in significant improvement to universities.

However, still more remains to be done. Yet how grossly accreditation can be sought is illustrated by excerpts from a letter to the president of a large private eastern university:

> . . . Would [your] University be interested in working with us to develop a western branch in Los Angeles? . . . We propose to start out as an accredited institution by existing under sponsorship of . . . an already established . . . university. . . . Your university, because of its outstanding reputation, would be an ideal choice for such a venture.

CODES OF CONDUCT

One promising response to such invitations to cheap compromise is an institutional code of conduct. Interest is growing in this idea, and several major associations in higher education are already using some forms of ethical codes. These include the Council for the Advancement and Support of Education and the American Association of Collegiate Registrars and Admissions Officers. The constant threat of further government regulation intensifies the pressure toward this development. In fact, some feel that promulgation of a good-conduct code by the higher educational community is the best answer to threats of further government intrusion because the code would represent another step toward more effective self-regulation.

To cynics a code of good conduct developed by, and applied to, the higher education community itself falls short of the desired accountability; nevertheless, such codes have been helpful in other areas of endeavor. Certainly such a course is preferable to placing full responsibility for accountability in the hands of government. Governmental oversight, supervision, and regulation, at any level, are actions viewed with increasing fear by many citizens; at the educational level they become particularly ominous because freedom of thought (including the right to criticize government itself) can be jeopardized.

The general public is aware that standards of ethical practice have long been recognized by many of the professions as important to the behavior of practitioners. Qualitative statements of performance have also become important, and the proverbial "would you buy a used car from this man?" is a common test. As a consequence, organizations have given serious attention to ethical codes in order that potential abuses may be policed and the public's confidence enhanced. With the growing strength of the consumer movement in American society, such efforts may be expected to increase. To assure institutional probity, a triangular compromise is needed among consumers, government regulators, and the professions or institutions.

In the case of universities it is no longer to be taken for granted that each stands for the highest levels of integrity; the careless behavior of a few has become the burden of the many. Faced, therefore, with more government regulations, sharper demands of the marketplace, and, above all, the fundamental need to rid itself of unbecoming conduct, the university may indeed appropriately turn to its own code of conduct as one mechanism for self-policing.

To rally support for self-policing, the university must show by actions that included within its own ranks are those best equipped to assess both the ends and means of the university and the will to discipline those guilty of irresponsible behavior. The general public may be persuaded to accept this voluntary approach because those in the university act with dispatch and responsibility. The public's confidence, lost in recent years, may be regained. One necessary step is to have incorporated in codes clear, careful, and honest statements regarding programs and activities of the institution; accurate information on costs and services; and reliable material regarding the neighborhood and area in which students will live and travel. Recruitment of students, services to graduates, quality of faculty, library resources, and intellectual level of offerings are but some of the topics which must be defined with objectivity and precision. It may well be that the university should state "disclaimers" as well as point out possible avenues of satisfaction and advancement. May the university, for example, claim that its program in liberal arts will lead to "a more satisfying life"? Instead, should not emphasis be on what the educational programs include rather than the effects they are presumed to have upon the students life?

Furthermore, efforts to write codes must involve experts from the various programs. Admissions practices will require input from experts in admissions work; similarly student advisors, registrars, professors, and research directors will contribute. It is no longer enough to describe university operations in platitudes and inspiring adjectives. Instead, it will be necessary to point out that enrollees may find themselves isolated in the rural area without adequate transportation or that class buildings are on the street corner of the inner city where students are beset with hassles of overcrowding, traffic jams, and no parking. These suggestions are far more revolutionary than may appear. But has anyone ever read a description by the institution of its own disadvantages or what it is pledged to do about them?

The general public, perhaps through the participation of consumer groups, has much to gain from the development of bona fide university codes of conduct. The lawmaker and government bureaucrat also profit. But the most important beneficiary of an effective code of conduct would still be the university itself. Self-policing can renew integrity, restore confidence, and offer a promising avenue for recapturing some of that already lost character of the university.

CHANGING OBJECTIVES OF REGIONAL ASSOCIATIONS

Colleges and universities sometimes point out that institutional accreditation tends to whipsaw their activities as social and political winds change. While numerous illustrations may be cited, some of the more dramatic concern admissions standards. As enrollments grew following World War II, educators participating in accreditation visits constantly urged faculties and administrators to raise admissions standards. A favorite stunt was to pull from files samples of the credentials of entering classes and to question, meticulously, judgments for anyone admitted who failed to meet announced grade and test levels. The institution was thereby put on the defensive. To admit a returning veteran whose credentials were not equal to those of students coming directly from preparatory schools was considered possible cause for censure. Such factors as "maturity and motivation" were then unrecognized as important factors. Similarly, when faculty qualifications were examined, sole interest was often in the scholarly training and publication record only. Little weight was given to such practical experience outside the academic world.

By the late sixties, however, the social climate had changed and campus recruiters were encouraged to look for high-risk students. Visiting committees now put institutions on the defensive by asking: "Why don't you accept more high-risk students?" "What special support programs do you provide for inadequately prepared students?" "Isn't the college failing its responsibility when high-risk students fail?" On the faculty side, accreditors have encouraged the university to appoint more staff who could bring a *practical* approach to the classroom, could better relate to students from all walks of life and, very particularly, who understood directly the psychological and intellectual barriers which minority students faced.

The university was thus caught in the shifting tides of social and political change. The strongest institutions, financially and academically, responded with little difficulty; the weaker ones, caught in conflicting societal goals, experienced periods of unusual stress and tension. The university is by no means "out of the woods" in its search for a full reply to these shifting pressures. But the point is this: as each group imposes its particular viewpoint on the institution, authority for decision-making spreads away from the campus itself. And too often is the university a silent or passive partner.

## Accreditation for Specialized Programs

### THE PROFESSIONS AND THE UNIVERSITY

While the clergy exercised a strong influence on the university early in American history, it was the medical profession which brought the influence of specialized interests to full realization. Other professions followed suit. The result is that specialized accreditation (technical, vocational, professional, and related interests) has become one of the most difficult of all challenges to institutional autonomy. The pressures gave rise to the creation, in the early 1950s, of the National Commission on Accrediting—an organization designed to brake the proliferation of specialized programs.

Unfortunately, special programs have continued to expand at an ever increasing rate. As fields of work and study have been divided and subdivided, more special interests have made greater demands on the university. Programs in engineering now number almost 1,800; dentistry reaches more than 1,200; and nursing almost 1,100. In such a broad field as allied health, we find almost 3,000 separate programs. Whether the field is chemistry, music, journalism, or social work, specialization piled upon specialization, and since accreditation brings prestige to all training programs, it is easy to see why "programmatic review" by accrediting bodies has become an almost continuous part of campus life.

IMPACT ON THE CURRICULUM

As each specialty becomes more precise in its requirements for entry into its area of work, pressures mount on the university to offer more specialized courses and programs, often of a highly technical nature. Such action requires, in turn, institutional employment of faculty who have the expertise and skill sought by the interest group. Effective working relationships among practitioners and faculty bring new demands for offering programs which "qualify" for graduation, certification, and licensure. At the undergraduate level the requirement of a common area of knowledge becomes increasingly difficult under the weight of continuing specialization. It is not uncommon to find practitioners, licensing authorities, faculty, and students within a specialty all aligned against the liberal or general educational requirements of the college, and as the university umbrella has been broadened to embrace more and more special interests, new coalitions have been created which work to erode the central unifying educational thrust of the institution.

As work-related programs brought demands for new courses, including specialized practicums and internships, the university has often been forced to take financial resources away from educational programs unable to marshal similar pressure. In such cases, *specialized accreditation directly collides with institutional accreditation because the latter places emphasis on the overall strengths and quality of the university's broader educational goals.* The pressures are money or prestige and the university's responses are too often opportunistic—or cowardly. We are witnessing a growing mobility to respond effectively to the more complex needs of the total society.

Institutional heads have grown accustomed to the litany of the specialized visiting committee's exit interview wherein the members preview personally with the chancellor or president the forthcoming formal report on the visit. After giving assurance that renewal of program ac-creditation is merely a formality, and that the institution is to be commended for the strength of its (specialized) program, suggestions invariably follow, which include:

1. more money should be allocated to the specialty from the university's budget for supplies, equipment, and facilities;
2. one or more new faculty members should be employed with special interests and/or expertise within subspecialties of the specialization;
3. more money should be found for student aid and for faculty research; and
4. the university must recognize that professional and technical people within the specialty command higher salaries in the marketplace than do faculties of the rest of the university.

All too commonly this shopping list has been developed with the active participation—and even connivance—of the professional school's faculty and administration. Here, indeed, is a thin line between responsibility and venality.

Since such recommendations often find their way into the hands of important practitioners within the community (trustees, legislators, alumni, and others) and since the network of interest in a particular program of the university includes everyone—from the beginning student stage to the licensing authority—new faculty, new courses, new library acquisitions, and new commitments to the program will be demanded of the institution. In many instances, this means less money and less support for essential but less politically potent areas of the university's total educational efforts.

ADMITTING THE STUDENT

A number of the professions have tried, with varying success, to limit the number of students admitted to special programs. The medical pro-fession has long been accused of this behavior in order to prevent too much competition among practicing physicians. On the other extreme, the emergence of the paraprofessionals (aides to dentists, lawyers, veterin-arians, physicians, and others) has often brought deliberate public rela-tion campaigns to the general public. The message is that fully licensed professionals will be aided in their work by well-trained paraprofession-als. To ignore the need is, according to the critics, irresponsible. Yet some of the training has no place in a university, and some universities are carving their niche in such narrow fields. As the various professions and subprofessions work to protect their economic interests by controlling administrations, it may be expected that the general public will withdraw certain prerogatives now extended to the specialized interests. But the university will be the likely battleground for such confrontations with all the tugging and hauling further eroding the autonomy of the institution because the institutions have been feckless in the past.

## PLACEMENT AND LICENSING

The public, through its educational institutions, has allowed, and sometimes welcomed, the award of a license to practice as a result of accreditation of a special program. An example is the pharmacist who, in most jurisdictions, is required to have a license. To get that license, the individual must either pass an examination or successfully complete a prescribed course in pharmacy. In some places, he must do both; but in other jurisdictions graduation from an accredited program in pharmacy is full qualification for licensure. The university with the program in pharmacy is therefore controlling practice in this field of work as well as prescribing the training.

New problems are appearing, however. Requirements of licensure are now being challenged in several areas of work through sharp questions which ask if the prescribed training is essential to successful performance as a practitioner. In a number of cases artificial barriers have been erected—with the university's tacit acquiescence—through this device. To limit competition (rather than to protect the public against malpractice) those who control accreditation, certification, and licensure have become the gatekeepers; as the suspicion of artificiality has grown, these gatekeepers are asked to offer proof that the barriers thus established do indeed guarantee a level of competence. On the other hand, some formal educational programs have been mainly used to "train for the exam"—without giving serious attention to other aspects of the student's educational experience.

With the placement of the graduate representing still another barrier, and with gatekeepers scattered at many points throughout our society, each special program of the university holds the ever-present potential of nibbling away yet another bit of the university's overall autonomy. The multipurpose institution becomes a standing target for every special interest group to lay claim to its piece of turf. When the claims are honored so often, is it any wonder that the university has become suspect?

PROLIFERATION OF SPECIAL PROGRAMS

New professions, new vocations, new technologies, new bodies of knowledge, and new combinations of both old and new knowledge are daily creating new special interest groups. As each strives for recognition, visibility, and acceptance, its efforts are likely to focus more narrowly upon the new entity itself than upon a renewed interest in the centrality of the university. In fact, each such group brings still new forces to pull away more of the total autonomy of the university. *The strongest, fiercest driving force of each new group is likely to be the interest of the group, not the institutional goals or public service.*

The development of special programs has become so routine as to produce a recognizable maturation process. Each begins with informal contacts among the few with similar interests, both within and without a small number of institutions. As common agreement is reached on a desirable core of knowledge and skill, an informal association, with rapidly growing inner communications, is established. Such informal groups, in the early stages of development, usually get together in annual meetings, workshops, and seminars to hammer out program objectives, course outlines, and core requirements. What is lacking in intellectual breadth is made up in professional zeal. Electives, loosely defined initially, become more narrow as plans develop and the network spreads. The informal association often conducts its own informal accreditation long before it seeks recognition from either established organized voluntary accrediting groups, state licensure agencies, or related federal agencies. By the time the central administration of a university learns about the new group—size of faculty, students enrolled, and other budget requirements—formal accreditation may be the only step remaining in the life cycle of a new specialized professional group.

Today's multipurpose university is a breeding ground for new groups. The virtues of the campus—openness to new ideas, receptivity for innovation, coupled with the ever-present search for new knowledge—encourage the very activities which tear away its autonomy. Whether or not such forces, moving in a centrifugal fashion, will create an intellectual vacuum within the university is a question that cannot be avoided.

There is, at least, one redeeming characteristic. As new professions mature, they seem to push prerequisites further up the educational ladder. For many years schools of law admitted students directly from high school, as did programs in business, teacher education, and a num-

ber of other fields. As such endeavors became more attractive to applicants, professional schools were created which, in turn, required two
years, four years, or some other designated college level program before
admission was granted to the specialized curriculum. A recent study of
the field of police education follows this example: it recommends that
academic programs emphasize broad training in the humanities before
specialization in the technical aspects of the work. Such an outlook can
be found in other fields, and this trend gradually turns attention back
to the parent university so that lost segments of autonomy are returned.

But proliferation of special interests continues to endanger institutional autonomy. The next decade will be a period of increasing difficulty because liberal arts colleges, in efforts to maintain enrollment,
may develop more and more job-related specializations at the undergraduate level. The fact that career education is one of the darlings of
the United States Office of Education makes the temptation harder to
resist. A college of liberal arts, therefore, with multiple special programs,
risks becoming a loosely organized holding company for the liberal arts
themselves.

SPECIAL INTERESTS AND DIVIDED LOYALTIES

An example may serve to illustrate the reality of divided loyalty
among teachers in professional schools. A professor of law, serving on
a university-wide committee charged with examining and recommending
tenure-tract quotas for the institution's various schools and colleges,
worked long and hard with his fellow committee members to give a
realistic projection of appropriate faculty size for the years ahead. Re-
alizing that the law school of his university must be a part of the total
institution, the committee's recommendation included limitations on the
number of tenured professors for its various schools and colleges, and, in
the case of the law school, a reduction of one faculty position. When the
law professor was informed by his dean of the accreditation standards
of the Association of American Law Schools and the standards committee
of the counsel on legal education of the American Bar Association, he
was faced with a dilemma: responsibility to his university or to his profession. The appropriate sections of the standards follow:

  A. *Association of American Law Schools*
     § 6.e *Tenure Quotas.* A law school shall not limit the number of full time
     faculty members who may be granted tenure.

B. *American Bar Association*

Memorandum 7879–11, Sept. 25, 1978

§ 405 The law school shall establish and maintain conditions adequate to attract and retain a competent faculty. . . .

Interpretation 1: Any fixed limit on the percent of a law faculty that may hold tenure under any circumstances is in violation of the Standards, especially Standard 405. Resolution of the Council of the Section of Legal Education at Cleveland, Ohio, meeting in 1973.

Regulations such as those listed above are not limited to law schools. They extend in varying degrees to most professional and specialized associations. Each takes its toll on the individual professor's loyalty and leads inevitably to a compromising of institutional integrity. Such intrusions on the autonomy of the university also guarantee a continuous struggle among the various specialized interests within the institution for financial support and favored academic position. All too often, victory goes to the element possessing the greatest political or economic clout and not to those forces committed to the institution's core purposes.

The point of greatest impact is the faculty where the professor is both a member of the university collegial body and a member of a discipline or professional group. Divided loyalty results in the faculty member supporting the activities of the university which employs him and the specialty with which he is identified. Frequently the good of the institution conflicts with the good of the discipline. In a period of high mobility, the professor may make unusual demands on the institution in order to enhance his service to the discipline; in periods of reduced mobility the professor may feel frustrated at being required to give more attention to the institution because his bargaining position is weakened. In either case the academic enterprise suffers.

A strong professional society, with broad programs of involvement for its members, often pulls the professor's loyalty away from the university. As research, scholarly publication, and public service are identified with the specialty, there is added temptation for the professor to bring the professor's views and values into the university rather than to take the university's position into the society. To put matters bluntly: we have too many faculty who are practitioners first and faculty second. And when most faculty hold membership in powerful groups, and when such groups take active part in *public* policy decisions (including the awarding of research funds to members of the society itself), it has become impossible for the professor to give undivided loyalty to the university. The best that can be expected is a balance which, to the professor, recognizes the opportunities provided by the specialized society and which, in turn, respects the integrity of the university. But doing the balancing act well is difficult.

The effects on students are predictable. By the time graduate or professional school is reached, students confront the same choices and absorb the same values as the professor; often they are easily persuaded to follow the mentor's example. And with one eye on placement of the graduate, it is easy for professional faculty to view the institution as a means for self-fulfillment. Particularly in a scarce job market does loyalty to an individual university become even more difficult. In sum: specialization attracts the loyalties of students as well as professors; by maintaining close communication with the practitioners, subgroups become committed to their own goals and loyalties. The university pays these Pied Pipers.

### Business, Industry, and Labor

When industrialization came to the western world the university was placed in a pivotal position between meeting the longer social good and providing human skills for economic advancement. It generated a debate over the very purpose of education. The debate continues at the heart of the academic enterprise. Social change is tied to economic trade-offs which come to rest at the university's doorstep. As industrial groups, business interests, and labor unions seek to use the university for their respective and, sometimes, selfish ends, conflicts have been sharpened. Those concerned with the Third World countries are vitally involved, too, with issues related to the interdependence of *education, work,* and the *quality of life.*

Philosophically, the question is this: should the university restrict itself to those universal, all-encompassing, and transcendent concerns of mankind (and if so, what are they)? Or should the university serve as the gatekeeper (certifier) to those who enter the world of work? More recently, the same debate has come to include the question of the most appropriate education for one who will be forced, by the nature of our rapidly changing society, to move through a variety of jobs during a productive lifetime. Then, too, there is the related question: are too many people attending college? Or too few? What happens when college graduates in large numbers cannot find jobs? The experiences of France and Italy are, in this regard, rather ominous.

MEETING MANPOWER NEEDS

What knowledge and skills are necessary to improve the standard of living? In various forms this question is asked of groups and peoples the world over. Standard of living, the good life, improving human conditions, and a myriad of other concepts may be injected into the discussion. But the question reaching the university remains the same: *what is the university's role in relating educational programs to work?*

Americans have wrestled with this problem before. The land-grant college system was created in the United States because society felt that the university was failing to relate its programs to the manpower needs of a growing nation. The philosophy of this movement has spread around the world; it has a special acceptance in certain American universities.

It is now accepted that the university shall respond to certain areas of manpower needs. If the world needs more engineers, the university will bring this to the attention of its students, will recruit candidates for the field, will train them to the level of the beginning practitioner, and will direct them to the job locations. The same may be said with regard to other fields. The real question relates to the fields which qualify for this level of attention; therefore the debate now centers on what vocational skills shall be taught to whom, and at what levels. While the university has entered the world of work by accepting a responsibility to meet certain manpower needs, the changing demands of the marketplace still pose vexing problems. How can we get flexibility so that obsolete jobs do not become critical entrapments for individuals? How can we make learning experiences more useful to performance?

PRESSURE TO PRESENT POINTS OF VIEW

That the campus has become a battleground of ideas is, obviously, a natural outgrowth of the fundamental search for truth, the university's basic purpose. So long as trained proponents of all ideas have equal access to the community of learning, and so long as those ideas can be examined through a free flow of study, experimentation, and debate, there need be no fear. However, when special interests force their particular needs and ideas upon the campus (or refuse to allow the admission of opposing points of view), the university fails its mission.

American higher education is filled with examples of the attempted imposition of a self-serving ideology—not only by radicals of the left or right, but by business, industry, and labor groups. From time to time, some universities have been captured by those who would present only one point of view—on religion, on economics, on morality, on health. Special groups, having their own ideas of liberal learning, demand to be heard: environmentalists, minority groups, historic preservationists, right-to-work advocates, liberationists. To listen is salutary. To become converts to ideology is tragic.

THE WORLD OF WORK AND THE UNIVERSITY

To tie the university to the world of work is an unacceptable restriction on its role. Nonetheless, pressures from that world are so many and so varied that they are a constant threat to the autonomy of the institution and to its real mission; there is danger that the university will capitulate to the temptation of some promising new "opportunity." When this happens, it is easy to put together a sequence of a few preparatory courses, add something called "practical" experience, and respond to a new job market overnight. With appropriate "electives" such an improvised program probably will be copied by other institutions interested in recruiting new students.

The prospects of a declining enrollment will intensify the pressures to accept job preparation as the university's primary function. But no matter how far the university extends itself to embrace, to accommodate, and to train for new jobs, it still will not be enough to provide every student with an entrance permit to a field of work. Over and beyond the job, the university must provide an educational experience that has value in itself. Its operating premise accepts the proposition that life offers enriching experiences beyond those provided by the job—and beyond those which the individual alone is capable of reaching! The automobile mechanic, the plumber, the lawyer, all benefit from a knowledge of mankind's heritage, from an understanding of the universe, from introduction to the arts, and an in-depth knowledge about one's own well-being. These are some of the common interests that hold civilization together. Contemporary man's intellectual capacity and curiosity are best addressed by the university. No other institution has yet appeared to compete for this part of the individual's attention.

### Faculty Unions

With the appearance on campus some years ago of the faculty union, another fundamental challenge to autonomy was posed. Without debating the merits of the labor union, it can be said that participation in union activities constitutes another inroad upon the energies and loyalties of the professor, generally instills an adversary mentality, and mechanizes decisions on salaries and ranks. But under the banner of *collegiality*, the creation of a *community* of *scholars* has been accepted as key to the protection of the university's autonomy. The professor looked upon himself not as a hired hand but as a partner. Upon arrival on campus, the youngest student, the most mature scholar, the researcher, the tutor, the advisor, the administrator—all are accepted into the "community of colleagues."

As professors have organized to bargain collectively for rights and benefits, that community has been threatened; adversarial relationships with other members of the campus community have even developed. Most directly, faculty is first pitted against the administration and/or the governing bodies. More recently, students in a number of public institutions have won the right to participate on the public side in negotiations with the faculty union. Clearly this tends to place the more mature scholars against the beginner. The collegiality of the campus is thus torn apart by the squabbling factions.

As unionization came to public employees across the country—cities, counties, and states—employees in public colleges felt the need for unions in order to protect their own interests against those of public workers. Faculty mobility being what it is, those who benefitted from collective bargaining in the public institutions have transferred such interests to the nonpublic campus when opportunities arose. As economic prospects become increasingly bleak for both private and public universities, unionization may look even more important.

One basic question of governance looms, and its resolution will have profound effects upon university autonomy: *should those protected by labor unions be permitted to participate in managerial decisions of the institution?* Universities have delegated extensive managerial powers to faculties; through various organizational arrangements, professors establish admission standards, prescribe the educational programs, determine graduation requirements; they exercise the decisive influence over the appointment, promotion, and tenure of faculty members and academic administrators. To decide that university faculty do not, in substance, manage the academic enterprise would be to say that educational programs are managed by others who are not the most mature, experienced, and knowledgeable academicians. On the other hand, to deny the right of collective bargaining to faculty in public institutions is to withhold a right already exercised by other public employees. This conflict is far from settled. Its resolution may have profound consequences for the university and for society.

## Influence of Foundations

The private foundation exercises a unique influence upon the university. Frequently the private foundation has at least two programs—one constructed on the perceived interests of those who control the foundation and a second which responds to a university seeking financial help for programs of its choosing. History includes many accounts of university acceptance of grants to programs designed to fulfill foundation objectives. Corporations have, at times, invaded the university through power of the purse; in some cases large foundations have established programs within universities which will survive after funds vanish. The dangers need not be detailed.

One private foundation is credited with remaking medical education in the early twentieth century by supporting studies which made visible the problems besetting the field at that time. Whether academic medical education was a greater threat to the autonomy of the university before Abraham Flexner issued his history report, *Medical Education in the United States and Canada* in 1910—or after—is still a matter of debate. It is true that the Flexner review, both comprehensive and hard hitting, resulted in closing many medical schools and in revamping the programs of study in those that survived.

Much later another large foundation undertook, through grants to colleges and universities, to open admissions to elementary and secondary school teaching for large numbers of graduates of liberal arts programs. Universities participated for a variety of reasons: some wanted to be a part of a promising new experiment; others were convinced that the result would be good for the lower schools; and still others simply wanted the money. Without debating the merits of the case, it is only necessary to point out that the foundation made the decision with regard to the program and then sought university acceptance, rather than vice versa. This is not to suggest that here is a classic case of tail wagging dog. It does suggest that foundation tails have wagged academic dogs. Many foundations have behaved like individuals—donors, alumni, trustees, friends—in using money to position on campus a pet idea or program, and, in all fairness, it must be pointed out that universities have rejected offers and overtures, sometimes with quite large sums involved, because the donor wished to impose conditions unacceptable to the institution. But institutions have been "bought"—and none of us are sure today that the "for sale" sign has completely vanished.

## The Future

Over the past half century special interest groups have made, in my judgment, frightening inroads on the university. If an institution of higher learning is supposed to be dedicated to the pursuit of truth, it follows that the unfettered search is compromised when a special interest exacts its tribute from the university. Academic freedom is the delicate balance of environment and intellect, and there is fear that this freedom, won from political despots and religious fanatics, is being lost to special interests whose ends are camouflaged by thousands of guidelines, conditions, goals, regulations, and statutes. In previous centuries, enemies of academic freedom were easier to identify and to combat; today's enemies are more subtle. They have learned to attack each grain of sand within every building stone of the entire institution. Grains are not missed until the cracks show.

On such a bleak note, what then may be done to turn the tide? About the only major recourse is renewed attention to liberal learning. In the lift of forecast demographic changes, many institutions will further compromise the liberal arts to maintain enrollments; it remains for a few bastions of liberal learning to keep alive the importance of university autonomy and the conditions necessary for the continued unfettered search for truth. Liberal arts colleges within major universities have a special responsibility in this turbulent sea of special interests.

Certain circumstances are propitious. Flexibility and adaptability are more frequently required of the individual in the rapidly changing world. All indications point to even greater change—more radical and more rapid. Liberal and general education offer the best foundation on which can rest each person's own adjustments—including adjustment to the next job. The university's autonomy can best be protected against inroads by special interests, or by governments, by a continued emphasis on liberal learning.

*Richard M. Cyert*

# 5

# Governance and Administration of the University

When two scholars describe the organizational structure of a university as "organized anarchy," as did Michael D. Cohen and James G. March in *The American College President*, two intriguing questions arise. Who helps make the university "organized"? Who contributes to the "anarchy"?

Despite this characterization, it can be argued that the problems of managing a university bear great similarity to problems of managing other organizations, including business firms. The lack of a well-defined hierarchical organization within the university, however, makes a major difference in the way it is governed. Since obviously all organizations, including universities, require managing, I shall discuss some of the ways it can be done and some of the problems inherent in the process. Before examining the issues in depth, it is useful to look cursorily at some of the participants in the university.

The trustees' role is analogous to the role of directors in a corporation —similar, but also different. Because a major function of trustees is to serve as a financial fiduciary for the organization, they must see that the university's fiscal integrity is maintained. This responsibility is usually

RICHARD M. CYERT *is president of Carnegie-Mellon University. Director of a number of boards in business and the performing arts, he has written widely on administration problems and is a former president of the Institute of Management Sciences.*

discharged through the formal committee structure of trustees and through reports by the president to the full board. Fiscal responsibility is a major legal responsibility of a trustee, and it is a function whose performance is easily measured.

But this is not all. Trustees must look to the maintenance and improvement of academic quality, and this involves subtle relationships with faculty whose powers are substantive. Therefore, to understand university governance, it is important to understand employment relationships; faculty members do not have the status of employees in a corporation, and their relationship is different from the employee-business firm relationship.

The reason for the difference is tenure, which developed to protect academic freedom. Tenure, literally a life-time job guarantee, holds except for behavior involving moral turpitude on the part of a teacher or in the case of financial exigency on the part of the university. Note that competency is seldom, if ever, discussed after tenure is granted and that the accepted two exceptions are not particularly well-defined. The result is that the faculty member with tenure has a long-run commitment from, and represents a long-run investment by, the university. He, therefore, cannot be treated as an ordinary employee. Further, because of his secure status, the faculty member makes efforts to have some voice in the decision-making process of the university.

While students are in the position of being customers of the university, they are different from customers of the business firm; they live on campus, consume services of the organization on the organization's property, and are, as a consequence, interested in decisions that affect their living, working, and learning conditions.

Finally, the alumni believe they deserve a voice in some of the decisions because they are not simply products but assets since they represent a potential for contributing money. Pride and purse provide twin courses for alumni claims to participation.

With this brief background it is now possible to look in more detail at the governance and administration of the university.

### Role of Faculty in Governance

The decentralized nature of the university means that colleges and departments are important units in the governance. The translation of this relationship makes deans and department heads particularly significant in the governance process, and this fact, in turn, means that the faculty play an important role. By necessity the faculty must play a role at the departmental level because there is little administrative manpower at that level; but their most important role is in the evaluation of other faculty for promotion. The universities are committed to peer review with respect to promotions and contract renewals.

### PEER JUDGMENT

At the first stage it is the tenured faculty members in a department who pass judgment on the others in the department who are eligible for contract renewals or promotions. Put another way, the university utilizes experts and specialists to judge others in the same field. This procedure clearly makes a great deal of sense; however, it is necessary for the department head to exert great leadership if this process is to be effective. It is always possible for the process, basically a good one, to degenerate unless the faculty involved are prepared to make judgments strictly on the basis of talent rather than friendship or other irrelevant criteria.

What, then, are the basic problems? First to be noted is that the process frequently makes changes difficult. The tendency for faculty members is generally to perpetuate themselves, and colleagues whose positions are regarded as unorthodox in a discipline often have difficulty in winning promotion. Thus there are impediments for interdisciplinary faculty members unless leadership is exerted from the top that legitimizes interdisciplinary work. And legitimization is not easily achieved because faculty invariably are conservative when a discipline is involved.

The degree of professionalism with which the faculty in a department discharges its responsibilities of peer review determines the quality of the department. To do the evaluation properly the peer group must read the research papers of the candidate being evaluated, find ways to assess the teaching, and then estimate the person's capacity for sustaining high quality performance. Guidance as to the proper weights to attach to each of these activities should come from the president with inputs from the dean and the provost. Ultimately the final decision on tenure appointments rests with the president, but he can make good decisions only if the faculty does its job well. In today's academic world, what happens— and too often—is that an offer from another institution of comparable quality galvanizes action for a faculty member whose prospects were deemed poor prior to the job tender.

## FACULTY SENATE *

In addition to their role in promotions and contract renewals, the faculty play a role in other aspects of university management, and this is generally fulfilled through a faculty senate. The structure of the senate differs from university to university; in some places it may be a convocation of all full professors or tenured persons; in others, the senators may be elected on the basis of some representational formula. In any event the senate tends to be a body through which the faculty attempts to make inputs to management.

There is usually no limit to the issues a senate may decide to consider. If the university is not unionized, discussions of salary and work-related conditions may not be proper because such discussions could lead to the declaration of the senate as a company union by the state or National Labor Relations Board. Aside from this restriction, however, the senate is generally free to discuss those issues that it considers important. The issues may relate to the budget (such as the amount of resources allocated to the library or to athletics), to the number of part-time faculty members employed, to the kind of salary information given the faculty. The senate may function in many different ways: it may elect members of a presidential faculty advisory committee; it may appoint members to trustee committees; it may stipulate procedure for faculty recruitment. There is relatively little the senate cannot make its business.

The basic question is whether the senate follows an adversary relationship with the administration or a cooperative one. In an adversary relationship the senate adopts the attitude that administrators are sometimes incompetent, sometimes untrustworthy—but always a fitting object for watchfulness. Rather than participate in the management of developing policy, the senate stands outside to let other hands work and to rap knuckles when it wills. It attempts to monitor the operations of the university and to find the means of mobilizing critical sentiment against particular policies of the administration. An adversary relationship does not mean one where the senate seeks to force a resignation of the president, although it can come to that; it is rather a particular attitude that attempts to get advantages for faculty through a policy of criticism.

* None of my comments on faculty senate should be taken as a description of the situation at Carnegie-Mellon University. Through special efforts of many people, particularly our outstanding scholars, we have been able to get a more representative senate than is usually the case. Nor is this necessarily the best model. Some institutions form university senates including faculty, students, librarians, and administrators.

In a cooperative mode the senate attempts to work with the administration. Problems it discovers are brought to the administration and attempts are made, in a mutual fashion, to resolve conflicts. The working premise is partnership, and the aim is to make the university a better place for faculty by working jointly with the administration. Whatever the model, senate actions invariably take the form of resolutions calling upon the administration for a particular action; they are attempts to force the administration into a particular action by mobilizing faculty opinion, thereby putting pressure on the administration.

It is important, therefore, that the senate, if it is to have any power, must be truly representative and must be able to speak for the faculty; unfortunately in most institutions it is the less able and less prestigious who participate in senate politics; it is unusual when a senate election gets a majority of faculty to participate in the election. Only when the administration or university is in difficulty does the senate become a rallying force. Thus one way to view the senate is as a mechanism that becomes important in emergencies; under normal conditions it may be difficult to involve good people, and the senate then becomes a place for irrelevant debate by academic politicians.

One reason the senate is unable to involve the most prestigious faculty members is that such faculty have access to the market. They are in demand by other institutions. Such people do not need the senate to play an important role in the governance of the university; their stature assures that department heads and deans pay attention to *their* needs. They also can get the president's ear for something of importance to them. Ironically then, the most prestigious professors are most often content to leave the management of the university to the administration, with confidence that their own particular environment will be shaped as they desire.

Nevertheless, it must be stressed that the senate is an important part of governance in the contemporary university. At all times, it should be understood that the function is advisory and that the decision-making power rests in the president and those members of the administration to whom he delegates power. Legally there is no other way in which the university can be governed since all legal power rests in the hands of the trustees who, in turn, delegate certain of these powers to the president.

There occasionally may be exceptions to this process. The faculty may become a pressure group protesting certain actions of the administration. Frequently such confrontations are conflicts over the abrogation of a "right" the faculty believes it has. The protest eventually reaches the trustees. Under pressure a board may well be tempted to resolve the conflict by delegating some of its powers to the faculty senate rather than to the president. In my view, such moves only postpone difficulties, never solve them. If a board feels it must yield to faculty by eroding the president's power, the best solution may be to fire the president; finding a competent successor then becomes a major problem.

UNIONIZED FACULTY

In institutions where faculty members are unionized many aspects of governance change. There generally is no faculty senate; the contract negotiated between the union and the university defines the faculty's role in the management process. Faculty meetings are generally replaced by union membership meetings. The main point is that the definition and description of faculty roles are described as part of the labor contract: promotions, contract renewals, teaching loads, office hours, outside consultantships, and a host of other issues. The relationship of the faculty member to a department and to the university is changed; no longer an independent entrepreneur, he is now an employee whose duties are outlined. Where his job was unstructured without a union, it now becomes structured and defined in the union contracts.

One of the most interesting elements is the union attitude toward tenure, and the following, from a union publication, illustrates it.

> For whatever reasons, history, tradition, or common law practice, the wedding of these two concepts [academic freedom and tenure] has engendered a discriminatory distortion within academe. That is, tenure, as a protection of academic freedom—delayed for years—in fact denies that freedom to nearly half of the scholarly community. Worse than that, it denies protection of academic freedom to most of the youngest and brightest scholars at the time they need it most—at the fresh, creative, and bold beginnings of their careers. As yet unattained by departmental, institutional, and intradisciplinary politics and intrigues, entrants into the academy are forced to conform, to play it safe, to be traditional in their teaching and research and postpone the development, practice, and publications of their theories until after they have been housebroken—that is, achieved tenure. (Alfred Loewenthal and Richard Nielsen, "Unions and Academia: A Bargaining Frontier," *AFL-CIO American Federationist,* April 1977)

The reason for this position, of course, is that the union wants to be the primary source of security for the faculty member, and it wants to have something to "sell" to the younger faculty member. It is a bit ironic to note that on this tenure issue, the businessman trustee and the union are in agreement in opposition to the concept, though for different reasons. The businessman, reasoning from experience with the firm, cannot understand how or why anyone in the society should be guaranteed a job until retirement. He sees only the evils associated with security because he lives under much greater uncertainty. Chief executive officers do get fired, and not infrequently. The union, on the other hand, has its primary appeal to those who do not have an alternative in the marketplace. Thus the union must stand for salary increases that are independent of professional competence and achievement and for such policies as cost-of-living increases that are across-the-board salary increases regardless of the individual's performance. Consequently one would expect the more mediocre members of the faculty to be the leaders in attempting to move faculty toward unionization. In terms of our earlier discussion it is clear that attempts for a cooperative relationship between the faculty and the administration are made difficult under a union contract whose rationale is an adversary relation.

Faculty members lose some incentive for further professional development under unionization since they are reasonably assured of standardized salary increases regardless of achievement. Thus one would expect to see under union conditions more individual faculty members reducing the intensity with which they work—just as some do when tenure is granted. In other words, the security coming from the union contract does bear some resemblance to the security coming from tenure. However, the pride of the individual faculty member and his own interest in this field will continue to stimulate the average professor to work for academic recognition.

Conflicts continue to arise with increasing regularity under unionization because the authority of the administration is no longer recognized. Issues of teaching load or special activities not clearly covered in the contract are protested and sent to arbitration. Attempts at forming new organizations for innovative purposes within a university are often frustrated unless there is a provision within the contract covering such activity. The extra efforts that faculty members make for the organization (such as speaking to alumni, spending extra time with students, heading various committees, participating in certain aspects of community life) will tend to be sacrificed. *In general, the union must weaken the loyalties to the total organization in order to be successful.* The union becomes a formalization of a phenomenon that is frequently seen in organizations. That phenomenon is the emphasis by a subunit on its own goals, even though these goals conflict with those of the total organization. It is difficult enough, even when all goals are in conformity with university goals, to run a university well; with a union it becomes extremely difficult for an administration to do a good job of managing since the major participant group, the faculty, will likely attempt to achieve goals that are inconsistent with the goals of the total organization. There can be exceptions to this proposition in the short run, but in the long run the proposition must hold or the union will cease to maintain its membership.

One situation that may be even worse than faculty unionization is having some subgroup of the faculty unionized when others are not. Such a state of affairs can arise when professional colleges, such as medical or law schools, are declared separate bargaining units in an election. If two or three such colleges vote for a union and the rest of the faculty votes against it, a great deal of faculty cohesiveness is destroyed. The administration must behave differently toward the different groups and must always be concerned that unionized members get no major advantages over the nonunionized faculty. The president winds up running two separate universities.

## Trustee Roles

Trustees are generally part-time people who donate their time to help a college or university. They are there generally because of their position in society and are expected to give generously and help raise money from others. But in the modern university their roles go far beyond these more easily delineated functions. They are expected to learn something about the university and to participate vigorously in the governing process.

### SELECTION OF TRUSTEES: A TYPICAL PATTERN

Selection of trustees is extremely important. In contrast to corporation directors, trustees are usually selected by a committee of trustees appointed by the chairman of the board. The president, being an ex officio member of the board, is on this committee, as is the chairman. Nominations may come from other board members as well as from the administration itself. While the president does not unilaterally select the trustees, it is clear that he must have an important voice in the selection process. He evinces his concern by the nominations he submits and by his actions within the committee. Nevertheless, it is the committee that, in the end, formally nominates the future trustee and the full board that finally must approve the nominations.

It should also be noted that there are two other ways in which trustees may be elected. A common practice in public universities is to have the trustees elected in a state-wide election or appointed by the governor. Still another form is to have the trustees elected by the alumni of the university. It is also not uncommon to have combinations of these methods. Thus, even where trustees are elected by a subcommittee of the board, the president of the alumni association may serve as ex officio member. In the case of universities that receive large amounts of public aid, but may once have been private, it is not uncommon for some proportion of the trustees to be elected as described above and for some portion to be appointed by the governor.

While qualities desired in a trustee vary by institution, there is ever-present the sweet smell of cash: will the trustee support the institution financially? And independent institutions are especially hungry. Most universities also look for trustees who know something about management, since universities, next to churches, have been notoriously mismanaged. Further, it is important to have the trustees represent a mix of the colleges on the campus; thus a university with a college of fine arts is interested in getting people from the arts on the board, and a faculty in architecture shows the same proclivity. Finally, it is desirable to seek individuals who are on other boards, either of profit or non-profit organizations, because they presumably are experienced in diverse endeavors. With criteria such as these, many boards are dominated by corporate executives who themselves are on different corporate boards. One study has found that of seventeen major university boards, the trustees included nine directors of Chase Manhattan Bank, seven of General Motors, eight of Standard Oil of New Jersey, five of Ford Motor Company, and eleven of General Electric. The inference, however, that the corporate mentality therefore dominates the university is not accurate, as we shall see below.

While terms differ, it is fairly common to have terms specified for trustees, and it is also usual to allow permanent appointments as life trustee for individuals who have distinguished themselves.

Occasionally a person accepts trusteeships from several schools, and if the schools are different, do not compete, and the institutions make only modest demands for time, energy, and money, there is no problem. To me it is improper for a trustee to act on two boards when the schools are in similar fields or attempting to raise funds from the same sources. If the trustee is insensitive, the president and the chairman should take action.

In some schools the ideology of the activist period for participatory management continues, leading to student demands for student representation or from faculty for faculty representatives. The history of such representations, when they have been allowed, is that they contribute very little. More importantly, acceding to such pressure is simply wrong. I am firmly persuaded that board members should be picked for ability to perform, not on the basis of political considerations. A university is not a democracy nor is it a political party, and those who would politicize the university must be resisted. Unhappily, we have examples where expediency has dominated decisions regarding board composition, and the sorrow is that no comparative studies have been made to show the relative effectiveness of different board models.

The president plays an important role in the selection of trustees because they are important and because he must work with them effectively. However, a wise president exerts his influence through a trustee committee and avoids giving any impression to a trustee that his appointment is owed to the president. Again it should be noted that this process is different from that used by corporations where, in most cases, the chief executive officer selects the directors, makes the approach, and lets the nominee know he is the prime mover. With emphasis on independence of the corporate board, however, changes are coming.

SELECTION OF CHAIRMAN

The selection of the chairman is a responsibility for all trustees. And, technically, the board must elect. In ongoing boards when the term is about to expire and the chair declines reappointment, a subcommittee (usually the outgoing chairman and the president) is established. But it could well include other trustees. Here again the president must play an important albeit not dominant role. Since the chairman and president must have a good working relationship, the president should have a strong voice in the selection of a chairman. Ultimately the authority is the board's, but unless the recommendation is completely contrary to the board's view, the recommended chairman is invariably confirmed—usually for a specific term. Since very good chairmen are priceless, they are not too common, and this may be one factor in poor performance by an institution.

## FINANCIAL DUTIES

As indicated earlier, a major function of the trustee is to maintain the fiscal integrity of the university. This fiscal integrity consists of two parts. First (and perhaps most crucial from a legal standpoint) is the investment of the endowment in a way that conforms to the "prudent man" rule. Traditionally this responsibility has been discharged by placing the endowment in a trust department of a reputable bank and on the assumption that if the endowment is invested in such a way that no significant loss in value of the principle occurred, the prudent man rule is being followed. Historically most endowments were invested heavily in bonds by bank trust departments, but in recent years a number of occurrences have changed this philosophy.

The first is the recognition of the concept of a "total return," defined as the sum of the yield (dividends and interest) plus the capital gains. In times past, the income from endowment has been defined only as the dividends and interest. With the new definition many laws were changed to enable capital gains to be expended, and the new definition made growth stocks (and similar investments that were more heavily weighted toward capital gains than yield) attractive. This development, and the generally poor performance of bank trust departments, led to the development of smaller firms that are investment managers and specialists in managing stock portfolios; many endowments are being handled by such specialists.

A concurrent development has been recognition by the Federal Reserve Board that interest rates are an important factor in controlling inflation. Through the operations of the federal reserve system, interest rates have been allowed to fluctuate over a much wider range than had been the case in previous periods; as a consequence the nature of bonds as an investment has changed, since significant capital gains are now possible through bonds as well as stocks. A group of bond specialists has developed, and many investments are managed by equity managers, on the one hand, and fixed investment managers, on the other. Where an endowment is handled in this fashion, it becomes incumbent upon the board to decide what proportion of endowment should be in stocks and what in bonds.

Policy on the endowment is usually handled by an investment committee of the board, and this same group makes decisions as to who should do the managing. While it usually avoids directing the manager to invest in particular securities, it does have responsibility for monitoring the investments and for establishing an investment policy to determine what income from endowment is needed for expenditure. All decisions of this committee must be approved by the full board.

The second area of significance for the trustees in discharging their fiscal responsibilities is approval of the budget submitted by the administration and stipulation of rules by which the administration operates under the budget. It is this critical point where trustees exert a form of financial control. Because many institutions face lean years ahead, the board's role here may be expected to increase appreciably, and control of purse can mean control of other things as well.

In addition to endowment and budget, trustees must look for other signs that the institution is maintaining its health. It must, in a word, look forward—even when indicators are uncertain. One key is enrollment trends. Are applications rising, holding steady, declining? Why? What are the implications of these developments for construction needs, present plant use, faculty? If enrollments are constant, is the "mix" the same or are some schools being bloated and others famished? Is the quality of the students being maintained?

Another method for monitoring the institution's viability is through long-range financial planning. Trustees must ask the administration periodically for long-run financial plans which include estimates of what is going to happen to tuition and other revenue, changes in expenditure patterns, inflation's impact, and so on. Since administration is in the position of absorbing uncertainty—that is, knowing where the figures are soft—trustees must ask tough questions to make certain that the quality of planning is adequate. Only when trustees have some idea of the future financial condition, as well as the present financial status, can they discharge their duties as fiduciaries.

From time to time political issues vex the finance committee. There has been agitation to use investments as a means to punish or reward firms for certain activities. The recent fuss over South African investments is an example. These efforts stem from the incorrect concept that a university, as an institution, can be an activist social reformer. That concept is incorrect and must be explained to students—and trustees, where necessary! A university has an obligation to get, legally, the largest total return that it can.

MONITORING QUALITY

At the heart of the university is, of course, intellectual quality. To find measures to detect changes in quality is never simple, and trustees who show themselves especially vigilant in this regard can readily run afoul of a president (who has played a major role in the trustee's selection) and faculty who are often prickly when so-called "business types" presume to judge faculty performance.

One way of doing this delicate task is through visiting committees, often created by a department, with the requirement that at least one trustee be on it. Visiting committees usually consist of academics and professionals in industry or government who produce a report for the president and the chairman of the board. The visiting committee at some institutions, however, is not expected to monitor quality but to help a department identify and meet new challenges as these arise within the discipline itself, with changing patterns of doctoral programs, and the like.

In addition to reports from visiting committees, trustees may require periodic examinations of particular departments by a committee of externs who might consist of faculty from different universities. The accreditation organizations also make evaluative reports, and reports are also available to the trustees. Finally, the president must, from time to time, make reports using objective measures of quality as much as possible. It is, therefore, through a combination of methods that trustees maintain a fix on the quality and discharge their basic responsibility. If both financial and academic areas are in good condition, trustees have assurance that the university is sound. In turn, the trustees are then discharging their particular responsibilities.

### SETTING POLICY

Always a major problem between board and president is the former's role in setting policy as opposed to managing the university where boundaries are not always clear. The distinction becomes particularly difficult during conflicts. In general, when conflicts between the students and the administration arise, the trustees rely on the administration to settle matters, and the problem is viewed as one of internal management. If the conflict so gets out of hand, however, that the viability of the university itself is threatened, the trustees must intervene. It is in the less grave conditions when the gray areas appear. Trustees may respond when students send petitions and make telephone calls to them; their rationale is that they must be responsive when large groups are dissatisfied with the president or when the issues are important and not being addressed forthrightly. What is needed at these junctures is close co-operation between the administration and the trustees. Conflicts between the faculty and the administration can be similar, although faculty carry greater clout. The president must be backed by the trustees as long as they have faith that he can handle the problem, and when confidence vanishes they must fire him. They cannot, however, attempt to manage the university.

There are areas in which the trustees may wish to establish a policy and make special allocations of resources to back the policy. In salary administration, for example, trustees may feel that a larger amount of funds should be allocated to salaries than that recommended by the president; in order to make such funds available the trustees may elect to allocate a larger portion of endowment income to salaries or a reduction in capital expenditures or another budget line in order to shift funds to salaries. In all such cases the policy positions should be taken only after review with, and concurrence by, the administration.

Because trustees rarely have knowledge of individual faculty salaries, the administration has a heavy responsibility to keep the trustees informed of the university's salary position in relation to the several schools. Essentially the power to set individual salaries is delegated to the president. It is incumbent upon him to recognize that this power is his, particularly in the face of accrediting agencies' encroachments. Some professional associations use the accrediting process as a means to raise salaries of faculty members and deans in their respective schools. Clearly a salary policy (for example, one that emphasizes merit and excludes across-the-board raises) developed by management and approved by trustees should not be abandoned in the face of threats from accrediting agencies.

The trustees also set the tuition level. The administration makes a recommendation and establishes the evidence for the recommendation, but the trustees formally approve the recommendation. There was a time when this decision was easily made, but escalating costs, inflation, shaky enrollment projections, and student consumerism make tuition-related decisions very sensitive. Matching what the university needs to what the market will bear is no longer an easy task.

Trustees also approve the administration's recommendations for tenure, and to take this action responsibly, they need a policy on tenure. Given present circumstances the policy should specify limits on the percentage of the tenured faculty, but such a policy cannot be developed in isolation. The administration must provide alternatives, specifying the policy it thinks is most desirable. Nevertheless, the policy ultimately has to be the trustees'—no one else's.

Similarly the trustees should develop a policy with regard to capital expenditures, and here difficult questions abound. Shall the administration cut back on maintenance and renovation to support a higher operating budget? University administrations in some financial difficulty know that brick and mortar do not threaten to unionize, draft manifestos, or write letters to the editor. The relevant trustee committee should monitor the physical plant and recommend capital expenditure policies to the board, this despite voices clamoring for other allocations. It is possible to decide, as policy, to let the university's physical plant run down, but everyone—president, faculty, students, and alumni—must be made to understand the price. As I view the maintenance problem today, it seems that we have accepted an *après moi, le déluge* mentality.

## FUNCTIONS OF THE CHAIRMAN

There is no need to rehearse the things a chairman is expected to do routinely: tend to the committee structure, appoint the members, oversee the agenda developed initially by the president, make his ex officio committee rights appropriate to the needs, arrange that the proceedings of each committee are given to the total board, review the minutes for accuracy, conduct the meetings.

Above all, leadership is required. And leadership requires capacity to get the facts as sensitive events develop with respect to the president or to other university business; it is important that the chairman get the right information. This cannot be accomplished unless the chairman develops a good working relationship with administration; he must know people personally so that he can telephone them freely and get frank answers. He must be careful in following such a policy not to intrude on the president's role or inadvertently erode the president's authority. Nevertheless, there are instances when the chairman, as representative of the trustees, must determine the nature of a conflict or the status of a particular department or college. He must be careful to talk directly to the president about his findings.

The chairman must also play a critical part in fund raising. It is far easier for trustees to be asked to contribute by another trustee than by the president or the development officer; the chairman can be helpful in requests made to corporations and foundations. However, the fund-raising role should not necessarily be considered a job requirement for the chairman. It is common to have a trustee development committee. The role of the chairman comes down to his own desires and talent—not always the best way to define it but certainly the most realistic. If the individual does not feel comfortable in the fund-raising role, he should see to it that there is an effective development committee and that other trustees are assisting the administration in its fund-raising activities. In other words, the chairman has some responsibility for the school's fund-raising activities but may discharge this responsibility by delegations.

### Administration of the University

SELECTION OF THE PRESIDENT

The chance for long-run success of the president begins with his selection. There are several constituencies of the university which must have a role in the selection process, lest any one of them take a hostile position toward the new incumbent. Thus the selection process should include a place for the trustees, who have the ultimate responsibility; for the faculty; for the students; and for the alumni. The participation of these groups can be handled in a variety of ways. A simple way is to have a special selection committee consisting of each of the groups, where each committee is selected by the relevant organization. Each committee should be allowed to determine its own definition of the job and the characteristics desired in the president. But the activities of the committee and the overall process must be managed by the chairman of the trustee committee, who would ordinarily be chairman of the board. Ultimately each group should focus on the same candidates, those entering the finals of the selection process. Prior to that point, however, each committee should have the opportunity to suggest candidates, and these candidates should be made into a common list and analyzed by each group. It is highly desirable that each group approve the individuals that move into the final selection process. The final list might consist of three or even six candidates. It is not necessary that each group agree on the preference ordering of the final candidates, but it is desirable to have each group acknowledge that each individual would be satisfactory from its point of view. With such a process the president finally selected by the board of trustees has the opportunity to carry the support of each group with him as he attempts to do his job.

When a selection committee becomes splintered, when leaks to the press occur so that reputations are harmed, when confidential information is carelessly handled, when divisions remain on the institution's future, then the results are calamitous. Unfortunately, the "whens" have often occurred.

## POWER OF THE PRESIDENT

The power of the president will vary from organization to organization and will be, in part, also a function of the individual's personality. The power of the president is, in part, limited to his influence on the behavior of others. Nevertheless, by using this influence in subtle ways he can make a significant impact on the organization. Specifically, by making clear where he stands on particular issues he can influence the behavior of the participants in the organization.

One example is in the setting of educational policy. Perhaps the most important aspect of educational policy, particularly in a research oriented university, is the emphasis that the institution is going to give to teaching. The president must work through his deans and his department heads as well as through direct communication with the faculty. He must clarify his own values to the deans and department heads. He must elaborate his reasons for believing that his particular position with respect to teaching is of significance to the organization. He then has to see that the reward system—salaries and promotions—does in fact reward individuals who are good teachers, as defined by the policy. The role of innovation in teaching is an area in which the president must make his position known. He must also find ways to implement this policy just as in the case of good teaching. One way is to make funds available for proposed innovations and education and to see that the innovators get rewards, making sure such actions are taken into account with the proper weight in salary and promotion decisions.

There are other important variables in setting an educational policy. There are mechanical aspects such as setting class size and quality of the student body. There are long-run considerations such as those involving curriculum changes. The tendency for a faculty is to follow the same curriculum until it becomes obviously obsolete. The president and his administration must set policies that will encourage more frequent examinations of the curriculum in the light of criteria specified in the educational policy statements of the president.

Educational policy and, indeed, any policy in the university cannot be established and implemented by the president alone. His deans and other members of the administration must serve as his advisors and critics. There must be a close intellectual bond between the president and the deans and between the president and the department heads. These interactions will most likely come in formal meetings that are scheduled on a periodic basis. Through this process a mutual understanding of goals and values will be established. Where there is failure in the process, the president must see that the faculty dean or department head is replaced.

GOAL SETTING

One of the critical functions within a university is the allocation of resources. This allocation determines the character of the organization. Those activities receiving resources are elected to live and function within the organization and, depending upon the amount of the resources in relation to need, to prosper or merely to survive.

Within any nonprofit organization the usual economic pricing mechanism is absent, and in its absence the allocation of resources tends to become a political process. In a university those deans who are most influential or most articulate may influence the president or the budget officer into allocating a larger proportion of funds to their units. No methods exist for making measurements such as the increase to profit that would result from certain allocations.

The reason for the difficulty is a lack of a clear-cut set of objectives and priorities for the organization. Without a clear understanding within the university of a set of objectives and a set of priorities designed to implement these objectives, there will always be ambiguity and arbitrariness in the resource allocation process. It is clear that a university must develop a set of objectives and allocate resources in accordance with this set of objectives.

There are frequent discussions in textbooks about the need for an organization to have objectives and goals, but little work has been done to describe a process by which these goals may be determined. All of the relevant constituencies in the university must somehow participate in the determination of its goals. The key, however, is that the administration must attempt to integrate the inputs from the various constituencies and develop a comprehensive set of goals.

The process should start with planning at the grass roots level, and this means at the departmental level. The central administration should provide guidelines concerning the nature of the planning process. Emphasis should be placed on involving all faculty members in the planning process and on the need to develop a strategy to achieve the goals of the individual unit. The president should also indicate to the departments and other planning units the goals with which he believes the departments should be concerned. For example, if the president believes that it is important for each department and college to determine those areas in which it has a natural comparative advantage because of location, individuals at the school, tradition, or particular strengths currently existing in the departments or related areas, he should so state in his planning instruction. The administration should also provide a broad analysis of the environment in which the organization is expected to operate. Each department should then develop its own goals and the strategy for achieving those goals.

The goals should then be analyzed at the college level where further refinements may be made, and then, perhaps, some provision should be made for developing intercollege and interdepartmental goals. It is desirable for the nonacademic units to develop a set of goals in a similar fashion.

All of these individual units must then go through the disciplines of discussing and defending their particular documents before the president and his long-range planning group. After all the individual plans have been discussed and defended, it is incumbent upon the president to make a first draft of the set of goals for the organization and to develop at that time a set of priorities for implementing the goals.

This draft should be considered, however, literally a first draft. The document should then be given to all the relevant constituencies in the organization. Within the university these would be trustees, faculty, students, and alumni. Within some organizations there may be other constituencies and within some colleges certain of these constituencies may not be a relevant group. Each of the constituencies should have an organized process by which the goals document is discussed. Well described channels should be developed for getting feedback on the recommended changes to the president. The president must then take into account these inputs and develop a document that is consistent with his concept of the organization's goals, but one that represents a workable consensus for the organization.

## BUDGETING

The most common procedure for budgeting in universities is to begin with the expense side. The position seems to be one of attempting to determine "the amount of expenditure that is necessary" for the organization in the coming year. Budget forms are sent to the units of the organization that are authorized to make expenditures. Some suggested guidelines on the desired limits to expenditures are generally given in the form of some percentage, such as "salary increases should not exceed 4 percent of last year." The attempt of the guidelines is to keep some control on budget projections.

However, it is well known both in the budgeting and organization disciplines that the budgeting process is one that can be described in game theory terms. The unit preparing a budget recognizes that the president will cut the proposed budget by some amount. Therefore, the tendency is to incorporate this knowledge in the budget and increase the proposed expenditures by something more than the expected cut; therefore, when the cut is made, the unit will have the funds that it desires. The net result of this process is invariably one in which the budgets are submitted at a higher level than the management desires. The usual procedure then is to iterate the process. The president cuts the individual budgets, usually at some conference with the deans of the individual colleges, and new budgets are submitted. Unfortunately, this process takes a great deal of time and leaves the budget for the coming period somewhat ambiguous. In universities, commitments for the coming year have to be made before the budget is settled. Thus, the president is confronted after some time with the argument that the unit can no longer cut its budget because commitments have already been made.

In a period when revenues are increasing, and perhaps expansion is expected in universities, such a process may well be a viable one. In fact, incentives to get increased funds may well result in the individual units developing some innovative ideas to justify increased budget allocations. The process is unsatisfactory, however, during a period when the organization is contracting or when revenues are expected at best to remain constant. In those circumstances a tighter rein must be kept on budgeting, and management cannot afford a large number of iterations with the concomitant commitments that will prevent budget decreases.

An alternate and more acceptable procedure is to begin the budgeting process from the revenue side. Revenue estimates are made by the appropriate unit in the administration. These estimates will be for the budget period and will become a guiding force in the budgeting process.

Once the revenue estimates are made and refined, it is then possible to begin the second step in the budgeting process. This step is to make actual allocations of the revenue to the operating units.

It is at this point that the objectives and priorities for the organization come into play for allocating resources. The allocation of dollars to the units can be made on the basis of the objectives. Though it is difficult to get objectives so specific that they can be translated into precise dollar terms, it is possible to develop a clear ordering of objectives that can be translated into the size of the allocations to the various units. It is desirable, however, to have the participation of the deans before the precise dollars for each unit are determined. It is also important, however, that the first attempt at allocations be made by the president. After the participation of the deans, the allocations are made within the constraint of the total revenue estimate. The third step in the process, the detailed determination of the individual budgets by each college, then begins. Each dean knows the total dollar amount that his budget must equal, and each has the freedom to allocate the dollars within his units in the fashion he believes will come closest to achieving the objectives of his college.

This process leads to a faster completion of the budget cycle because it eliminates the various iterations. At the end of the process the budget is balanced, in surplus or deficit, depending upon the target the president had at the time the revenue was allocated. The success in terms of reaching the target is dependent upon the quality of the revenue estimates and the quality of the control mechanisms within the organization.

## LONG-RANGE BUDGETING

Despite the difficulties of making estimates far in advance, the university should also make rough budgets for at least five years ahead. This type of budgeting is important because of the longer period of time it takes the university to free itself from contractual commitments to individual participants. An obvious example is the multiple-year contract with faculty members. If a university were to decide to reduce the size of its faculty. it would clearly take a number of years to do so because of the varying lengths of the contracts of its faculty. Similarly, if a university decided to abandon a certain program, it would take about four years to execute the decision because of commitments to students already in the program. Thus, only by setting targets for the future can the university attain a different disposition of its resources and move into significantly new kinds of activities.

In order to do long-range budgeting, it is obvious that a strong set of goals must be available. In other words, long-range budgeting requires some specific guidelines as to the directions that the organization is heading. Such directions can only come from the goals statement. The long-range budget is an attempt to translate the goals into a set of monetary requirements for achieving the goals or putting the organization on the track of achieving these goals at some later point in time. Each year the budget must be revised in the light of changing environmental conditions and in the light of changing goals.

By applying "backward induction" it is possible to develop a series of operational plans for each of the years. By specifying the position at which the organization wishes to be five years from now, it is possible to work backwards and determine where the organization must be at year four if it is to achieve the goals posited by year five. Similar reasoning applies for year three, two, and one. In this fashion the organization develops a basis for steering itself toward particular positions. In the absence of such a budget the tendency is to make decisions on the basis of goals that remain implicit or short-run. Further, when the organization changes personnel, there is great difficulty for the new decision-maker to understand the past, and the ability to maintain continuity in the organizational strategy is destroyed.

INTERNAL MANAGEMENT

Because of the nature of a university, the word *management* tends to be a "dirty" word. Not being an employee, the faculty member wants to avoid the notion of being managed by anyone. In addition to this psychological element, it is also a fact that the university has tended to be a decentralized organization. Colleges and departments operate relatively independently from the central administration. In some older universities the various colleges are so well endowed that the bulk of the funds go directly to deans rather than through the central administration.

As Alfred Sloan showed in the 1920s, however, it is critical that the central management have a financial control system if decentralization is to be effective. The university cannot operate as an effective organization without a central management unit exerting significant control over the university as a whole. The central university management must determine the way in which resources are allocated. Aside from questions of fiscal integrity, it is impossible for a university to prosper unless there is a central management. A university must be more than a collection of colleges. If it is not, then the organization is missing a number of opportunities to capitalize on its comparative advantages.

In addition to resource allocation, the management of a university includes many other responsibilities. It is not possible to discuss all of them in a short space. It should, however, be understood that a university president must operate through the provosts, deans, and department heads on the academic side and the vice president for business affairs on the nonacademic side. Both sides are obviously crucial since all schools must operate under financial constraints.

A dean plays a leading role in the academic development of the institution. He must work closely with the president and be his representative within a college. The dean generally has a great deal of discretion in allocating the resources he receives from the central administration as well as in other aspects of the management of the college. The degree of his discretion will be a function of the decision by the president on the way he wants to manage the university. The more decentralized he wants the organization to be, the more discretion the dean will have.

The importance of department heads in the management process is generally not well understood. Department heads, in many respects, have the hardest management job on the campus. They are expected to exert peer leadership, the most difficult leadership role to perform. Without a strong department head, it is next to impossible to build a strong department. The department head must be a strategic planner and must be able to lead his faculty into the areas that seem most promising for the department. He is the major faculty recruiter for the department. Unless he is able to attract some of the best people in the field to the department, there is little chance for developing a department of high quality. In short, department heads are the first line of management, and it behooves the president to know them well and to have a strong voice in their selection.

One of the important tasks of the president in internal management is the development of policies on difficult issues such as salaries, tenure, and educational level. To give a better appreciation of this area we will look at some of the problems involved in developing a salary policy.

Salary policy is set by the president in conjunction with his deans and vice presidents. With inflation in the economy, the development of a salary policy presents some difficult problems. Most major research universities attempt to follow a policy of giving salary increases on merit rather than giving across-the-board increases. A salary policy then would consist essentially of specifying an average rate of increase. The dean would have the responsibility with his department heads of determining the distribution of increases, subject to a final central administration review. With inflation, however, the university is in effect cutting the salary of those who do not receive increases equal to the inflation rate. Thus, the central administration must decide how severe it wishes to be in this regard. More generally, it must participate with the deans in determining the distribution of increases within each college. In statistical terms, the salary policy must specify the variance as well as the mean.

A salary policy must also face the question of the importance of the market in determining salaries. In most universities the salaries for the same rank differ among colleges. This difference can usually be explained by differences in the opportunities in the outside world and in other universities. Physicians in a medical school earn more than English professors in the liberal arts college, even though they are at the same university. A salary policy must grapple with the question of where gaps should exist and how large they should be.

## ADMINISTRATION OF UNIVERSITIES OF CONSTANT OR DECREASING SIZE

One of the problems that university presidents and their administrations grapple with is the expected drop in the pool of students eligible for colleges. The effect of the reduction in the student pool is expected to put most universities and colleges into a contracting state.

For any given organization, the opportunity for promotion for participants decreases as the rate of growth decreases. The low probabilities of progressing in the organization considerably decrease the organization's ability to attract first-rate participants into the organization. This difficulty is compounded when there are organizations in the society that are in an expansionary phase. When an organization is unable to attract outstanding new participants, it suffers a reduction in the input of new ideas and in the supply of future leaders. As a result, the cadre of experienced people available for promotion to the top position in the organization may not contain the number of high quality individuals desired. The university may be forced to look outside for individuals for top professorships, for example. Thus, the probability of attaining a top post for those within the organization is reduced further, and the job of attracting bright young people into the organization is made even more difficult.

In fact, the university community must try to avoid the vicious circle which is characteristic of a contracting organization. The trick of managing the contracting organization is to break this vicious circle which tends to lead to disintegration of the organization. Management must develop counter forces which will allow the organization to maintain viability.

FINANCIAL DETERIORATION

A good example of the vicious circle exists in the financial problems inherent in the private university. The university begins to suffer financial reverses because of a decrease in the student body, and its only recourse is to increase tuition. An increase in tuition itself will eventually lead to a further reduction in the number of students coming, and so a vicious circle begins. In order to justify a higher tuition the private university must achieve a level of greater excellence than the public university. To reduce costs, university managers reduce the salary increases paid to faculty and the number of outstanding new faculty hired. Then, gradually the university's excellence will deteriorate, and it will no longer be in the position to justify the higher tuition cost.

In all of the cycles involving financial deterioration one obvious solution to breaking the negative loop is to find more resources. Such resources are hard to find. The best resource is improved internal management. The technique is to find ways of achieving approximately the same quality level of education and research that has been achieved, but to achieve it with fewer resources. Achieving that result means that management, someplace within the system, has increased productivity.

INFLATION

The problem of the survival of a university that is not growing is exacerbated when one postulates an inflation rate of 5 to 7 percent within the environment. The inflation factor means that the organization must continue to get an increase in its total revenues equal to the rate of inflation if it is to achieve a constant dollar equilibrium. It is clear that economies due to management cannot achieve continued savings. Inflation means that certain expenses continue to increase and that the organization can meet them only by acquiring additional revenue. If the revenue is not acquired, the university eventually becomes bankrupt. If the revenue is acquired by continued tuition increases, it is likely that the organization will be forced into a vicious circle of the kind described earlier.

There are other aspects of remaining a constant size in an economy that is experiencing inflation that plague the university. One of these is the role of outside activities of the faculty. It is common practice, which most universities encourage, for faculty members to have outside consulting arrangements. The consulting should be in the form of challenging assignments that will increase the faculty member's professional skills and lead to research and publication. Most universities have some limitation on the amount of time a faculty member may spend on such assignments, but the faculty member is given the responsibility as a professional to police himself on both the amount of time spent and the quality of the assignments. In the best of times, there are faculty who behave unprofessionally. In a period of no growth and falling real income, the temptation to increase the amount of time spent on outside work will tend to become overwhelming. Faculty who have the opportunity will focus on the income involved rather than the intellectual quality of the assignment and will, in effect, become part-time faculty. There is an obvious source of potential conflict here if the university management attempts to correct the situation.

## STRATEGIC PLANNING

A university that cannot operate successfully in the conventional way may need to reexamine the areas in which it is offering educational services. It may be possible to develop a plan for operation that would eliminate some of the educational areas where the university is losing money and move into other areas in which the organization has expertise, such as research. Stated more succinctly, it may be possible for some private universities to operate more as a mixture of a research institute and an educational institution than is currently done. Since such universities now offer both educational and research services as part of their product package, the strategy seems feasible. The examination of a new strategic plan would reduce the emphasis on producing educational services and increase the production on research services. Thus students would become less important and outside research contracts and grants more important. This example illustrates only one strategic alternative. More generally there is a need when an organization is contracting to find a new mix of services that can allow it to attain an equilibrium position. Some universities will disappear because there are no services or mix of services that can win support. A good strategic analysis should uncover such a situation and allow the organization to close its doors in an orderly and dignified manner.

It should be clear that this type of strategy is only one of many possible for a university. Nevertheless, it is worthwhile discussing because it does carry with it potential danger. That danger stems from too great an emphasis on survival—survival at any cost. It is probably always possible for a university (or any organization) to survive if it is not committed to a set of guiding principles that prevent it from being infinitely flexible. The university seeking alternative strategies must be wary of being seduced into becoming an applied research institute with no standards as to the type of research it does. The path to such a position is characterized by an increasing emphasis on contracts and a decreasing emphasis on grants. The contracts tend to prescribe the type of research that must be done, and faculty members soon find themselves, in essence, doing research that is not of basic interest to them. Its only virtue is that it pays part of the salary of the researcher. Such a strategic path must be avoided. The university must not only survive, but it must survive fruitfully.

Strategic planning is generally difficult to do within universities, but it becomes more difficult during a period of contraction because certain functions may have to be eliminated. Planners must change their orientation to think in terms of attaining an equilibrium by contraction rather than growth. In addition, financial criteria must be given a heavy weight in developing criteria for eliminating activities, and such an emphasis is contrary to academic thinking. In short, the type of planning that is necessary for survival requires a significant change in thinking. Clearly, strong leadership is necessary to produce meaningful strategic plans under the circumstances.

Where solutions are hard to find—and they are harder the greater the contraction—the danger is that aspirations for the organization and for the individual will be reduced in the minds of faculty members. The real danger in contraction is that individuals who by nature desire excellence will settle for mediocrity.

### MISCELLANEOUS PROBLEMS PLAGUING PRESIDENTS

With all that the president has to worry about in order to make the organization function, it might be thought that he has little chance to get himself into trouble on other issues. Unfortunately, there are many traps awaiting the unwary. A president has many opportunities to insert himself into controversial public issues. In general, the president should avoid public issues that do not involve education or the welfare of his university. He should have the right to speak on foreign and domestic policy as a citizen, but no one can separate him from his role as president. Thus when he speaks, it is as though he were speaking for the university. He should, therefore, avoid public statements on controversial issues while president.

He should play a role in the large number of organizations involved in education. It is desirable to have presidents, who can spare the time, involved with such organizations as the American Council on Education. He should have a role in civic organizations which attempt to improve the community in which the university is located. Above all, he should use every opportunity to tell the story of his university, its goals, its strengths, and its accomplishments, to the public.

It has been said that the day of great college presidents is past. No one in the present can approach some of the giants of the past who single-handedly built great institutions and were leaders of society. The reason given for this view is that the current job of president turns respectable academics into grubby beggars. The implication is that presidents must spend their time raising money, and thus they have no time for the important things of the mind. Every president must answer these comments for himself. Personally, I get a great deal of satisfaction out of raising money, as much as publishing research papers. It may well be that the day of great presidents is over, but if so, it is not because fund raising is too time consuming. Perhaps Cassius gave the answer when he said, "The fault, dear Brutus, lies not in our stars, but in ourselves."

*Roy E. Licklider*

# 6

# Faculty Ethics in
# an Academic Depression

College faculty are professionals employed by institutions. As such they have significant obligations to at least two separate constituencies: the profession or discipline which they represent and the institutions which employ them. In addition they may feel obligations to their students, to organizations and individuals within their schools, to the people or institutions who ultimately finance their institutions, and to American higher education in general. Each of these obligations is perfectly legitimate, so a forced choice among them is particularly difficult.

The primary professional challenge of college faculty is to organize their time appropriately in terms of these conflicting obligations. By the nature of their job, they often have a good deal of flexibility. Much of their work cannot really be supervised directly; many, for example, work at home, set their own hours, and define intellectual standards.

Neither these loyalties nor their potential conflict is new, of course. Over time, faculty have worked out a number of accepted solutions to the problem. Different institutions structure incentives to produce different mixes of faculty loyalties; while most liberal arts colleges reward teaching and institutional loyalty, research universities look for work

Roy E. Licklider, *associate professor of political science at Douglass College, Rutgers University, has written on a variety of academic subjects, including educational innovation, graduate programs, and the ethics of research.*

within the discipline. Moreover, each institution has a mix of faculty, often working under a set of tacit agreements whereby some teach large classes, others spend much of their time working within their discipline, and others work within and outside the school to strengthen it. Even the focus of an individual faculty member can change. These solutions have become so accepted that even the resulting problems seem clichés: teachers complain that researchers get excessive rewards; faculty promotions are given to good administrators; and "upgrading" an institution shifts the reward structure to favor research and attract scholars with a national reputation.

The approaching academic depression will force every school to reopen these questions. When resources were increasing, faculties could be changed simply by adding new people, producing institutional change without hurting anything but the pride of the old guard. Many schools will have to reduce faculty, and competition among faculty and departments will escalate. Some institutions will have to close, increasing the competitions between schools and between different sectors (such as public and private). Students will be caught in the middle of all this; the same people who advocate increased enrollment to keep the institution running will often be unwilling to do anything extra to help the resulting underprepared students. Faculty will be hard-pressed as their separate loyalties counsel conflicting actions with increasing strength.

In order to begin some serious thinking about these problems, I shall discuss briefly the pressures stemming from these different loyalties and the sanctions by which they are reinforced. In the light of this background, we can then analyze some fairly typical problems.

### Loyalties, Pressures, and Sanctions

The academic discipline or profession shapes college faculty profoundly, often more than they consciously realize. Its pressures to communicate research results have produced an explosion of journals which even university libraries increasingly cannot afford. Its impulse to clone scholars makes a graduate program a potent status symbol for faculty and institution alike. The drive for greater specialization makes communication difficult even within departments, much less among them. The dominance of the discipline-based department has largely been responsible for reducing general education to a shambles at most schools.

Disciplines, however, are not only a necessary evil. On balance they have done more good than ill to American postsecondary education. They have allowed new knowledge to grow and develop, despite their formal strictures, since new disciplines can be formed when necessary; they allow scholars at thousands of different schools to communicate regularly with one another, and they give rewards to those who communicate best. Moreover, the peer pressure which they exert remains the single most important force for retaining academic quality—even when institutions are increasingly prepared to lower standards to maintain their existence.

Loyalty to one's discipline produces pressures for several different types of behavior.

1. A faculty member is pressured to maintain standards of certification. If you are producing a Ph.D. in chemistry, there is a general sense of what such a person should be able to do. Faculty at schools which fall conspicuously below that standard will suffer a loss of prestige.

2. Faculty should communicate research results to a national community. This encourages faculty to push for more time to do research, presumably resulting in less time spent in teaching, public service, and institutional maintenance.

3. Graduate programs remain almost exclusively based on separate disciplines. Junior faculty, coming out of these programs, are given neither motivation nor preparation to do interdisciplinary teaching or research.

4. The low rewards for both teaching and interdisciplinary work create an extremely hostile climate for general education programs at most institutions.

5. The prestige pecking order dictates that graduate programs carry more weight than undergraduate programs and that doctoral programs are more impressive than master's concentrations. Thus colleges and universities are under pressure to develop the most advanced programs even when their graduates are unlikely to find jobs.

6. Disciplines pressure people to specialize, particularly graduate students. The result is young faculty incapable of doing interdisciplinary work and, even worse, so tightly concentrated in a particular area that they sometimes cannot teach the introductory course in their own discipline.

The sanctions to enforce these pressures by the discipline are invariably informal. There is no provision for depriving an individual of the right to practice, as in some other professions. Accrediting procedures make institutions as a whole accountable to outside professionals, but the procedure tends to be *pro forma*. Moreover, most disciplines do not separately accredit institutions; obviously in an institution-wide survey the impact of disapproval of a single discipline will be significantly diluted. Effective sanctions, then, are essentially the disapproval of professional peers. However, this informality should not be confused with inefficacy. Social pressures are, in fact, the primary sanction for most professions, and people shape much of their behavior in response to them.

To an outsider the relationship between schools and their faculty is much clearer: they pay their salaries. Many faculty, in addition, put considerable effort and emotional commitment into their institution. As the depression deepens, faculty will be less able to move from school to school. This may strengthen both the material and emotional ties.

As resources become scarcer, schools will increasingly focus their demands on faculty in areas deemed necessary for institutional survival. These come down to three: getting and retaining enough students, cutting costs, and pleasing certain significant outsiders. Of the three, the struggle for students will be the primary concern of most schools. Students are the financial lifeblood of colleges—whether they fund the school directly through tuition or indirectly through enrollment-driven budgets from state governments. Professor Ernest Bloch of New York University sees each school trying to retain or increase its market share. The result is a market system where the student is king. Not surprisingly, this results in administrators pressuring faculty to "give them what they want," whether this involves less complex readings, vocational programs, credit for life experience, or impressive-sounding new programs empty of significant academic content. A few schools are reputed to have experimented, for example, with turning over curriculum decisions to public relations firms. This concern with short-range desires is reflected also in distribution of resources within the school, as popular departments are allowed to maintain their current level of funding while unpopular ones are cut back. One result is pressure to inflate grades to encourage students to take your courses; another is the development of more "relevant" courses where relevance exacts an exorbitant price from content.

Another, and more sophisticated, strategy for dealing with the problem of market share of students is to establish a unique identity for the school, thereby presumably staking a claim to a group which may be a small percentage of the national population but is quite sufficient to keep a few schools going. The various religious schools have always done this, and some which secularized themselves a few years ago are now trying to turn back the clock. A distinctive curriculum is another technique and examples include St. John's College, John Jay College of Criminal Justice, and the American Institute for Foreign Trade. Women's colleges are enjoying a new burst of popularity, and the black colleges, as ever, contrive to survive in adversity.

This strategy is attractive in general terms. Yet it is difficult in practice to imagine each of the roughly 3,000 colleges and universities in the United States finding such a niche. Indeed economic theory suggests that schools which do find such a special group of students will induce others to compete for the same group. Moreover, to the extent that these special identities are taken seriously, they exert pressure to modify the curriculum. This development raises a fundamental question: will such tightly focused institutions give their students an experience that can be called a liberal education?

In turn, two other questions are raised. What do students really want? And is what they want really what they need? It is often assumed that students are primarily interested in easy courses on topics of current interest. This is by no means always true. Good students, in particular, find such experiences boring and depressing. They sometimes also have a remarkably clear view of what they need. A case in point is the Yale English department which recently asked entering freshmen to pre-register; almost 100 percent signed up for a basic English course even though none was required. Despite the evidence, some administrators and faculty are likely to continue to believe that novelty and ease are important ways of increasing the numbers of students, and, for the institution's survival, quantity of students is more important than quality.

All schools will have to consider how to cut costs as a matter of survival. Since most costs involve personnel, this means firing people or not hiring replacements. As Professor Bloch noted, because tenured faculty represent fixed costs, the brunt of cost-cutting will fall on non-tenured junior faculty who represent variable costs. The results of such cuts can be seen in the English department at the City College of New York, which has over seventy full-time members, only one of whom is not tenured. Costs here cannot be cut much further without making fundamental changes. Clearly the institution of academic tenure will come under increasing pressure from institutions struggling desperately to survive.

As funds become more limited, the impact of even small amounts of outside money becomes greater, since these may be the only discretionary funds available. This further complicates the old problem of the appropriate relationships between schools and outside donors. Recently, for instance, there has been considerable discussion over chairs of free enterprise, over contributions and students from Arab oil countries, and over federal aid to medical schools tied to admitting quotas of American transfer students who begin their study abroad. The potential impact of cutting off federal funds in affirmative action cases poses the problem in rather stark terms. As money gets tighter, institutions will pressure faculty, and faculty themselves may scurry to do whatever is necessary to get external funds. Outside pressures will accordingly be harder to resist. Of course, all such pressures should not be resisted; external funds are one of the few incentives for major changes in schools. Unfortunately it is difficult to tell in advance whether the proposed change will be beneficial or not. At any rate, the balance of influences is clearly tipping toward the donor.

A school has two sanctions to persuade a faculty member to respond to these pressures. As a first step it can fire individuals, but this is effective only against nontenured faculty. Firing tenured faculty usually requires eliminating an entire section of a school, so it is difficult to use this sanction against individuals. The second route is to go bankrupt. This threat of going out of business will probably be the institution's main sanction to press faculty to respond to its perceived needs.

Faculty certainly feel other loyalties as well, but none is so institutionalized as the two just noted. The welfare of students is an important consideration for many faculty. However, this obligation is, in one respect, more difficult to satisfy than the others. Whatever one may think about them, the goals of the discipline and the school are usually clear; the debate is over how they should be weighted versus conflicting interests.

Of course if one argues that students know what they need, they will presumably tell you what you should be doing. But if you believe that students do not necessarily know what they need, there is no single external standard. The faculty member must decide what students need, and faculty themselves do not agree. Do students need mechanical skills or experience in critical thinking? Do they need training in logic or emotional stability? Should they be closely guided in their work or allowed to make their own mistakes? Should they get education useful in their first job or over a lifetime? Advocates for all these points of view can be found on the typical college faculty.

As a result of this lack of consensus, the pressures are diffuse. Depending on the mood of the time, the pressures may suggest that requirements be dropped or added, that new programs be evaluated in terms of their vocational or educational utility, that marginal students be admitted or refused admission, or that discretionary funds go to remedial or honors programs. The result is more often to raise troubling questions than to give clear guidelines for action; student needs are thus at a disadvantage compared to the clearer dictates of discipline and school.

The sanctions of student needs are entirely moral. Moreover, they are often individual. A professor gets no punishment from a national peer group for shortchanging students; at worst, some of his or her institutional colleagues may express disapproval. Generally speaking, however, individual conscience is the only guide. Similarly, for faculty who devote particular attention to students, there are few institutional rewards and none whatsoever at the national level.

Historically American college faculty have responded to all of these forces in varying degrees. The discipline has been the dominant force, particularly in the prestige universities. Institutional pressures and obligations to students have been in uneasy balance at a lower level of priority. As faculty become less able to move among schools, and as schools increasingly see themselves threatened, institutional responsibilities may well become the dominant factor.

### Hiring New Faculty

The process of hiring new faculty illustrates some of these conflicts. As knowledge explodes, new faculty represent the easiest way to keep departments up to date. At most schools, moreover, their selection is largely controlled by faculty. Faculty hiring also represents an important affirmation of the professional status of faculty in that they set the standards for admission to their ranks.

Pressures from the discipline encourage hiring individuals with the most impressive scholarly credentials; often this means selecting relatively senior scholars who have done some significant work. These people are usually specialists in a relatively narrow, albeit mainstream, area of the discipline; they are disproportionately white males, and they may not have much interest in teaching. Increasingly the institution is likely to hire no one at all in order to keep costs down. The point may be reached where institutions cannot hire any new faculty at all, and this problem will disappear. My own sense, however, is that there will always be some turnover, but the hiring will often be temporary replacements or part-time faculty.

Assuming some hiring continues, nontenured appointments will be preferred by schools. If the total number of faculty is reduced over time, preference may be given to candidates who are versatile and have a broad background. Current interests of students probably do not precisely mirror the current scholarly fads, and institutions are likely to push for people they think will attract students—as will worried department chairs. In many cases this may mean interdisciplinary training. Outside pressure will make the institution more concerned to enforce affirmative action guidelines of various sorts. New minimum standards requirements may encourage institutions to hire remedial teachers of various types rather than products of the conventional academic disciplines. Unorthodox viewpoints may be seen as threatening outside financial support, both public and private.

Concern for students suggests it would be salutary to hire people who like to teach, who are good at it, and who will keep developing intellectually over their careers (one reason for requiring some research). The areas of specialization may be what scholars or students want; alternatively they may be unpopular fields which need to be part of one's education.

I am not suggesting that we used to hire paragons who simultaneously satisfied all these needs, but in the past these conflicts could be solved by using different criteria for successive appointments. As appointments become scarcer, the trade-offs become more difficult.

The situation is also complicated currently by the desperate problem of academic unemployment. This has several consequences. The number of applicants mushrooms, so that it is common to have several hundred people applying for a single position. Interview decisions, which reduce this number to four or five, are therefore crucial and are made on the basis of paper records. Unfortunately documentary records are becoming less reliable. Precisely because of the tight job market, authors of letters of recommendation feel obligated to write, as one said by telephone, "the best letter possible." Reviewing recommendations is becoming an esoteric art; employers look for what is not said and for the faint praise that damns. It is commonplace to find that the person, when interviewed, does not reflect the paper record. The combination of unclear criteria and imperfect data for selection makes the hiring process look ominously like a lottery. But the stakes are high indeed for the many applicants competing for very few jobs.

Some of us see another element in the problem of faculty hiring. We believe that graduate schools are not producing as many top-quality students as they did a few years ago, particularly in the conventional disciplines. While there is no hard evidence to support this conclusion, and it is, therefore, necessarily tentative, the suspicion persists that we are now seeing the first graduates who knew, when they entered graduate school, that academic jobs would be scarce and insecure. We suspect that this has caused more outstanding students either not to go to graduate school at all (presumably improving the quality of students in professional schools) or to choose nonacademic careers whenever possible. This produces the interesting phenomenon of having many applicants who seem qualified but few who are really worth hiring. If this is true, it represents a serious threat to the future of American higher education and raises the question of how to attract high quality young people into a declining industry.

### Promotion and Tenure Decisions

Like the selection of new faculty, the peer review process by which promotion and tenure decisions are made is an important symbol of professional status, and faculty generally control the process. But these decisions are also becoming increasingly difficult, particularly because we make them about people whom we know personally.

Loyalty to the discipline dictates that promotion be based primarily on the quality and quantity of scholarly work. But it does not specify just how good someone must be to get promoted. Even if this nebulous criterion is used, however, standards at most universities have risen over the past few years; thus we have the anomaly of senior faculty, who could not have achieved their present rank under current scrutiny, rejecting junior faculty with better qualifications than their own.

In the past a faculty member who did not get promoted at one school had a reasonable chance of finding a tenured position at a school looking for a different set of characteristics among its staff. As senior positions become scarcer, a negative promotion decision increasingly means that the person will either have to change careers altogether or start over by applying for another entry-level position. Doing this to one's friends is not a pleasant experience. Moreover, under regulations at most schools the person who has been dismissed will stay in the same place for anywhere from one to two years after the decision has been made. This can be demoralizing for all concerned.

Institutions have always had varying standards for faculty promotion, but the prestige universities have enforced the scholarly criteria of the disciplines. Two factors may change this in the future. As the need to attract students increases, institutions may become increasingly reluctant to promote good researchers who do not draw large numbers of students or who are in unpopular departments. Secondly, the pressure to cut costs means that a larger and larger percentage of faculty will be tenured. In order to keep costs down and retain some sort of intellectual liveliness, tenure quotas will become inevitable; thus nontenured faculty will be dismissed regardless of the quality of their performance.

The pressures on the academic tenure system as we know it will become very heavy, and I myself do not see how it can survive another twenty years. A positive tenure decision by a major university may commit a million dollars over thirty or forty years. Increasing the mandatory retirement age from sixty-five to seventy, with no obvious reason why it should not escalate further, increases the obligation. We have not yet devised an alternative to tenure which will safeguard academic freedom at less financial cost. Without such an alternative financial arguments will undoubtedly be used to justify firing faculty who take unpopular positions.

As the academic depression deepens, tenure will come under fire for ethical as well as financial reasons. Is it right to use tenure to effectively deny a generation of graduate students access to teaching and research positions? Do we have any way of encouraging a significant number of senior faculty to leave the university, thus opening up both new positions and realistic hopes of promotion? Research suggests that early retirement plans do not make much difference. Faculty retraining for nonacademic jobs has not yet been seriously tried. There is some suggestion that nonacademic internships encourage tenured faculty to leave the university, but do we want to do this if it results in the brightest people leaving the university?

### Graduate Programs

Graduate education has become an important part of the American system of higher education. In many cases graduate students serve as the primary link between teaching and research; they are at once students who must be taught and potential colleagues, useful critics, and research collaborators. In many institutions they are also very important as teachers of undergraduates, particularly in discussion sections of introductory courses. Lastly, of course, they are the future faculty and thus, in some sense, our constant hope for immortality.

The relationship between faculty and graduate students is one of the last holdovers of the apprentice system. Ideally one learns by observing masters performing their trade and then by undertaking projects of one's own under their supervision. The advantage of the system is the close personal contact which, in some cases, makes teacher and student see one another as colleagues.

However, this strength is also its weakness, and graduate students are uniquely vulnerable to the irrational whims of their mentors. Maintaining this relationship in a university bureaucracy has never been easy; increasing economic pressure will subject it to more severe strains.

American graduate education burgeoned in the 1950s and 1960s. The attractions of academic life, bright job prospects, and disillusionment with fields such as business attracted a disproportionate number of the nation's brightest young people into graduate school. The number of schools offering such programs exploded, particularly in the public sector; so many teachers colleges turned themselves into state colleges and universities that they formed a separate pressure group in Washington. Whole new state university systems were built, most notably in California and New York. New programs increased the demand for new faculty, which in turn encouraged more people to enter graduate school. The euphoria of a boom period was everywhere.

The boom is clearly over; we now must deal with its consequences. College faculty in most fields on the average are relatively young; so the vast number of graduate students now in the pipeline will have to rely primarily on new positions rather than replacement jobs if they are to work in the academic community. But, in fact, we face a situation where old jobs will have to be eliminated as the number of undergraduates declines. The result is a massive unemployment problem.

The first signs are clear. New York City, for example, has a group of academic lumpen proletariat, Ph.D.s from top schools who struggle frantically to get one or two part-time teaching jobs which carry no prospect of continuation or promotion. Similar groups can be found in other intellectual centers. Since we have not yet seen the impact of the decline in the college-age population, things will be much worse as we move from "steady state" to depression in a few years.

Faculty control over the introduction, continuation, and termination of graduate programs is less strong than for the issues previously discussed; the decisions involve substantial resources, and administrators, trustees, and significant outsiders often make the choices. Nonetheless, faculty usually have a significant role, particularly in the initiation of change, and they exercise almost total control over the content of the programs. The apparent inability of American higher education to react to this problem is due, at least in part, to the lack of incentive for faculty to recommend that graduate programs be significantly altered, reduced, or shut down altogether.

As noted previously, the disciplines award prestige to graduate programs over undergraduate ones, doctoral programs over master's programs, and discipline programs over interdisciplinary ones. This is only partially offset by concern for quality; in general it is better to participate in a poor graduate program than in none at all. Moreover, graduate programs do seem to encourage faculty to do research, which the discipline rewards. Nor is there any sanction if your graduate students are unemployed.

The institutional picture is somewhat more mixed. Because graduate programs tend to be expensive, some schools are reducing them. The usual pattern is to cut back "weak" programs but to keep others; relatively few schools are interested in moving from university to college status. Indeed most schools find considerable incentive to retain and even increase their graduate programs. The programs are often the major justification for giving state universities higher assistance per student than state colleges. Specialized programs serve as the basis of funding requests by private universities. Again the school does not suffer if its graduates are unemployed. Thus, for the moment, the incentives for graduate programs remain strong at the institutional level. However, they are subject to drastic change if important outsiders become disenchanted. For example, if state boards of higher education start giving less money per student for graduate students or outside funders focus their grants on undergraduates, this pattern could change very quickly.

Discipline and school thus both pressure to keep or possibly increase graduate programs. The dilemma for faculty arises when they contemplate the morality of training students for nonexistent jobs. What is the obligation of faculty to graduate students? One school of thought holds that students are adults and are entitled to attend graduate school if they want to go, are intellectually competent, and can pay the necessary fees. Another group argues that, at a minimum, all entering graduate students should be systematically informed of the academic job situation and likely future prospects; very few schools now do this. A third position is that the lack of available jobs lowers both the quality of incoming students and the morale of those enrolled, significantly lowering the quality of education, and that the programs for both educational and moral reasons should be eliminated until some sort of balance between supply and demand is reestablished.

Foreign students represent a possible bridge for this period, but they raise a number of troubling questions as well. On the one hand it seems fortuitous that at precisely the time when Americans have a surplus of faculty and facilities, foreign countries have a surplus of students. By bringing these students here, we can keep our schools occupied and at the same time allow foreign countries, particularly those in the Third World, to increase their intellectual capital without having to build expensive new schools.

Nonetheless there are problems. Foreign students are not equally distributed across the curriculum. As one might expect, they tend to specialize in engineering, science, business, and economics. Should we cut back on other departments because the latter do not get as many foreign students? Moreover, as foreign students become dominant in particular fields (e.g., about half of all doctoral degrees in engineering awarded in the United States are now given to foreign students), we face the question of whether we should alter the program to fit their special needs. Are such changes appropriate for the American students still in the program? If not, how do we balance our obligations to different sets of students with different needs?

Foreign students are economical to a school only if their marginal cost does not outweigh the extra income they generate. Thus many schools are reluctant to spend much money on altering programs or improving living conditions for these students. Is this fair to the students? Moreover, since tuition does not begin to cover the full cost of education, foreign students are being subsidized by someone (a state government or the endowment fund). From both an ethical and political viewpoint, this can be a dubious undertaking. Since this is in effect a form of foreign aid, we may want to ask the federal government to contribute something. This, however, raises the delicate question of whether these students really need the education they are receiving.

If foreign students are not the answer, perhaps the solution is to develop new graduate programs which can use existing faculty, maintain intellectual standards, and prepare students for nonacademic positions. Such programs would indeed solve many of these problems, but it is unlikely that they will ever exist in any significant numbers.

There is, after all, no reason to suspect that graduate schools in arts and sciences can do a better job of training business executives than business schools. We do not know what people with Ph.D. degrees need to succeed in nonacademic careers, but it probably involves skills and knowledge which current faculties do not have and cannot communicate. Academic skills may be potentially useful to business and government, but students must learn how to translate these skills for these very different kinds of institutions. Who will teach them?

Successful new programs of this type will require significant new resources, which will make them unattractive to many schools. They will also probably require existing faculty to significantly alter their current activities in ways that will not be rewarded by their disciplines. The result is likely to be a plague of programs whose novelty resides mostly in their names. They can be recognized by the lack of new faculty, the lack of changed behavior on the part of old faculty, and the production of people with conventional graduate training under a new label. By undermining the credibility of the effort, they will seriously increase the problems of the few institutions willing to seriously tackle this difficult and important problem.

Yet another complication is that the quality of graduate students may be declining, as mentioned previously, as high quality students quite sensibly prepare themselves for careers with better prospects. At what point should a faculty member recommend dissolution of his or her own graduate program because it is educating rather unimpressive people for nonexistent jobs? What kind of information should he or she make available to influential outsiders who may be paying the bills?

One reason this problem is so difficult is that we have, in industrial terms, a long lead time. Students now entering graduate school will be on the job market in about five years. We can make guesses and projections, but these have been mistaken in the past. We ask a great deal of faculty if they are to deny themselves an important part of their professional career, with no offsetting compensations, on the basis of a guess about the future.

Another view of the problem is the collective goods approach. It is clearly in the interest of American higher education *as a whole* to reduce graduate education significantly. However, as we have seen above, there are few incentives to *particular institutions or individuals* to do this themselves and no central authority which can decree it. The lack of central control in the American system, which Joseph Ben-David among others sees as an intellectual advantage, makes the response to any problem of this sort slow, halting, and inadequate.

### *Undergraduate Curricula and General Education*

Undergraduate education remains the major function of most institutions of higher learning; its importance is demonstrated by the fact that a decline in undergraduate enrollments is expected to cause an academic depression. The need to attract and hold such students has raised again the perennial question of what they should be taught, which for most schools means reopening the issue of a liberal arts education. Are there certain things that "every educated person" should know or be able to do? If so, should they be imparted in special courses designed for this purpose (general education courses) or should students be required to take conventional courses in various areas or disciplines (distribution requirements)?

The disciplines are not averse to distribution requirements, but they penalize faculty involved in general education courses. Such people are usually not working exclusively within a discipline; if they do do any research, it similarly will probably not fit within the mainstream approach of a field. Even people who focus on teaching introductory courses in a discipline can expect no support from outside their school in this role. Moreover, junior faculty are uniquely unprepared by graduate school to teach general education courses; the tight focus on discipline-based research rather than interdisciplinary teaching guarantees that any school starting a serious general education program will have to teach its faculty first. Usually, of course, this is done on the job and at the expense of the first set of students. The bad performances which result seem to justify the original opponents of the scheme. Disciplines thus push for distribution requirements.

Institutions are often indifferent as to which alternative is selected. Many schools developed general education courses and distribution requirements in the 1950s, dropped all requirements in the 1960s, and are now moving back again. Institutions with a clear mission may prefer general education courses which will let them focus on appropriate themes and materials ("ethics for engineers," etc.). However, this general indifference may change because important outsiders are increasingly becoming concerned with the question. Businessmen, who hire college graduates and find that many of them do not know about supply and demand or American history, may make their concern known to schools to which they give money. As a result, money is often available to support new programs in general education for undergraduates.

However, the central problem in establishing such programs is not money but whether an institution can create an incentive structure so that faculty will be attracted to teach the courses and rewarded if they do the job well. The history of general education suggests that it cannot survive in a school dominated by disciplines; faculty attached to the program will simply not be retained. Establishing it in a school or department of its own, on the other hand, results in stultification and separation from the rest of the institution, since there is often no research tradition attached to it. Thus many programs are started with fanfare but die out. Distribution requirements are easier to establish and maintain, but it is unclear that they really do the job; are some courses in science fiction and Zen Buddhism sufficient background in the humanities for a college student? The tension between what students want and what they need is very important here, and faculty remain unable to agree on a single set of requirements. Moreover, as resources contract, any department whose courses are required has a tremendous political advantage, since it is guaranteed lots of students. Thus faculty are reluctant to require many courses in any single department (unless it is their own) because of the impact on the internal allocation of resources. Distribution requirements thus seem likely to become more popular, for better or worse.

### New Types of Undergraduate Students

Compared to European colleges and universities, American higher education reaches a remarkably broad spectrum of the population. However, we have increasingly become aware that schools are geared to serving a particular sort of student: full-time, between the ages of eighteen and twenty-two, resident on the campus or in the community, with certain basic skills, and possessed of higher than average intelligence. Perhaps the most exciting educational experiment of the past few decades has been to reach beyond this group to other sectors of our society. As the process has gone forward, debate over its wisdom has increased. Do these students need anything other than the traditional curriculum? If so, what are our obligations to more traditional students?

The disciplines pressure faculty to encourage students to study within established fields. However, if a field is important and generally needed, it can become a new discipline of its own. This seems to be happening with the teaching of basic skills, particularly composition. Increasingly students at all schools arrive unable to write standard English. Pressure from important outsiders and from faculty who find themselves unable to teach such students has resulted in schools establishing new programs to teach these skills, even under conditions of financial stringency. These fields are now developing into subdisciplines, with journals, national organizations, academic conferences, and specialized graduate programs of their own. This may seem silly; in fact it is crucial, since the people who teach such subjects can be promoted within their institutions only if they can establish the academic legitimacy of their work by developing a research tradition of their own. In practice this means that they will have to be established as de facto separate departments, although many may nominally remain within major disciplines, such as English, for a long time.

From the institution's point of view, the number of students is more important than their other qualifications. Therefore, as students become scarcer, many institutions will broaden their search for potential bodies. Most schools now take part-time students, even in their graduate programs; the effect on the general intellectual climate of other students who are less involved in outside activities is unclear. Attempts to reach students older than the conventional age group have had some success, and their addition to the classroom often is helpful for younger students as well. However, neither group is likely to solve the problems of most institutions; it requires several part-time students to replace one full-time student.

Attempts to reach students who do not reside in the immediate area have also not been particularly successful. A series of attempts to do this by electronic means remains very much in the trial stage. One interesting result has been the establishment by many schools of separate programs located literally thousands of miles away from the home campus, usually to provide courses for a particular consumer like a corporation or a military base "on site." In 1978, for example, college courses were being offered in Seattle by Southern Illinois University, the University of Southern California, United States International University of California, Chapman College of California, Antioch University, Columbia College of Missouri, and Golden Gate University of California. Many are skeptical of the academic quality of such programs, particularly over the long run.

Extending college education to students whose intelligence would previously have prevented their admission is a sensitive issue. There is no question that a lot of this has gone on, and many students are now in college who do not by any stretch of the imagination belong there. On the other hand, our ability to select students to enter college is not particularly impressive, particularly among minorities, in part because motivation has more to do with success than sheer intellect. At some point it becomes an economic problem: should we encourage ten students to enter, knowing that only three will graduate but being unable to predict in advance which three? Colleges have traditionally admitted on the insurance policy, taking students who were most likely to graduate. Are these the students who need college most? Is our assumption correct that students who do not graduate represent personal and institutional failures?

The efforts by institutions to reach more students in order to keep their enrollments up will continue until halted by the outsiders who finance these activities. In fact, this is happening as state governments attempt to cut back expenses amidst charges that money is being wasted in higher education. Nonetheless the pressure from schools on faculty is likely to be toward taking more students who do not fit the traditional mode. Again, however, this is only economical if the marginal costs of such students can be kept low. Thus schools are often reluctant to expend resources in meeting special needs of such students; basically they expect faculty to do whatever is necessary on their own time. The development of ethnic studies programs was one effort to meet these needs; with some exceptions it produced a series of programs which cannot hold their own with other academic departments and which now face severe enrollment problems. This experience suggests the hazards of altering curriculum to fit current fads. On the other hand, the expectation that any college student will find the current course menu appropriate also seems unlikely. Some of the most significant changes will take place within existing courses, as faculty struggle to shift the content of their

courses to meet the perceived needs of new students while continuing
to serve the old ones. They will in general not be rewarded for this activity by either the discipline or the institution.

## Outside Consulting

Most colleges and universities allow faculty to work for outside employers part-time while drawing full-time salary from the school. Increasingly there is some sort of general guideline which is usually not
enforced (a limit of 20 percent of total salary or one day a week or both
is common).

From the viewpoint of the discipline, this practice has mixed benefits.
It can offer faculty unusual opportunities for professional development;
particularly in the more applied disciplines, off-campus experience can
catalyze academic research. Indeed, if research becomes less popular on
American campuses for reasons discussed earlier, the function may have
to migrate off-campus into research institutes and corporations, as it
already has to some extent. The risk is that much consulting amounts
to routine repetition of earlier work, presumably using time which the
individual might have devoted to something more original. In general
this has not been an important issue for most disciplines.

Although outside consulting is a more serious problem for schools,
they, too, have mixed feelings. Professional development may improve
teaching and research, possibly attracting students concerned with getting
jobs after graduation. The contacts made with important people off-
campus sometimes are helpful to the school. Some of this can be called
public service and viewed as assistance from the university to the community at large. Faculty find this sort of freedom (and the money associated with it) an attractive fringe benefit which does not cost the school
any money.

However, because the benefits are distributed so unequally among
faculty, it can also be a terribly divisive issue within an institution.
Some disciplines routinely do a lot of consulting (engineering and psychology, for example); others do almost none (classics and English). Departments that consult not only get consulting fees in addition to their
salaries, but ironically their salaries are often higher to begin with, since
they can argue that their services are highly valued outside of the school.
Not surprisingly there is much resentment by other faculty who perceive

themselves, sometimes quite correctly, as getting less money for doing more work within the institution.

Conspicuous consulting can also make important outsiders uneasy. It is sometimes hard to persuade legislators and businessmen that college faculty, many of whom teach only nine or twelve hours per week and do not keep regular hours, are really working full time. A few examples of faculty spending a great deal of time off-campus working for someone else can make fund raising very difficult indeed. However, policing these rules tightly is not easy to do.

The problem is likely to become more severe in the next few years. The real income of college faculty has been declining since 1972–73, according to the American Association of University Professors; by 1978 it had dropped over 10 percent. This decline will probably continue, as the excess supply of college faculty becomes evident and as funding agencies find it difficult to keep up with inflation. Indeed, it may be many years before college faculty return to the level of real compensation they enjoyed a few years ago. Faculty will thus have a strong economic incentive to seek and retain outside consulting jobs, and schools may be prepared to turn a blind eye to it, since this may be the only way they can effectively raise the salary of faculty who have outside market value. At the same time the problems of inequitable distribution of outside employment will become correspondingly severe.

### Faculty Unions

Faculty unions on American campuses are a relatively recent development, and they have generated a remarkable amount of concern and controversy to which I feel inadequate to add much. For our purposes they are interesting because they represent a potential new loyalty for faculty, conflicting with the others we have discussed.

Disciplines have shown relatively little concern for them, but academic administrators have more than made up for this indifference. Two serious problems are raised. Faculty unions bring onto campus the whole panoply of legal apparatus associated with collective bargaining, thus altering the power balance in unpredictable ways. More importantly, the determination of university policies by collective bargaining undercuts the traditional role of the faculty in university governance. If the concerns of the faculty have become exclusively personal, will they do whatever is necessary to help the institution (taking a salary cut, for instance), or will they prefer to drive it to ruin? What remains of the ideal of the university or college as a community of scholars working together for common purposes?

These are serious concerns, and we have had so little experience that it is difficult to persuasively refute them. Moreover, as the academic depression increases, the economic conflicts within institutions will intensify. One can, of course, argue that these problems have been overstated. Unions have not yet wreaked havoc with universities. In many cases collective bargaining is limited to compensation issues, and recent court decisions also restrict the issues on which schools may bargain. Indeed, sophisticated faculty quickly discover that their real adversary on these issues is not the administration but the trustees or the state legislature. Thus it is not surprising that unions are increasingly cooperating with administrations on matters of common concern, something for which awareness of industrial relations should have prepared us.

The general discussion of unionization assumes that all unions are the same. In fact, the three different, competing national faculty unions may have significantly different impact on institutions. On the other hand, economic stringency and union competition may force the demands of different unions to become more similar. Again, we have too little experience to determine which of these alternative theories is correct.

At a deeper level, one can argue that unions are the effect, rather than the cause, of tensions between administrators and faculty. Research indicates clearly that unions are not spreading uniformly throughout American higher education. They have been most popular at large public institutions and community colleges where faculty have not been heavily involved in governance and where the image of the school as a community of scholars has had little relevance. Many schools which have maintained close ties between administrators and faculty have successfully resisted demands for unionization. Viewed in this light, faculty unions become epiphenomenal, a distraction from the real problems which American higher education faces in the next few decades.

### Participation in Institutional Governance

It is clear that important changes will have to be made in many American colleges and universities over the next several years. However, the process of change itself is costly, regardless of the substantive result.

If major changes are to be made, faculty must be involved in the process. However, there are relatively few incentives for them to participate. One of the most confusing aspects of American higher education is its authority structure. At the risk of oversimplifying, there are two parallel authority structures at most schools, each dealing with somewhat different issues and relating to one another uneasily at best. The administrative authority structure is a conventional bureaucracy. We know that the actual control of top-level officers in such organizations is materially limited by subordinates' monopoly of vital information, outside political contacts, and internal alliances. Nonetheless the system is fundamentally hierarchical. This structure deals with problems such as fund raising, financial control, accountability to the outside world, and generally facilitating the interaction between faculty and students which is the heart of the operation.

The faculty authority structure, on the other hand, is fundamentally egalitarian. Obviously there are exceptions here as well, such as the position of nontenured faculty and occasional dictatorial department chairs, but the generalization holds. Individual faculty have remarkable freedom to do as they wish in both teaching and research; the almost total exclusion of administrators from direct control of the central activities of the organization makes this a very unusual arrangement which outsiders find difficult to comprehend. Group decisions on issues such as courses, selection of new faculty, faculty promotions, graduation requirements, and often student admission standards are made in a legislative setting whose chair must persuade rather than dictate.

An individual faculty member certainly wants *some faculty* involved in major decisions of the school, but there is little reason to become involved personally. Certainly the discipline will not give any such incentives; the time used in committee work might otherwise be spent doing disciplinary research. Some schools have informally given rewards for such work, but as faculty unions make all such processes more formal this will become more difficult. (One pernicious effect of unionization may be to hinder institutions from developing incentive structures to offset those of the disciplines.)

Faculty are asked to participate in a number of different institutional committees often with varying membership and uncertain powers. At the end of it all, they will probably be unable to say with confidence what difference their presence made to the final result. Since you cannot tell whether you had any impact, you cannot justify participation as a defensive maneuver to protect particular interests. Often discussion is dominated by administrators who talk their own language about financial affairs, and faculty suspect that their views are not being taken seriously and that they are there to ratify rather than make decisions. Nor will they get much support from their colleagues; when the decisions concern reducing budgets, everyone is sure they could have done a better job, although few volunteered to help. Moreover, in an interesting paradox, both faculty and administrators want faculty who are respected by their colleagues to participate; thus precisely the people who are already deeply committed to other activities are most in demand, while those who could more easily participate are often less desirable.

Given these uncertainties, does it really make sense to a faculty member to participate in such decisions? Many will do so, either because of loyalty to their institution or because they get other rewards from the process. But in the long run, charity and side payments are unstable foundations for something as important as faculty participation in institutional governance, and it is important that we somehow develop new means of making it worthwhile if we are to get the most satisfactory results from what will be in any case a difficult situation.

### Conclusion

These are examples of the kinds of ethical problems faculty will face over the next two decades. All represent the most difficult kind of problem, conflicting demands by worthy ends. None of them is new, but all of them will have to be thought through again as the academic depression makes them all more difficult to deal with. What are we to make of them?

One response is that they are separate issues, and the only problem is to suggest the best response to each. It is easy to set forth my own opinions.

1. Standards for hiring and promoting new faculty should be shifted somewhat to reflect the new needs of institutions while maintaining as best we can the high standards demanded by the disciplines.
2. Conventional Ph.D. programs should be cut back extensively, and innovative new graduate programs which claim to prepare students for new jobs should be viewed skeptically.
3. Faculty should be rewarded for high-quality work in general education and remedial education. However, like other academic fields, neither should

be regarded as a life work by anyone not doing substantial research in the area.

4. New students should be brought into a school only if they can do the usual academic work required or if the school provides adequate remedial assistance to bring them quickly to that point.

5. Consulting should be both encouraged and strictly policed by faculty committees.

6. Unions are a distraction rather than a major problem.

7. Faculty should make a serious effort as individuals to take part in institutional governance if they think they will be taken seriously.

Any such list is implicitly a set of recommendations to faculty, but all of these opinions are oversimplifications of important problems, and none is much use as a guideline for people wrestling with comparable problems in environments ranging from community colleges to research institutes, all of whom have different priorities, pressures, and possibilities.

At another level, it is clear that American higher education must make radical changes in the next two decades. It is important for those who wish to facilitate such changes to remember that the incentive structures of faculty will influence how change is implemented, regardless of fancy titles and impressive sets of rules. This is less a problem for college administrators, who grasp it intuitively, than it is for outsiders such as government, corporation, and foundation officials who deal primarily with administrators and sometimes adopt their attitude that they represent (as one university president put it) the "operating sector" of the school. General education is a good example of an area where lots of money will be spent on new programs which will not have much long-term impact because the donors do not focus on the real problems of general education, particularly the lack of incentives for faculty to take it seriously.

This is not another plea that college personnel know best and will solve these problems if just left alone by outsiders. College faculty and also administrators have been painfully slow to react to these kinds of problems; their tendency is to keep doing what they have always done and hope things will work out. They resist taking a broad view of education, and they do not work well in groups. The necessary changes will certainly come in large part because of outside initiative, as they have in the past. But if this intervention is to be effective, it must be done with serious consideration given to the motives and interests of the people who will have to carry out reform in the classroom, to what a colleague in sociology, Robert Parelius, has called "faculty culture."

There is another, more optimistic view of these problems. The challenge of most human endeavors centers on finding a point of balance between incompatible pressures, whether it is the choice of spending your recreation time with your family or alone, or the tension of the statesman to select between national interests and universal norms. Making these choices and living with them is an essential part of being human, and sometimes they make us reach within ourselves for hidden resources. Our challenges are not new. They will take on new dimensions as financial stringency increases, but in one form or another we will grapple with them forever in American higher education. The best we can hope for is to reach temporary accommodations which let us get on with our work but do not deprive us of the nagging dissatisfaction which is the spur to human greatness.

*Willard F. Enteman*

# 7

# The Integrity of the Student:

A Normative Approach

The integrity of the university is tested by the way in which it treats people connected with the university. Students constitute the largest single group within the university. Thus, integrity will be a direct function of how we think about students and how we act toward them.

Our thoughts about students have usually been expressed through various conceptual approaches which, quite naturally, have leaned upon related metaphors. These concepts and metaphors should bear examination before we may proceed very far in understanding how the university can maintain its integrity and the integrity of the student. At its base, integrity means honesty in the most fully developed sense of that term; it implies not merely refraining from deception but so understanding others that we award them their fullest dignity.

We should look at the conceptual structures and metaphors which have dominated our ways of thinking about students in order to keep such dominance under control and in order to know our students more

WILLARD F. ENTEMAN *is president of Bowdoin College and professor of philosophy. In 1972–78 he was provost of Union College. Dr. Enteman has been a consultant to state education departments, accreditation committees, and foundations on many problems of higher education, including tenure, management systems, and planning.*

fully, more directly, and, finally, nonmetaphorically. It is only through a full vision that honesty and integrity are possible.

## Concepts of Students

### STUDENT AS CHILD

Our thinking is so dominated by the notion of the student as an undergraduate that we lived far too comfortably with the concept of the student as child. Parents were content to send their children off to college because they thought the college could, rightfully, act in place of the parent and enforce rules and regulations for the student. It is a matter of some irony that often parents expected colleges to insist upon stricter rules and regulations when the colleges were acting *in loco parentis* than when the children were home. Of course, the colleges acquiesced and even seemed to relish their role as surrogate parents; the list of rules and regulations never seemed to be too long or too petty to be enforced.

Actually, it is misleading to speak of the concept of the student as child in the context of metaphors. The adherents of this image probably did not think of it as a metaphor at all; as far as they were concerned the student was, indeed, a child. Having thought of students as children and, consequently, having treated students as children, the students obliged and acted as children. The rules and regulations were not seen as reasonable devices for enhancing the education at the college. They were seen, rather, as arbitrary devices for furthering the paternalism of the authorities and as devices to be challenged, evaded, and compromised much as a child constantly challenges his parents' rulings for a bedtime hour. There is a lesson to be learned: once established as the conceptual framework, the metaphor takes on a priority of its own and is treated as axiomatic in debates about institutional development. The student of integrity would be conceived as one who obeyed the rules and regulations no matter how senseless. The college of integrity would be one which had clear and distinct regulations enforced firmly and without exceptions.

Informative concepts can be extended beyond the legitimacy of their realm, as is shown later with other metaphors; they can also live beyond their time of usefulness, as is the case with the concept of the student as a child. Serious commitment to graduate and professional education combined with early developments in "adult" education and returning veterans using the G.I. Bill began to put an end to the childlike concept. It is instructive to note that much of what was later called continuing education started by being called "adult" education, thus emphasizing a distinction between the predominant children-students and the newly emerging adult-students.

The concept of the student as child is no longer entertained seriously by anyone. So many social forces have led to its demise that, apart from a complete social history of the United States after World War II, it would be difficult to know what particular forces to identify as most significant. One might point to two institutional forces in higher education, though, which, while in conflict, served to alter the *in loco parentis* imagery radically: 1) the increasing educational and academic seriousness of faculty, especially those in the leading liberal arts colleges, and 2) the increasing formal participation of faculty in college and university governance. These two forces are ultimately in conflict, and that conflict still seeks resolution.

As presidents and deans lost their authoritarian power with respect to a faculty and as faculty began to assert a stronger, more meaningful, and more formal role in governance, faculty had to participate increasingly in the construction, enforcement, and even defense of the multifarious rules and regulations. Previously, the authoritarian dean, backed by an equally authoritarian president (and, if challenged, an acquiescent court system), could make the rules, enforce them, and distribute punishments as he saw fit—all rapidly and with little concern for what we today call "feedback." As the dean lost his authority, it gradually became lodged in a faculty committee where the academics' penchant for talking and arguing from absurd extremes would know no limit. In the meantime, however, the faculty, especially in the best colleges, were collectively taking their scholarly lives more seriously. Serious scholarly work demands time: time to do research, time to write, time to be psychologically free of trivia to consider scholarly issues, and time to be in active participation with the field. However, participatory governance (committee work) also requires time: time to listen to colleagues, time to write new legislation, time to persuade, and time to learn about allied aspects of the issues under consideration. These time demands were in ultimate conflict.

A partial resolution would be to abandon the *in loco parentis* concept, to treat the students as adults (no matter how much they continued to act like children), and, thus, to be free of a whole set of problems. In a celebration of "liberalism," students and faculty could be freer. The faculty problem of the conflict between professionalism and participation was partially resolved. Even that partial resolution is short-lived. Committee work will always expand to fill whatever time people will give to it. However, through it all, the concept of student as child was abandoned.

STUDENT AS POLITICIAN

Group interest political theory has become the conventional wisdom among political scientists, and it should not be surprising that a political metaphor would be imposed upon the university. As national decisions are imagined to be taken as a result of the negotiations of various special interest groups, so it was thought university decisions should arise from the negotiations of special interest groups within the university.

It has never been clear who the special interest groups were. Alumni? Taxpayers? The public? Governing boards? Administration? No matter for our purposes. Two groups would be in all models: faculty (they were advocating the model) and students (newly emerged from their cocoon). Student governance would take on a new and more serious role. No longer would it be the game of "dress-up" which was given in patronizing fashion to old student governments. The stakes were made real. Real political conflicts could be negotiated.

Students could serve on faculty committees, attend faculty meetings (to the mutual embarrassment of students and faculty), serve as voting members on campus legislative bodies, and meet with governing boards and their committees. Students could negotiate for increased "student services," for decreased course requirements, for the promotion of popular professors, or for anything students felt was important. Students could even attempt to negotiate for an expression of university opinion on a wide range of national and international political issues. It does no good to protest that on some occasions, expression of university—or student—opinion on external political issues is irrelevant or inappropriate. In group interest theory, an expression of opinion is relevant and appropriate if the group says it is.

As might be expected, the student-politician would be successful to the extent to which he or she could appear to marshal student support and—in the spirit of negotiation—garner support from the faculty interest group or the administration (conceived as an interest group). Logrolling could take place, votes could be traded, and a university's future could be determined as a vector consequence of conflicting political forces. The "model" and the metaphor are popular. They are, nevertheless, inappropriate for several reasons. In the first place, while they grant the dignity of an adult political animal to the student, they deliver that student to mere manipulation. The student is to be courted because votes can be delivered, and whatever other special interest groups want can be given greater chance of achievement if students can be manipulated into throwing their political weight the "right" way. The concept is not one which grants the student integrity. The student survives the suffocating paternalism of the student-as-child metaphor only to be suffocated by a metaphor which construes the student as a political pawn in the limited-stake game of politically motivated academic governance.

In addition, the student-as-politician metaphor leads to absurdities. For example, students may sit on faculty promotion committees as voting members. On what principles should they vote? They cannot really vote as a result of a knowledgeable evaluation of a candidate's credentials. In the best of circumstances students can tell whether or not they like a candidate, but since that is only a portion of the information which should be at the base of a decision to grant tenure, they cannot rationally vote on such a decision. Knowledgeable professionals have a difficult enough time attempting to estimate a candidate's potential. If the student cannot be expected to cast a rational vote, he or she must be expected to cast a merely political vote. What then? Should student representatives trade votes? Should student representatives tell a faculty representative that if he or she will vote to grant tenure to candidate X, who is popular with students, then the student representatives will vote for candidate Y, who is desirable from the faculty point of view? The potential scenarios are so numerous and frightening that we need not carry this analysis further. The absurdity of the student-politician model is there for all to see.

In addition, the student-as-politician metaphor simply will not work. Group interest theory depends upon relative stability in the groups and relative stability in group leadership. Otherwise, long-term compromises and agreements among group representatives cannot be made. The student body membership changes regularly. Leadership views may change radically. The student government of one year cannot bind the student government of the next year. Long-term negotiating and long-term planning are impossible. As a consequence, the newly conquered "student power" is delivered to consideration and serious participation for only short-term issues.

Finally, the student-as-politician metaphor will not do because it is dishonest in representing the student. The student is not primarily a politician but a learner attempting to grow, develop, and acquire better values. The group interest political process manipulates individuals and hopes for their stagnation so as not to disturb the "equilibrium" of the special interest group and of negotiated settlements. Groups must display cohesiveness and loyalty (whether honest or not) to leaders if they are to be victorious in the decision-making process. Education requires disequilibrium, honesty, and a positive approach to nonconforming opinions.

### STUDENT AS COMMODITY

In a society dominated by economic imagery, it is not surprising that economic metaphors would arise. We consider two: the student as commodity and the student as consumer.

Perhaps there is no more dramatic way in which students are used as commodities than in the advancement of athletic programs. Students are recruited, persuaded, bribed, coerced, deceived, and bought in an effort to be sure the team in question, which, by the nature of the process, is atypical with respect to the rest of the students is victorious. Somehow, it is believed that one university is better than another because it can beat its competition on a Saturday afternoon. The instrumentality of no-need athletic grants represents the actual but final absurdity in the whole process. No-need grants are, in short, payment for services rendered. They often cease if the student becomes too interested in his or her studies and decides to withdraw from varsity competition. The athlete is, quite simply, purchased in the same way other commodities are purchased, and the athlete is equivalently expendable. A service is rendered—athletic activity—in return for payment. With the Internal Revenue Service interested in closing loopholes, surely here is a hole large enough safely to run through even the slowest back. The purchased athlete is not a student in any substantial sense. Attending classes and taking examinations, all is incidental to the primary purpose. What of the integrity of the university which engages in such practices? We need not bother to look. It has lost its soul by treating some students as objects to be manipulated, as commodities to be bought and sold. There are excuses offered for such disreputable behavior.

In the private sector, it is assumed (usually without much evidence) that alumni demand winning teams, that they were not well educated about the institution's values while matriculants, and that they cannot be persuaded of the need for a university to focus its energies on education. The public universities blame legislators; teams must be developed so as to allocate scarce and desirable tickets among supporting legislators. Through it all, the university allows itself to be manipulated, and the students allow themselves to be manipulated.

To be the willful object of manipulation may be superior to being a coerced object of manipulation: the fact remains that one is an object of manipulation and, thus, has lost integrity. I speak of the extreme case of no-need financial aid here. It should be pointed out, however, that between the extremes of no-need financial aid and financial aid without regard to promised athletic performance is a long continuum, and many institutions which reject no-need financial aid still find ways to achieve much the same end and, thus, conceive of students as commodities.

If the only way students are viewed—and treated—as commodities is in respect to athletics, we might ignore the issue as lamentable, but aberrant behavior. However, we cannot be so comforted.

Brains are bought quite as much as bodies are. Merit scholarships, so-called, represent little more than a blatant attempt to purchase student services. There is usually much less faculty objection to the purchase of brains than there is to the purchase of brawn, but the principle of commodity treatment remains the same. It is presumed that the alumni want athletic teams while the faculty want young scholars. The best way to appease both groups is to purchase some of what they want. In addition, students are admitted and, in some cases, graduated because of parental standing (real or imagined) as alumni, as government officials, as fund-raising prospects, etc. All such actions fall within the conceptual framework of the treatment of the student as a commodity.

Furthermore, the relentless search for marginal enrollment-driven revenues and the willingness to accept full-time enrollments (FTEs) at virtually any educational cost represent the purchase of a student-commodity. The primary purpose is net revenue production. It is frightening, but realistic, to recognize that there is probably no subject so trivial and no treatment so substandard academically that we could not find some college or university somewhere offering a course in it. The marketing hype which is going into selling "educational" programs and courses at colleges throughout the country is distressing for those who, without being trapped into providing operational definitions, know there is a difference between college-level work and education outside that domain. Admittedly, the boundaries are difficult to define. It is also difficult to define precisely the difference between a good teacher and a mediocre teacher. Difficulty of precise definition does not warrant the conclusion that there is no difference. Unfortunately, the substandard programs are frequently justified and maintained on the basis that they are net revenue producers. The long and short of it is readily comprehended: educational goals have become secondary to financial objectives.

The public institution which is not tuition-bound is FTE-bound since FTE counts form the basis for public funding. Thus, the search is for marginal FTEs. The private institution which is tuition-bound searches for marginal tuition revenues. Both effectively purchase students and manipulate them as if they were commodities. Continuing education programs which were, perhaps, originally founded on sound educational principles, are construed as net revenue producers, and the corruption threatens to infect the whole campus.

STUDENT AS CONSUMER

Perhaps one might expect that, within the confines of economic imagery, a national response of students to being viewed as commodities would be to establish themselves as consumers and demand all the "rights" consumer movements insist upon. But the fact is that others acting in the name of students, and not students themselves, advanced the consumerism movement. Whatever its historical origin, the logic of the movement seems clear. Since students pay for education, they are to colleges and universities what customers are to corporations. The colleges and universities *produce* courses, credits, and degrees. Students *purchase* courses, credits, and degrees. While the logic *seems* clear, it is based upon an analogy—and the analogy is fallacious.

Students are not consumers. The economic meaning of the concept of consumer derives from the economic function of producers. Firms produce goods and services; they offer them for sale at full price market value; consumers purchase those goods and services at full price fair market value. Emphasis is on a value that is fair market value, in short, a price arrived at through open and unfettered competition. It is also important to emphasize that the value will be full price (i.e., will cover all costs). If the sale price is not full cost, the producing firm will either have to raise the price to full cost, if the market will bear that, or go out of business. We may presume this is the context in which the student-as-consumer advocates want us to understand the movement. The student as consumer deserves all the rights which belong to other consumers.

The student, however, fails to meet a necessary condition for being a consumer: he or she does not pay a full cost fair market value for the education provided. In the public sector, which accounts for almost 75 percent of all enrollments, the price is not arrived at by anything approaching open market conditions. Furthermore, the price is well below full cost. It has been estimated that tuition in the average public institution covers only about one-fifth of its stated educational and general expenses. If, as economic theory would have it, one acquires consumer rights because one had paid full value for a service, then the student does not have consumer rights. The other suppliers of funds acquire stronger rights: donors, taxpayers, the public-at-large, etc. In the private sector, while the student comes closer to providing full price, it is nonetheless estimated that tuitions meet only 60 percent of stated educational and general expenses. Endowment income, gifts, bequests, government grants, and (all too frequently) deficit spending make up other sources of revenue.

As I compared tuition revenues to expenses, I carefully used the term "stated" with respect to expenses. There are large segments of unstated expenses which, if they were imputed into the stated expense budgets, would diminish even further the proportional contributions students make to their education. For reasons I find insufficient, college and university accounting systems will neither state nor fund depreciation. Whether stated or not, the facts remain that buildings and equipment do depreciate and deteriorate. That depreciation (however estimated) is a real cost of "doing business" and the failure to state and fund it merely hides real costs. In addition, colleges and universities have enjoyed the advantage of tax-free property. The money which is forgiven to colleges and universities must be raised elsewhere by taxpayers. As a final example, consider compensation for the faculty and staff at most colleges and universities. Even faculty who are indisputably successful in their professions are paid—relative to other professions—either as if they were unsuccessful professionals or successful nonprofessionals. Faculty and staff have made enormous collective contributions to the education of students by foregoing the kind of compensation enjoyed by their professional peers. Far from being presumptive consumers with presumptive consumer rights, students are beneficiaries of enormous charitable munificence and, thus, owe a deep debt of gratitude.

Before leaving the concept of student as consumer, it is important to mention its most pernicious consequence. By the nature of the concept, a consumer has no responsibility toward the producer or seller. If I purchase something, I usually have the right to use what I have purchased however I wish. The seller has no justifiable claim on me. The consumer is a *taker* in the marketplace. However, if education, especially liberal education, is to fulfill its mission, it should educate students to be *givers*, not takers. The student has responsibilities toward the educational enterprise because of the benefit derived therefrom. The student should not be a passive recipient and taker in the educational endeavor; it is only through active participation and active giving that the process of growth and development can take place.

### THE REAL STUDENT—THE STUDENT AS A PERSON

Hopefully we have examined enough metaphors to support the point that we should stop using metaphors and consider our students directly. By so considering, we find, not surprisingly, that students are real and genuine persons.

When we start with the premise of the student as a person, interesting results follow. Degrading references to people tend to be self-confirmatory. People who are treated as children, as politically motivated, as commodities, or as consumers tend to validate the role into which they are cast by acting out those roles. An analysis of the concept of person will reveal the importance of the conceptual shift. The analysis cannot be exhaustive and may even appear diversionary, but even a cursory analysis will be revelatory, and it is central to my theme.

A person is a center of values. As long as we merely receive our values from others, as long as we subscribe to a set of values because they are given by others, we deny ourselves the dignity of being a person. As a person, I may, of course, decide to accept the values of another person because I think those values are right. However, it is I who decide. If I agree to accept the values of another—parent, teacher, or the political system—because of the "superior" standing of that other, I am dedignified and lose my status as an independent and value-creating being. On some occasions, it may make most sense to do as another says. The other may hold power or control over me. When someone threatens to shoot me if I do not hand over my money, I may sensibly acquiesce and give up the money. However, it is not surrendered because I think the other has a right to it; I give it up as a direct consequence of my loss of dignity. My position is not morally inferior; it is inferior in terms of power. By contrast, recognizing some cause to be admirable and morally worthy, I may agree to give some of my resources to it. I do so out of a sense of my worth and a sense of the worth of the cause. My dignity is not only retained, but it is increased because my actions give my values concrete expression.

There are more complex cases. One may freely join an organization which requires obedience to its regulations, existing and potential. Or so it appears. The appearances are deceptive, however. One cannot, with dignity, agree to join an organization that demands dedignification except, perhaps, where exit from the organization is easy and without coercive restraints. Furthermore, no organization can have its integrity or legitimacy if it demands obedience merely as a consequence of its power. Some organizations, and even some individuals, may legitimately demand obedience of another if that other human being does not have a legitimate right to status as a full person. Parents have a legitimate right to demand obedience of children because children are not full persons and have not acquired the right to be treated as full persons. Parents must be careful lest the recognition that children are not full persons be maintained beyond its justifiable range so that the offspring who are full persons are continually treated as children. Children have "rights" which derive from the nonfree derivation of their status, and parental obligations to children are more severe than to other persons with whom something closer to a free relationship is established.

We are led, then, to more direct consideration of the university and its integrity. The central purpose of education should be to enable people to become free. If we abandon the concept of students as children, we are impelled to adopt a concept of students as persons whose freedom and dignity are to be celebrated. It would represent an obscene twist on mission and relationships to persons if universities—the source of freedom—should treat their own members as objects to be manipulated.

Students do have rights as persons: the right to be treated with honesty, integrity, dignity, and full recognition that they are the center and source of value. They rightfully expect the suffocating and patronizing paternalism (which has historically characterized university-student relationships) to be obsolete. They rightfully expect universities to be committed to the development of freedom for each student. They have a right to expect universities to resist attempts to command obedience. They have a right to be treated as free members of a free community. They have a right to expect university officers will deliver the best they can in terms of educational program in order to get students to take an active part in their own growth and development toward freedom. They have a right to ask us to set high standards and evaluate student performance in accordance with them.

High standards and insistence upon quality are not inconsistent with student freedom. In fact, they are the only criteria which are consistent with recognizing the student as a person with dignity and integrity. The view that professors know nothing more than their students is simply fake humility (or the professors need to return to school). The student should seek to learn in order to become freer. The professor who does not demand the best potentially commits students to ignorance and corresponding enslavement. A faculty which does not recognize—and insist upon—a difference between a college-level course and a course below college level engages in patronizing behaviors quite as much as those who see students as children. The line is not easy to draw, but it can and should be drawn, and that can only be done, finally, by a professional and concerned faculty. The fact that people disagree on standards does not provide evidence for the view that there are no standards. When we abandon standards, we abandon the concept of the student as a person. Students should expect to be held to standards and evaluated in the context of them. The student who wants to perfect an ability to play the violin expects the instructor to set high standards and evaluate performance in the context of them. Anything short of that is a fake; it is dedignifying and lacks integrity on the part of the instructor and the student. Novitiate violinists do not seek to be told their playing is good (unless it is); they seek the truth in the context of appropriate standards. Why should we assume other students seek anything less?

*Obligations of Students*—Persons have rights; they also have obligations. Students have rights; they also have obligations. One of the more unfortunate aspects of the metaphorical treatments of students is that most such treatments tend to eliminate or reduce the obligations students have beyond what may be recovered in a quasicontractual relationship. The obligations of children are quite limited by their status. The obligations of human commodities and consumers are limited by their mere quid pro quo relationship to the other party.

General human obligations flow from a general concept of integrity and honesty through which it is dictated that one should accord to another the respect and dignity one expects for oneself. The university has an obligation to treat its members with respect, dignity, and complete honesty because that is what is required in moral relationships between human beings. Members of the university have an obligation to treat each other (and, so, the university) with honesty and integrity.

There are special forms of dishonesty which are particularly pernicious in an educational setting: plagiarism; cheating; submitting work not one's own; desecration of scholarly, educational, and artistic materials. Such acts are not only an offense against any human society, but constitute a particularly grievous assault against the heart of the institution. College and university officials should get clear on their procedures and principles with respect to academic dishonesty before the courts take away all the initiative. Unfortunately, the pseudosophistication associated with using legalistic terms has led campus guard-house lawyers to use phrases such as "due process," "prima facie evidence," "burden of proof," and other legalisms in setting up and carrying forward procedures. Having invited the legalistic wolf into the hen house, we find now he wants to take over.

A faculty member who thinks a student has committed a breach of academic honesty feels increasingly as if he or she, not the student, is on trial. Endless hours can be spent on defining plagiarism and proper footnote procedures where the issue is simple: was material presented such that a reasonable person might assume the student intended the teacher to consider it the work of the student whereas the student should have known it was not his or her work? In brief: was the student dishonest? Breaches of academic honesty should be dealt with swiftly, surely, and severely. If the courts wish to tie the university in knots, let the courts rule explicitly. In our frequent efforts at assuming what courts will do or in settling out of court until the procedurally perfect case is presented, we may overcompensate and, thereby, lose integrity by incremental concessions.

While academic honesty is necessary, mere academic honesty is not enough to encompass the broad range of obligations assumed by students. As we turn to a consideration of a broader range of student obligations, we continue to speak in a moral context. In a society which sometimes seems to want to legislate and regulate morality, it is well to remember that what is legally required is only a subset of what is morally right.

The educational enterprise is, essentially, a cooperative and giving enterprise in which people are called upon to work with one another. The university which is dominated by combative, contractual, and taking relationships cannot fulfill the promise of its mission. The external world of clawing and grabbing is not an appropriate "model" for the university. A student who enters a university acquires obligations to other people in the university to become a giver, not a taker. Participation and cooperation in the classroom, the laboratory, the studio, the dormitory, and collegial governance are obligations students acquire by virtue of their status as persons who are students.

## *Some Issues Considered in Light of the Student as Person*

In recognition of the student as person, we should be careful not to exaggerate the claims made. Students are not faculty or administrators or governing board members. Since other members of the university are also persons, they should be respected as such. Perhaps one of the most destructive interpersonal consequences of the student-as-consumer metaphor is the apparent justification it grants students to treat other university members as people whose primary role is that of servants. This dual understanding of students as persons and as students may shed light on certain issues which have vexed higher education.

### STUDENT SOCIAL LIFE

Because a person is a total integrated and organic being, it is senseless to divorce the student's social life from the student's academic life. We do, of course, live in a fragmented society, and we do carry out different roles in different places. Ultimately, however, we are one—and only one —person: we are thus called to integrate our lives into a more or less coherent whole. The residential colleges originally recognized the totality of the educational experience and took concerns about students' social lives very seriously. A combination of the growth of nonresidential colleges, graduate programs, and increasing faculty self-consciousness about scholarly professionalism led faculty to divert themselves of responsibility for students' social lives through turning control over to students themselves or by promoting the creation of "student personnel" officers. Students who had been treated as children reacted like children with their newly established freedom. (I do not mean students acted irresponsibly; that implies an excessively pejorative view of children.) The students supported the faculty's abandonment; in many cases, students even persuaded, cajoled, and pressured faculty into such abdication. Unfortunately, the movement was mainly correct in its conclusions but fallacious in its reasoning.

The view of the student as child was never really faced and destroyed on its own merits. Instead, an implicit argument was developed which claimed that the student had two lives: one social and the other academic. Faculty, so the argument went, had proper control only over the academic life. Someone else, or some combination of people, would have to see to the social life. The more liberal administrators, faculty, and students, of course, argued for student control. Conservative faculty, administrators, and parents argued there had to be a strong measure of institutional control. It is no wonder student personnel offices grew so rapidly. The new deans did not simply have a different job, they had a fundamentally incoherent one: to provide control, restraints, and restrictions, on the one hand, and, on the other, to meet student demands for services and a voice of advocacy in the higher counsels of administration. Having bifurcated the student, companion institutional structures had to be created to administer this conceptual incoherence.

The initiation of a process to find answers seems fairly simple. The student is a whole person and should be viewed as such. There may be little we want to do or can do about overseeing some experiences students have, but students will have them, and the experiences will have an impact upon our students. Education is an enterprise designed to provide freedom for people. If our students are not children, our job is to give them as much freedom as possible. There are consequences which flow from misspent freedom, and there is little reason to shelter students from those consequences.

In addition, our strength and our resources should be focused on academic programs. It is perfectly proper to observe that much education goes on beyond the confines of the academic program, but our strength lies in the academic program, and we threaten our integrity and the students' when we divert too many resources from the academic program to ancillary enterprises. Our focus should be on the academic program; that is where our ability lies; all other programs should serve the academic program. The student should be provided maximum freedom and held to rigorous standards.

ADMISSIONS

Few areas of university life provide a more accurate or sensitive barometer than admissions. There was a time, of course, when the basic decision for some universities was whether or not the candidate could complete the academic program successfully. Others decided to admit all —or at least most—applicants and effectively did admissions screening during the first year. Other alternatives appeared, but it should be recalled that, for many colleges and universities, survival has been a genuine concern, and new students were therefore vitally important. With the close of World War II, a number of forces came into effect: the G.I. Bill was passed, the "baby boom" started, the public sector grew dramatically, and the political rhetoric changed to advocating college education as a right.

For a brief period, the major admissions problem was finding ways to choose among overwhelming numbers of qualified applicants. Some institutions simply increased size to accommodate. Most of the prestigious colleges and universities erected all sorts of barriers: "aptitude" test scores, high school grades, high school class standing, quality of high school, admissions interviews, extra-curricular activities—all were used as filtering devices. Individually the devices were all known to be very poor predictors of student performance. However, a kind of perverse fallacy of composition made us believe that a collective analysis composed of individually inadequate parts would, somehow, prove sufficient. Since the stakes seemed so high to so many students, it would be inappropriate to call the whole process a game, but leaving aside the seriousness of the issue, students responded as if it were a game. Courses—whole curricula in some cases—were reoriented around preparation for aptitude tests. High schools and private secondary schools were selected with an eye on admission to the favorite college or university. Reputation of the secondary school had to be balanced against level of expected performance of the student in the secondary school. Students were driven (figuratively and literally) by parents to piccolo lessons, to science clubs, to Boy Scouts, to athletic practices, all in an attempt to add that dollop of unusual flavor to the transcript.

As if foreshadowing a deep depression and stormy weather, the admissions barometer fell precipitously. The overbuilt, overadministered, undermaintained, and "underfacultied" universities were delivered to a period in which first student applications and then student enrollments would slide downward at an accelerating rate. The public universities had argued their growth case before legislatures on an increasing FTE enrollment basis. Elaborate enrollment-driven simulation models became part of the jargon of the trade. As enrollment declined, or threatened to decline, legislators who had been persuaded with the FTE calculations in ascendancy could not understand why those formulas should not be used in decline. The answer was quite simple. Facilities which are built to accommodate marginal increases in the student body cannot be destroyed when there is a marginal decrease. Private colleges and universities were slightly more careful about overbuilding, but the fundamental argument for governing boards was the same: increasing numbers of students. Presidents gained prestige by persuading boards and legislatures to embark on major construction programs. Buildings were for presidents what books, scholarly articles, and consultancies were for faculty members. The fixed costs in universities were enormous and not only, or, perhaps, even primarily, a function of the favorite target: tenure.

If the fixed costs are really fixed (and with undermaintained facilities, increasing energy costs, unfinanced government requirements, and extraordinary inflationary pressures, it seems that it is not the base which is fixed but the rate of increase), if the institution is really labor intensive (it is), then the only viable response seems to be the maintenance and increase of enrollment at all costs (even academic costs). Institutional survival, not educational quality, becomes *the* criterion. Admissions offices, which previously had to be gatekeepers, are now required to become the institution's lead marketing arm; universities clamor for mention in the national media; curricula are restructured, reordered, and reinvented in order to lure marginal enrollments; academic departments, even individual faculty, are evaluated on their ability to draw students.

Admissions officers are given quotas to fill, and the concern is more with admitting warm bodies than with providing an education for appropriately selected students. Huckstering becomes the norm; insistence upon standards and quality evaluation becomes deviant, when not self-defeating, behavior. Promises which will not be kept are made to prospective students. The analogy is to the caricature of a used-car salesman or politician. Needless to say, the integrity of the university is being lost. In the current environment, it seems somewhat quaint to raise an issue about university integrity—like asking whether we should restore required chapel attendance. The issue is there; a long history of a tradition says it should be taken seriously; conferences could be developed in which each person might treat the topic in somber tones, but would anyone *really* take it seriously?

In many admissions processes, students are indeed treated as consumers, and, if careless, we shall find ourselves with politically imposed standards and regulations where we refuse to impose our own educational standards. It is too easy to say we shall get what we deserve; *we* shall not get much of the negative consequences; rather they will be left as an inheritance for our successors, and the momentum will make it virtually impossible to reverse course.

Our job is not to maintain existence at all costs but to provide a service of educating people and enhancing their freedom. If society does not value our services, we should close doors and dissolve our universities. If we sacrifice educational integrity by contorting ourselves and our admissions processes beyond recognition, we save only the shell of the university. Lost is the integrity which makes the service worthwhile.

Financial aids, which are related closely to admissions policies, are also subject to the same pressures. The simple concept that students who could not afford college because of personal financial difficulties would be helped has now been extended to include a multitude of questionable practices. Many qualified students cannot afford the charges of the university they desire to attend. Yet those same universities can be found using financial aids beyond student needs to entice athletes and other specially selected students to their institution. Is it any wonder students and other people become cynical listening to high flown academic rhetoric about institutional integrity? In many cases, the argument no longer is whether universities are losing integrity. The argument is only over the price.

STUDENT PARTICIPATION IN GOVERNANCE

A very controversial area which calls for further analysis is the area of student participation in university governance. As pointed out earlier, many university officers accepted a bifurcated view of students and gave them a large measure of hegemony over their own social lives. Few wish to return to the days of paternalistic involvement in students' lives Their reasons may be open to question, but their conclusion is acceptable, and the issue is not a live one for most. The cutting edge of problems lies with other more central areas, and we should turn our attention to them. Consideration of four critical areas which are qualitatively distinct may yield enough principles to allow further extrapolation.

*Governing Boards*—In some ways, student participation on governing boards seems to be the most troublesome concern. I think it is the easiest to resolve. Those who do not serve on governing boards imagine them to be the real source of power and decision-making. They are not and cannot be. I speak here with special reference to the private sector where we may presume the vast majority of governing board members hold the interests of the university as central to their concerns. In the public sector where board members may be appointed for narrow political reasons and often come with an independent political portfolio, the analysis may have to change.

The task of the governing boards is largely one of oversight designed to insure that administrators and faculty deal directly with issues. Governing boards sometimes attempt to define their roles as policy-making and planning roles. However, governing boards cannot do either realistically. They can endorse, amend, or reject suggestions. They can mandate studies, and they can direct the college to develop recommendations and alternatives, but they cannot do those things themselves; when they attempt to do so, the signals are clear that there is a lack of confidence.

The real functioning power lies with the administration and the faculty; governing board power flows from its legal authority, and that is enough to put a check on administrators and faculty who make recommendations without sufficient good reasons. The governing boards cannot make policy. However, they can decide whether the administration and faculty have justified the policies recommended with good reasons. In this context, students can and should participate on governing boards. If the students abandon their status as full student-persons and adopt, rather, a role as student-politician, their participation will be ineffective and counter-productive. If students are encouraged to act as delegates from the student body or as group interest politicians, they do not belong on private governing boards because of obvious conflicts of interest. If, however, the student acts as a person who is a student, the perspective brought by the student may help test whether the administration has presented good reasons for its proposals. Students should participate because, as persons, they are an important part of the university. Similar arguments could, of course, be made about faculty participation, assuming faculty have not entered into a collective bargaining agreement.

*Budget and Financial Planning*—Another area which seems controversial with respect to student participation is the financial area. Here, again, I think the solution can be arrived at fairly simply. Students have every right to be concerned about financial plans of their university and to participate in the shaping of those plans. Even though financial planning is not the most important aspect of planning for the university, it is extremely important, and in that planning many values are tested and given concrete formulation. Again, assuming the student is not an interest group representative in the process, it would seem that students' perspectives, concerns, and endorsement should be sought by active participation of student members of the relevant budgetary committees.

*Educational Planning*—The heart of the enterprise is education, and it might seem that if students are to be treated as persons they should be deeply involved in this central process of educational planning. While I concur finally that student involvement is advisable, I am more ambivalent about this case. As pointed out earlier, students are persons, but they are students, also. To put the matter simplistically, we might ask how the uneducated can participate effectively in establishing the conditions for education. It is difficult enough for those professionally trained to know what directions various disciplines might take and, further, which of those directions should be pursued. It is silly to think students, who may still be struggling to understand present courses, can make rational judgments about future developments beyond their ken. To think otherwise is to invite, once again, the fake humility which concludes professors know nothing more than students. Professors who are scholars should be at the cutting edge of their disciplines. None but the advanced graduate students can be at the cutting edge of the disciplines, and graduate students have precious little experience with teaching.

Nevertheless, perhaps we are too harsh. Our job is to teach, to persuade, to lead, to educate. It certainly would be an ironic twist if we were to allow students to participate in other processes while denying them access to the most central planning process. Perhaps we should have more confidence in ourselves and our students. We can answer reasonable questions, and we can persuade where persuasion is appropriate. Students will recognize their lack of expertise and defer to expert opinion where that is not merely a cover for prejudice or arbitrariness. Planning is a process. If it is to be a meaningful process for the institution, it should involve all those members who will be affected. Students constitute an important ingredient, and while I would not advocate a majority of students or student veto power in the educational planning process, I would recommend meaningful student voting participation on the basis of our understanding of students.

*Faculty Promotion Decisions*—The educational planning process should yield policies with respect to faculty promotion, especially in the context of tenure decisions. Promotion decisions are not planning decisions; they are implementation decisions. Thus, our arguments for involving students in planning are not sufficient in this area; furthermore, the dependence upon expert opinion is even greater. Systematic student opinion should be sought with respect to a candidate's teaching ability and, while substantially positive opinions may rank as a necessary condition for promotion, they cannot rank as sufficient in a college or university which takes itself and scholarship seriously. Once student opinion is gathered and systematically evaluated, perhaps with the participation of other students, the final decision should be made by professional peers.

Unhappily, under the current prevailing tenure procedures, the logic of the situation will almost guarantee that negative tenure decisions will make students unhappy. Universities which are doing their job with untenured faculty, evaluate them carefully and constantly. Poor teachers will be discovered in the early probationary years and, thus, will not be reviewed for tenure. The teachers remaining will almost always have a more or less strong student following, and rejections will often turn critically on evaluations of scholarly potential. Those evaluations can only be made by peers and, as a consequence, it will appear again and again that the institution does not care about teaching. A short-term political solution may be to invite students into the peer review process, but that is a baldly political solution which dooms us, once again, to a bankrupt view of the student. Our alternative, a difficult but correct one, is to be ready to explain again and again why the process should be a peer review process and to hope eventually that students will respect us for respecting them.

### Conclusion

What, then, of the future? The future for higher education is not a bright one, but not for the reasons usually mentioned. Prospective financial conditions set a context to which we are invited to react. It is not the conditions, but our reactions which lead to a dismal picture of the future.

It is always dangerous and statistically fallacious to merely project from the recent past to the future. Whatever else we know, we can almost always predict safely that the future will not be precisely like the recent past, so there is some hope. However, actions do establish habits and incremental concessions at the margin of academic standards can establish procedural habits which allow us to leave unquestioned further erosions which would have been questioned and dismissed earlier. If recent practice has established new conceptual habits, we should conclude that the future is bleak, indeed.

As the next few years pass, one is driven to the conclusion that adversarial relationships will tend to dominate campuses. The lawyers, the bureaucrats, and the social scientists increasingly set the tone for campus debates. All too frequently, their conceptual habits are adversarial and lead to negotiated settlements in which reference to principles is just part of the rhetoric of the debates. Collegiate education still has not gained the confidence to view itself except through analogies. As there are student analogies, so there are institutional analogies to business, to politics, to cities, to families, etc.

Thus far, the financial crises have not driven us to examine what is of central importance; they have driven us to survival tactics and, not infrequently, survival at all costs. The future is not very promising. Alumni and legislators are too distant and have too romanticized a view to be of help. Governing boards' members confine their attention to budgets. Administrators are confined to crisis management (when they are not looking for appointment elsewhere), and students are confined by various metaphors. If there is hope, it lies with a professional faculty, but those ranks grow slimmer. By a professional faculty, I mean one which accepts collective responsibility for the educational program and academic standards.

A university in which faculty are not effectively "more equal" than all others is a university which has lost its central mission; it has become merely a social organization which incidentally is involved in education. Herein lies the threat of faculty collective bargaining to the university. A faculty which endorses collective bargaining becomes an adversarial unit within the university. Ironically, faculty collective bargaining does not legitimize faculty power; it finally legitimizes the administrative role as the only role which, as an instrument of the governing boards, can lay claim to total institutional interests. It is not out of self-interest that faculty should exercise its leadership. It is out of faculty expertise and professional responsibility. Our hope is that faculty will come to recognize these responsibilities and, thus, establish a dignified attitude toward students. Our fear is that faculty have been so worn down and have been so forced into expressions of narrow self-interest that the recent habits will prevail into the future. Speaking realistically, our fears have more justification than our hopes.

Through an honest appraisal of students as persons, we learn about the integrity of students and about the integrity of a university of students. We must hope that we shall be able to put this understanding into effect. We must do more than hope; we must act.

*Elizabeth T. Kennan*

# 8

# The Curriculum

My message, deceptively simple, is this: the explosion of knowledge and the concurrent growth of specialization are more to blame for the current state of curriculum in higher education than economic pressures. And, ironically enough, the financial austerity occasioned by these economic pressures may indeed provide an opportunity to reexamine and reform what we educators are doing—and not simply what we are spending.

I propose to look at some of the problems—and possible responses thereto—as these touch doctoral programs, master and professional education, and general education at the undergraduate level. In each instance, I seek not only to offer answers, but to indicate what some institutions are already doing, successfully, to provide answers.

### Departments and Doctorates:
### The Management of Reduction

Discussion of the shape and philosophy of "general education" within the colleges has been intense in the past year. This concern is a timely and, indeed, necessary consequence of the abandonment of traditional structures of distribution requirements and mandatory courses

---

ELIZABETH T. KENNAN *is president of Mount Holyoke College. A graduate of that college and Oxford University, Dr. Kennan is a specialist in intellectual history. She is a consultant to the National Endowment for the Humanities and a board member of the Woodrow Wilson International Center for Scholars.*

over the past decade. But the curriculum in American colleges and universities has always placed its heart in the departments, in the undergraduate concentration, and the major field in graduate study, and it is here that inquiry must begin.

The "major" in practically every college in the country is built in the image of a graduate program. Departments teach the hermeneutics and the history of their own field. Even at the undergraduate level, faculty are anxious to insure that students have at least an introduction to all the subsets of their disciplines, so that historians in their earliest twenties will have an acquaintance with the *Annales* school, with prosopography, with intellectual history, with Weberian analysis—not to mention acquaintance with the traditional chronological divisions of European and American history. As a result, the bachelor of arts or sciences has become a miniprofessional. This tendency has intensified recently as the breakdown of prescribed general education programs has permitted students to choose freely among all the courses provided in college and overwhelmingly to add more credits in their own majors. Nor is this trend entirely a matter of free choice: the graduate and, particularly, the professional schools have encouraged and, in some cases, required a pinpointing of undergraduate preparation. Medical schools of course are a prime case in point. So comprehensive are their requirements in chemistry, mathematics, biology, and physics that they virtually blanket three years of an undergraduate's experience. Law schools are not nearly so arrogant, but they tend nonetheless to tilt undergraduate preparation into an intense concentration in the social sciences. Inevitably these requirements and the examinations which enforce them cause students to concentrate on what they can know in a very narrow spectrum at the cost of the larger questions of how man learns and what it is, after all, that is worth knowing.

The constant intensifying of major fields has professionalized undergraduate experience everywhere. And professionalization in academic subjects is a contagion which colleges have almost certainly caught from the graduate schools. Intense concentration within a field is, of course, the hallmark of American graduate education in the twentieth century and is surely responsible for much of the research capability we have attained, especially in the physical sciences. But in some fields intense specialization at the graduate level has come to postpone if not to prohibit adequate intellectual training. In medieval history, for example, requirements of the history doctorate have crowded out opportunities to study ancillary fields essential to scholarly pursuits, such as ancient, modern, and medieval languages; theology; philosophy; literature; and paleography. Knowledge of these fields, which, in fact, is fundamental to research, has become esoteric. In most cases, postdoctoral study is required to attain it. Nor is this paradox limited to so notably intricate a field as medieval studies. In anthropology, for example, scholars require a considerable range of knowledge in comparative social institutions, international relations, economics, comparative religion, and psychology. Few of these are likely to be included in their departmental requirements. The situation of doctoral candidates is made worse by their undergraduate preparation which, having emphasized a single field at the cost of study in languages or mathematics or philosophy, leaves basic skills in these fields to be picked up during postgraduate study—too little and too late.

Overspecialization, a fundamental and pervasive curricular problem in American universities, has traditionally been blamed on pressures scientific and scholarly societies have brought to bear on undergraduate departments. No doubt there is some truth to this accusation for departments, particularly graduate departments, seek to provide students with credentials for membership in just such societies. But to place on professional societies sole responsibility for the whole development of the university curriculum is to exaggerate their importance and to ignore the interests of the universities themselves in the growth of specialization. It was, after all, President Eliot of Harvard and his colleagues at the beginning of the twentieth century who popularized the elective system and the division of faculties into departments for the purpose of concentration. Universities have fostered their departments ever since and have been justly proud of the research institutes which they, in turn, have engendered. There is no question of the achievements attained under this system. The difficulties which remain, however, are the side effects of narrowing individual scholarship and of dislocating undergraduate programs.

THE ECONOMY AND THE OMNICOMPETENT UNIVERSITY

Surprisingly, the current stringency of the national economy may provide conditions in which such side effects can be diminished. Part of the problem in the twentieth century has been competition among the various universities, each seeking to become omnicompetent, to replicate the strengths of all others. At the height of their powers in the 1960s, there was hardly a university in the country which did not offer a doctorate in Victorian literature as well as one in astronomy and nuclear physics. Almost every department gave a graduate degree and most permitted specialization in the various subsets of their discipline. Administrations and legislatures poured money into the creation of a complete university, sometimes several complete universities, in every state.

In this period of intensely competitive growth, departments were extended in a linear fashion as their fields grew. In part, this occurred because no university wished to neglect an area of specialization in which others might excel. In many instances departmental requirements for advanced degrees simply followed growth. They came, without explicit intention, to engulf the entire curricular life of graduate students, until there was very little time left to master related fields which have always been the support of true scholarship.

It is now clear that we have passed the time of luxuriant growth. Even if the economy were buoyant, costs of ever more precise instrumentation, the radio telescope, for example, would diminish the number of universities capable of maintaining complete graduate programs in some of the scientific fields. But in this period of apparently permanent retrenchment, departments may be forced to reduce their programs even when equipment costs are less spectacular. At Bryn Mawr, the question of whether all departments offering a doctoral program should continue to do so has already been raised. At The Catholic University of America, one department has been eliminated for reasons of cost. Private graduate universities may face the prospect of disbanding whole schools in order to maintain others with quality intact. Legislatures, impatient of rising costs, are capable of forcing retrenchment even in the state universities.

If the reduction of graduate programs across the country occurs in haphazard fashion, there will be cause for alarm. But careful pruning could actually be beneficial. Overall, our aim should be to retain our capacity to support research at the edges of knowledge in every major field. This implies that we will maintain not only research facilities, but also curricular programs to train coming generations of scholars in each field. This is not to say, however, that each university or even each state should maintain this capacity. Constant replication is a luxury no longer affordable. But reduction is notoriously more difficult to manage than growth. Faculty are notably and properly suspicious of administrative decisions to eliminate or even to restrict seriously any given academic program, particularly at the graduate level. They realize, often better than planners, the implications of decapitalization in an academic field where the costs of recouping a library collection or rebuilding an inventory of scientific equipment could well be prohibitive. And if administrative decisions to trim graduate programs are likely to provoke real resistance, faculty themselves are an even less adequate guide in these decisions. The natural tendency to protect one's field can prove bitterly divisive if the matter of curriculum reduction is left to faculty debate alone.

In this situation, the national scholarly associations, far from threatening an administration, could prove an invaluable guide to economies of scale. Within their sphere of competence, they are in a position to recognize which university programs make a unique contribution to their field. What is more, they tend to conceive goals on a national scale, to be more interested in maintaining a research capacity than in reproducing it. In a period of scarce resources, when some programs will have to be excised, universities should maintain or enlarge just those departments or area studies which have unique strength. If they must reduce commitments, they should eliminate those best served elsewhere. To make these distinctions can be very difficult for a particuar administration, but with the advice of the scholarly associations taken in conjunction with that of their own faculty, a university should be able to identify those programs of quality to be preserved and fostered.

Any attempt to select and prune within a curriculum, however, will be sure to meet objection from the departments themselves. Almost every department which offers a doctoral program expects to offer comprehensive coverage of its field. How could a doctoral program be given in English literature, for example, in a department which did not maintain a post, or even a series of posts, dealing with the Victorians? To counter objections which stem from such expectation of completeness, one needs either a new set of departmental standards at the doctorate level, or else a new set of strategies for attaining them—if not a combination of both.

Without question, graduate schools should reconsider their departmental requirements for the degree. It is probably true that a candidate in English can do an excellent course of preparation without study in one or two subsets of the field. For some, Victorian literature could be replaced by comparative work in another literature or in metaphysics, theology, history of science, or music. For others, a concentration in the Victorians could be supported by course work in history, economics, and, perhaps, aesthetics. There is less need for interdisciplinary *courses* than for individual interdisciplinary *programs*. These would allow students to prepare themselves in ancillary fields to support their understanding of their major or to extend the tools they bring to their research. Students can accomplish this end often by taking rather fundamental courses outside their own departments. This allows the university both to reduce selectively the list of specializations in a department and to increase the use of a variety of rather fundamental graduate courses.

COOPERATION AT WORK

It is not all that easy, however. In every discipline, there are probably some subfields or methodologies which should always be studied for adequate mastery of the whole. Some of these may be very expensive to maintain. In such a case, a university facing curricular reduction might consider sending its students *extra muros*. Separate universities can supplement each other's programs by the simple expedient of encouraging students to visit another campus or research center for a semester, a summer, or even a year. This is frequently done among undergraduate colleges, but on the whole, graduate schools have been slow to enter regular arrangements for exchanges among students working at the doctorate level. Yet in some areas it has been done with great effectiveness. Harvard, UCLA, The University of Chicago, and The Catholic University of America, for example, have in alternate years offered special programs for doctoral candidates in the languages and critical tools necessary for research in various medieval fields. In doing so they have intended to serve a national constituency and have planned programs on a scale which no single university could hope to maintain. What is more, the separate graduate schools now rely on these national institutes in the basic disciplines and build them into individual student programs.

In these institutes for medieval studies each university relies in turn on another for support and planning of the program in successive years. However, it is not so unusual, for research purposes, for universities to join in a consortium which involves mutual support and planning. An interesting model for such cooperation involving curricular instruction has been established in Washington, where a constellation of universities joined through a subdivision of the Folger Shakespeare Library has created the Folger Institute of Renaissance and Eighteenth Century Studies. The Folger Institute now enlists a membership of thirteen universities whose graduate students and younger faculty are thereby enabled to receive instruction at the seminar level in history, literature, art history, archival studies, and other related fields pertaining to the English and European renaissance and enlightenment. Each university contributes financially to the cost of the institute, and, where personnel permit, each may also contribute teaching faculty from time to time. In return, approximately a dozen students per year receive fellowship grants from the institute to support them as they participate in Folger seminars. Others may be admitted to the seminars on a competitive basis.

The key to the importance of the Folger Institute lies clearly in the general access which membership allows to participating universities. It permits them to promise both students and faculty regular participation in a program of highly specialized renaissance and enlightenment studies. The program enhances regular departmental curriculum on a scale appropriate to demand for such instruction. No university participating in the Folger Institute thus far has yet experienced real inconvenience from a demand for Folger seminars in excess of what the institute could accommodate. Yet student participation has been steady throughout. As graduate programs in the humanities shrink, the Folger Institute provides an important model for the maintenance of truly advanced instruction. The fact that a major research library is cooperating with universities in this effort enormously enhances its value. The Folger collection is always used as the principal resource for course work, and it provides the necessary definition of its curricular programs.

This is a crucial point. General consortia among universities for cross registration and for pooling certain other resources, such as access to library collections, have long been established. But their impact on graduate curriculum has been minimal. In large part this stems from the fact that departments have been tenacious of their responsibility to provide complete access to their own fields. To relinquish a subfield to another university has been seen as a surrender of autonomy and of obligation. This has not been the case in the Folger Institute, however. The clear dominance of the Folger Collection is everywhere recognized. But beyond this, the explicit recognition of the limited aims and specific curricular competence of the institute has also been decisive. It would seem that if universities are to cooperate in their curricular programs, they will have to define the areas of the cooperation specifically and narrowly so as to strengthen rather than to threaten their departments. And very little other than course work should be accomplished under the umbrella of this consolidation. If cooperation is seen as a cover for merger, in the larger sense, it will be everywhere opposed—and justifiably.

It may be said in conclusion that the private foundations and the national funding agencies can be extremely influential in fostering this kind of coordination. Program support to enhance jointly offered seminars is only slightly less important than fellowship support to defray the cost for students of travel and living at a distance. The value of such expenditure both in terms of consolidation of effort and improvement of programs can be enormous.

Doctorate programs are reducing themselves as enrollment shrinks with the decline of job opportunities for degree holders. The burning question for planners is how reduction can take place not only in an orderly, but an imaginative fashion, while preserving the quality of our advanced education intact. Creation of doctoral programs with greater interdisciplinarity is the crucial first step in this process. But selective cooperation among universities for specific curricular programs will also enable us to preserve, in nationally recognized programs, all the essential curricular specializations we need. Furthermore such cooperation will enable us to pool our diminishing number of students so that they can have the stimulation not only of fine teaching, but also of intellectual camaraderie with others studying in their field.

If departments can also be encouraged to reconsider their requirements for undergraduates, with a view to strengthening their outside preparation, a major step will have been taken toward achievement of a liberal education. This, however, is a matter which must be addressed in conjunction with the general problem of undergraduate curriculum.

### *Master's Degrees and Professional Certification: The Management of Proliferation*

If enrollment patterns and the scarcity of college and university teaching posts necessitate a careful reduction and consolidation of graduate programs leading to the doctorate, almost the opposite effect is true of master's and vocational certification programs. Such degrees or certificates, earned as they are by course work in classes of moderate size and limited specialization, offer an important source of potential income to a variety of colleges and universities heavily dependent on tuition for income. What is more, they offer an important service to the general public.

It would be ungenerous and probably unwise to complain of this development. A number of liberal arts colleges, located in urban or suburban areas, have already survived the decline of their traditional liberal arts population in undergraduate programs by offering a curriculum which serves the vocational and paraprofessional interests of the surrounding community. The process is, of course, one of certification. But it is not necessarily a process without broader educational merit. In Livonia, Michigan, for example, programs in criminal justice and fire protection have been established at the undergraduate Madonna College. They have brought participants from fire and police departments from the larger Detroit metropolitan area. In addition to professional courses, however, the Madonna curriculum requires some general education, with traditional distribution among the humanities, sciences, and social sciences. What is more, special courses in the philosophy and history of justice, and in the concept of community, have been designed by college faculty for the program. As a result, the curriculum arches well beyond the training to be obtained at a police or fire institute. As long as the market exists for these programs, they will offer a genuine educational service.

At the very best, this should be said of all educational extensions in what is now generally known as continuing education. We are living in an economy which, as Matina Horner predicts, will require most persons to change jobs several times in a lifetime and careers at least three times. In such an economy there is positive need for continuing education to facilitate these demands for personal flexibility. Undergraduate education for many people will have to be supplemented by later programs which enable them to respond to the changing demands of the job market. And, this is especially true of those whose initial education was specifically vocational in nature.

Even though continuing education offers an important service to the adult public and a welcome source of tuition for colleges whose undergraduate population may shrink in the next ten years, these programs can, nonetheless, place considerable strain on curriculum. This strain is reflected in both the nature and the scheduling of courses. Working adults can seldom afford the daytime schedule of undergraduates, and in meeting their needs, colleges are often forced to revise patterns of teaching. Weekend programs, such as the HERS curriculum which introduces working women to administrative skills on a series of weekends, are useful extensions of the regular schedule.

Few colleges have the scheduling flexibility of Smith which permits its continuing education students, the Ada Comstock Scholars, to reside on the campus for three consecutive weekdays and complete all their week's classes and laboratories in that time. Most colleges are driven to evening courses, indeed a very old method of extending educational opportunity, or to special summer programs to accommodate continuing education. In many cases, courses in these extended hours are given away from the main campus in centers convenient to the working public.

There is a tendency, especially in programs developed for an extension center, to offer curriculum entirely designed for the market without any integral relation to the normal programs of the college. When this occurs, questions may be raised about the extension process itself and the point at which it becomes an overextension of resources. This is a serious matter, for the pressure to diversify in order to accommodate the market can be both compelling and confusing. If some care is not exercised, an extension program can divert the resources of a university or deflect faculty effort away from its central teaching mission.

In general, new, extended programs are most successful when closely allied to the established purposes of the institution and fitted to the needs of the community it serves. The Radcliffe Institute is a case in point: designed by President Mary Bunting at a college dedicated to the education of women and located in Cambridge where numbers of women were seeking new directions and career opportunities, the institute extended Radcliffe education to a group of women older than, but not substantially different from, traditional Radcliffe students. Instead of diverting the energies of the college, the Radcliffe Institute strengthened them.

Although considerably more modest, the new program at Madonna College is similar in its suitability to the college. The Livonia area is a residential community for numbers of municipal employees. The police and fire programs which have been designed for them at Madonna exactly serve the local community at the same time that they draw on the college's Catholic tradition in the study of philosophy and in community responsibility.

Extension into continuing education can often be done with a minimum of dislocation at colleges where resources are limited and the sense of distinct institutional identity is cultivated. The scarce resources of such colleges force selectivity in new curriculum, and there is frequently a considerable investment in planning programs before they are launched.

It is the universities, with their history of omnicompetence, which are most liable to overextension. With a large and complex faculty and a physical plant capable of a wide variety of uses, a university is capable of an almost endless proliferation of courses and vocational programs, each one able to shift and adjust as demand changes.

But there is a point when investment in part-time, continuing education students will unbalance any department. These students are almost always intensely vocational and highly mobile, so that they provide no core of ongoing academic study in the department. What is more, their demand for courses can be volatile, and overinvestment in offerings tailored especially for them could threaten the stable core of a curriculum. The universities, as much as the colleges, must assess their own educational goals and bring them into balance with the service they provide the adult community. Otherwise, continuing education will have to be a separate function of the university with its own faculty and its separate rationale. Planning courses in such a situation is a function of marketing, not of curriculum.

Aside from the problems of shifting schedules and designing new courses, continuing education has brought new problems in assessing academic credit. Anxious to complete their work for certification and often genuinely schooled in the practical world of experience, these new adult students have brought demands of credit for work and competence attained outside the classroom. Consequently, colleges and universities face the extremely delicate task of evaluating "life experience" and of testing competence for credit. A host of tangles follows. What portion of one's work for academic certification or degree can be permitted to take place outside the classroom? What shall be the method of integrating experience so gained into the academic program? At what cost shall credit be assigned to a skill or to an experience gained on the job rather than in the university?

Needless to say, the dust has not yet settled on costing procedures or on the whole question of the integration and evaluation of work experience in an academic program. These questions will have to be settled according to the conditions and the assumptions of each separate university or college. But there are a few general principles which apply to all. In degree work, or in work for academic certification, practical experience is no substitute for theory. The insights it offers are always partial, and, indeed, it is the limited nature of understanding gained solely from experience which leads people to seek the integration of academic knowledge. Therefore, to allow "experience" to account for anything like 50 percent of a degree program undercuts the reasons for certification and endangers the validity of the program itself. What is more, a standard test for "competency" introduced as a formula for transmitting the experiences of life into the skills of scholarship is as suspect as any other alchemical device. Credit for experience is one thing, to be rejected or accepted by a given university on its own merits. But tests which pretend to equate the attainments of that experience to the quite separate attainments of scholarship are quite another. Let us not confuse the business of the university just at the time when its doors open to a wider public.

## Undergraduate Curriculum: A Management Problem for Faculty

The tendency of graduate education throughout this century, and of all education in the past ten years, has been to tilt ever more sharply in the direction of professionalism. It is not entirely unfair to accuse universities and, now, the colleges of producing technocrats, persons with the special skills and finely pointed knowledge which can make our complex society work. We have seen that even at the graduate level this tendency can be self-defeating, either because it deprives a scholar of supporting sets of knowledge necessary to profound scholarship or because it provides a graduate with technical expertise which itself may be obsolete in a few years. But if narrowly professional education for graduate students is self-limiting, for undergraduates it is a bitter cheat. It deprives them of the one opportunity they have to master a wider variety of intellectual skills and to develop the capacity for critical judgment, without which they are truly helpless in our technocratic world.

### HARVARD'S UNDERGRADUATE PROGRAM

This, of course, is why the debate over general education has ranged so widely and attracted so much attention in the past year. Thoughtful scholars are troubled by their own students' deprivation, and the nation is appalled by the evidence on all sides of public lack of judgment. It is not often that there is such a confluence of public interest and university concern in curricular matters. Perhaps not since the "Redbook" of 1945 has the Harvard undergraduate curriculum been a matter for headlines in the national press. In a sense, the 1978 "Harvard Report on the 'Core Curriculum' " is a statement, if not as elegant, at least as searching as the 1945 *General Education in a Free Society*. The new report presents an examination of general education and a program to achieve it for the post-Vietnam years. It is a program important to the rest of the country principally for its philosophy. It was not designed, this time, for export from Cambridge. Indeed, its proposers make no secret of the fact that its elaboration will require time and attention from a powerful Harvard faculty now partially freed from their traditional teaching by declining enrollment in the graduate schools. In its detail it is predicated on a curriculum rich enough to offer undergraduates choice from some 2,500 courses. Few universities, not to mention colleges, will be able to muster the resources to duplicate its components. What is more, as debate in the press has shown, few faculties in the country will agree to the exact balance of skill and substance which Harvard has accepted.

Nonetheless, the Harvard Report is of general significance. Its very first precept puts great weight on *literacy* as the first requirement of a liberal education: "An educated person must be able to think and write clearly and effectively." To guarantee that achievement Harvard will require a program in expository writing, designed to improve the clarity and precision of writing style of each student. This instruction will be linked to the required courses in the curriculum. A writing teacher will join the other faculty in these courses to aid instruction and to help grade written assignments. Although this insistence on exposition is central, it is not, perhaps, the most impressive requirement of the Harvard program. Far more novel, although equally as necessary, is the stipulation that every student become literate in mathematics. Part Two of the report states:

> All students will be expected to demonstrate competence in algebraic manipulation and quantitative reasoning. This includes arithmetic, the use of symbols and simple algebraic manipulations, basic geometry, graphical techniques and the ability to translate verbal statements into mathematical notation.

In support of this requirement, the report further notes that "35 percent of freshmen entering Harvard in 1977 failed to achieve a score of 50 percent on the placement examination covering arithmetic, algebra, and basic precalculus mathematics." This condition, which is shared at colleges all over the country, poses grave problems to faculties concerned for the literacy of their students in a technological society. Harvard has attacked the problem directly. Not only has it prescribed the creation of new courses in mathematics for general students, it has also declared that the courses required of all in the sciences shall depend in their assignments on competence in algebra. Although achievement of these aims may be expensive of faculty time, they deserve the careful attention of every other liberal arts faculty in the nation.

To complete its requirements in the basic skills, the Harvard Core Curriculum will require competence in a foreign language sufficient to gain access to written materials in that language. This is not, in itself, a startling or even a new requirement, although it does set the face of Harvard against the general trend of the past ten years.

The Harvard Core Curriculum lays great stress on the skills of literacy in exposition, in mathematics, and in foreign languages. But it also addresses the large question of the literate or educated person. It recognizes that literacy exists in every intellectual activity, involving both the means by which to know truth and the means to express it. To become truly literate, one must enter into a vocabulary not only of language, but also of symbols and events; for literacy is built upon a shared body of reference which is the sum of our historical experience—our scientific observation and our artistic creation. To the end of creating such a vocabulary among its students, the Harvard guidelines establish a group of substantive courses, the "Core" itself. At Harvard they happen to be defined as literature and arts, history, social and philosophical analysis, and science and mathematics. There is nothing sacred about this listing of fields; they are always liable to modification according to faculty competence and interest. The Harvard list, however, represents a significant departure from the last generation's tripartite division of necessary fields into humanities, social sciences, and natural sciences. On this ground alone, they merit close consideration.

The "Core" designations also represent an ambitious attempt to convey a variety of methods of proceeding in intellectual discourse. But in the Harvard plan, the techniques of critical thought, per se, do not have centrality which they are given in other schemes for curricular revision. Other colleges propose to focus change in the curriculum on the techniques of thinking rather than the substance of knowledge. Their position has been eloquently stated by Margaret Ferguson of Yale in the November 1977 *Yale Magazine and Journal.*

. . . from the twelfth through the early twentieth century, the curriculum of the western university put great emphasis on the arts of argumentation—the arts Aristotle called dialectic and rhetoric and distinguished from all other branches of human knowledge on the basis of their capacity "to draw opposite conclusions impartially." Teachers and students, people at every level of the university hierarchy, were continually practicing, and developing, argumentative skills. . . . The university provided a forum in which critical thinking (within certain limits) was not only allowed but encouraged.

Professor Ferguson goes on to observe:

The problem we face today . . . is that the enabling conditions of debate are atrophying both within the university and in its relations to society. . . . What I propose is that the university should spend time and some of its dwindling money on devising ways to preserve genuine intellectual debate. . . .

Although Professor Ferguson can wryly accuse herself of tilting at windmills in her effort to foster critical thinking as the chief aim of the liberal education, she has allies. The new Amherst curriculum is grounded in the effort to create a certain intellectual predisposition, even more than to transfer a body of knowledge. It aims to induce critical mindedness, "the capacity to doubt, not cynically, but in a way that preserves openness of mind." This critical mindedness is defined as "an appetite for the new and the different, and a willingness to believe that the last word is never said, that new and more interesting possibilities always exist."

To achieve this habit of mind, Amherst challenges each student to choose his own course of studies, choices not only of the traditional major, but also of an adjunct field which is to be designed by the individual student. The aim of the adjunct program will be less to support the major field than to pursue "a common theme or question of the student's own devising." The freshman curriculum, especially designed and required of all students, will attempt less to convey a body of information than to provide information about the college, its faculty, its departments, and their methods of thought. The experience of these courses will enable the student to pose informed questions and make calculated selections. What is more, designed in an interdisciplinary format, the courses themselves will pose problems and instill critical habits of thought. The core courses will be far fewer at Amherst than at Harvard, for they will teach a method and provide an introduction to the college rather than passing on a defined body of knowledge.

The Amherst and the Harvard curricula are not entirely antagonistic. But the differences are, nonetheless, real. Amherst lays its stress on choice and on development of that critical judgment which is essential to it. Although Harvard does not neglect the matter of choice, it poses the problem in a different context. The Core Curriculum is, in fact, very much concerned with choice, but in its ethical and moral context. Perhaps one of the most compelling aspects of this new curriculum is the conviction, refreshingly renewed, that the development of virtue has a place in the college curriculum. As part of the requirement in philosophy there will be a course which addresses the problem of ethics, not to teach a system, but to address the steps by which critical judgment can be made.

The efforts to define and establish a program for general education has occurred not only at Amherst and Harvard this year but at Middlebury, Cornell, Stanford, Johns Hopkins, and a host of other institutions. As a result, the nature of the first two years of college education is bound to be significantly revised. But, as with graduate education, the undergraduate curriculum is dominated by the major field or the concentration. The major, bolstered as it is by the requirements of the graduate and professional schools, has not yet been challenged. Perhaps the major is necessary to convey the method of critical thought within a single discipline. Perhaps it is the indispensable route to a career or, at least, to a place in graduate school. But perhaps it is also far too dominant in today's curriculum. Perhaps our work will not truly begin until we raise questions about the departmental concentration.

Clarence C. Walton

# 9

# Reflections (or Fantasies?) on the University

In light of those tumultuous events which convulsed American society during the past quarter century—when pied pipers for all sorts of quixotic causes often attracted bizarre followings—it is perhaps inevitable that one, whose academic activities spanned this time frame, should experience a certain loss of innocence. Indeed some of the nonsense then paraded before us as serious intellectual fare seemed enough to fracture optimism irreparably. It is, however, a mistaken notion to believe the problems of higher education are caused by the student tumults of the 1960s or the financial crunches of the 1970s, and that a return to civility and prosperity will dispel the demons. Even before the days of Berkeley and Columbia riotings, a reviewer of K. E. Eble's book, *The Profane Country* (*Saturday Review*, 6/16/62), said that "only in a secular paradise (a leading college or university) could one find the bitchiness which often marks faculty relationships, . . . the maneuvering for position and power, . . . the mild corruption of human values which

CLARENCE C. WALTON *was president of Catholic University of America, 1968–78. Formerly a Penfield Fellow at the Institute of Advanced Studies (Geneva), visiting professor at the universities of Helsinki and Buenos Aires, and dean of the Duquesne University Business School, Dr. Walton is now professor of Business at Columbia University. He is director of several business corporations. A student of ethics, he has written* Corporate Social Responsibilities, Big Government and Big Business, Ethos and the Executive, *and* The Ethics of Corporate Conduct.

power and high position and rare intellect can bring." More recently, Charles Owen Rice, a respected Pittsburgh priest-journalist wrote: "The academic community is a feuding, backbiting, double-crossing snake pit."

Surely not snake pits. But, just as surely, the universities no longer seem as they once appeared to be—sanctuaries of stability and gentility. Realities, of course, never really matched the vision. Professors were sometimes spiteful, and students, often rowdies. Indeed, the larger intellectual community has never lacked the feuding, back-biting elements of Rice's profile; representative is Marx's description of Jeremy Bentham as "that insipid, pedantic, leather-tongued oracle of the vulgar bourgeois mentality."

Yet the public at large accepted the petty spitefulness with good humor and responded with such generous support to the academy that it was soon evident that what shrines and museums were to old Europe, colleges and universities would become for new America—showplaces of the nation's culture.

Today's climate is different. While public interest is still high, public confidence is less so—and for good reasons: more dollars are required by higher education, more social causes compete for scarce resources, more students are enrolled, and more professionals are dedicated to it. Vast numbers—of dollars and of people—provide good reasons for popular critical interest so that warts are as often noted as beauty marks.

Public skepticism is intensified by stories of irregularities within academe as it adjusts to prospects for declining enrollments and scarcer dollars. There are newspaper accounts of grade inflation even in the face of declining student performance as measured by standardized examinations; on televised talk shows the public hears of tenure problems and asks whether tenure has not simply become a device to protect jobs for incompetents; the young become embittered when they are encouraged to follow academic programs leading to no work; professors rail against sex and race discrimination, and yet the public knows that few women and few from minority groups hold faculty or significant administrative posts.

Because my focus is what is wrong within the academy, it is important to maintain perspective. As professor, dean, and president I have, in a sense, looked at the university from the bottom up and from top down. What I carry away from those experiences is captured in a quaint question once posed by Gilbert Chesterton: "How can this queer town, with its many-legged citizens, with its monstrous and ancient lamps, how can this world give me at once the fascination of being a strange town and the comfort of being my own?"

The university, too, is an amalgam of strangeness and familiarity for those involved, and the alma mater is a strong mother in her demands for respect and love. Buoyed by her—or suffering from her—it matters not. We respond, loyally. Perhaps that is why the late Richard Hofstadter was only half right when (at a Columbia commencement during the dark days of 1968) he said that a university is the most fragile of all institutions. It is also the most resilient and most durable. It shrinks. It retreats. It submerges. But it never really disappears. In moments of deepest peril, somehow and somewhere, a voice speaks up, a claxon sounds—and divided men unite to support the university. A common instinct recognizes that great universities are built through prodigious labor, bold imagination, considerable risk—and over long decades. The thought of destroying such an entity is so repugnant an obscenity that even the Mario Savios and Mark Rudds stop short of the final destructive step. If there are enemies on the outside, there are also enemies within, and their ranks include the irresponsible, the incompetent, and the indifferent —each of whom tarnishes education's good name.

### The Analytical Framework

To provide background for recommendations designed to correct certain deficiencies, I shall cursorily review three broad facets of university life as these touch on—

1. the university's basic purpose;
2. the state of liberal learning; and
3. the human dimension of the university.

### The University's Purposes

The American university is understood in diverse ways. To start with the concept of liberal learning envisioned by John Henry Newman's *Idea of a University* in the nineteenth century is to anticipate Robert Hutchin's efforts for undergraduate reform at Chicago in the twentieth. If, on the other hand, the model is von Humboldt's Berlin of a century ago, one moves quickly to 1930 and Abraham Flexner's prescriptions for a research-oriented institution outlined in his influential work, *Universities: American, English, and German.* Differences of purpose have led to such a variegated system of higher education that it is difficult to treat each segment adequately. The focus of this paper is on the university and the four-year college.

Recently, in a graceful little book titled *The Ideal of the University*, Robert Wolff of Columbia outlined four models of the university: as a *sanctuary* of scholarship, as a *training camp* for the professions, as a *social-service station*, and, finally, as an *assembly line* for the establishment. Those who prefer the *sanctuary* model are inclined to create an institution that is small, informally organized, weighted with tradition, and distant from the hurly-burly life around it. Wolff offered the University of Chicago as a paradigm for this type—and then pilloried it for its alleged aloofness. In his second model, Wolff speaks of the *training camp* university which prepares for the professions; except possibly for medicine and law, he would exorcise professional schools from the university setting. So to proscribe, however, runs contrary to both tradition and current needs. The tradition was expressed by de Tocqueville when he wrote: "In America, the practical side of science is cultivated admirably. . . . But hardly anyone devotes himself to the essentially theoretical and abstract side of human knowledge." Since practical knowledge is usually professional knowledge, and since the number of professions has grown rapidly, it is unlikely that American universities can ignore—or should ignore—the environment in which they operate. The new need for professional education is intensifying because of the marked change in the work force from blue to white collar perceptible in 1954 and clearly visible today. The work force is, by this definition, given to practical affairs and heavily inclined toward professionalism.

Dangers exist. Deans and faculty of professional schools have been known to play foxy games against their institutions by using accrediting associations as pressure groups to achieve what has not been forthcoming from administrators or approved by the faculty at large; they have behaved as imaginative entrepreneurs by securing short-term funding for special programs that are then left on the institution's doorsteps when the funding well dries up. Each profession pressures schools to provide for its particular needs; each jockeys for its own curriculum, its autonomy, its licensure systems. Interprofessional strife is common and its spillovers disrupt the university: doctors fight off claims by chiropractors; business schools fend against demands by accountants; registered nurses build walls to separate themselves from therapists—and so on. The new realities may eventually justify Wolff's pessimistic views, but, for the moment, the university simply *cannot* ignore the demands for professional education.

The *social-service station* university is also repugnant to Wolff and to the degree that energies are given to these purposes (by institutions like Cornell, Wisconsin, and California), to that degree is the university's mission distorted. Finally, there is the university as an *assembly line* which produces the establishment man; here the university is an instrument helpful in perpetuating the status quo—and destructive of its own sacred nature. Having rejected the four models which most generally characterize university activities, Wolff leads one to the conclusion that a university best fulfills its mission when it serves as critic of social ills and catalyst for social reform; a good university, therefore, is one whose professors are "engaged."

SCHOLARSHIP: OBJECTIVE AND ENGAGED

A major difference exists between those committed to scholarship based on "objective analysis" and those dedicated to the "engagement scholarship" which Wolff prefers. In the former, the assumption is made that the scholar is so obligated to his subject and discipline that the injection of values is quite unscientific. Tools of great sophistication emerged from this style—from psychoanalysis to atomic fission, from analytic cubism to analytic philosophy, from the New Criticism in literature to the digital computer. And, clearly, profound values exist in this approach: commitment to rationality, the importance of evidence, and the need for competition in the marketplace of ideas.

The "engagement" style, a newcomer on the university block, goes beyond the traditional approach. Stimulated by writers like Herbert Marcuse, Norman Brown, Marshall McLuhan, and Herman Hesse, engagement scholars ask for commitment to specific values and espousal of causes, for relevance and principle, for general education over specialized education (because only through generalization is the common ground of a common humanity made visible), and for fiery conviction over cool detachment.

While a distinct minority, the "engagement" style professors show increasing strengths in competition for dominance in the intellectual life. The contemporary university has not resolved the differences. A major problem is to encourage a dialectic between the two styles to make students aware that such a debate is being conducted, with important consequences for the kind of education they receive. My worry is that universities are dodging the issue, with the result that serious implications inherent in the debate are being papered over; needed, therefore, is a sharp statement of purpose by each institution.

## Liberal Education

Liberal education is in trouble. It has always been in trouble. For over thirty-five years I have heard the same lugubrious theme. With a drum beat so insistent, who dares cotton-wad the ears? What is really troublesome, however, is that so few significant efforts are being made to translate diagnoses into prescriptions and prescriptions into practices. The 1978 Carnegie Foundation report on the "Missions of the College Curriculum" underscored the point when it noted that "no curricular concept is as central to the endeavours of the American colleges as general education, and none is so exasperatingly beyond the reach of general consensus and understanding."

There is—sad to say—insufficient willingness by professors to ask themselves three simple questions. What are the particular resources of my institution? How may these resources be used to provide a challenging route to liberal education? How do we go about identifying our own weaknesses, and correcting them? Harvard's recent reform effort, the most publicized, is freighted with mischief—and not of Harvard's doing. When Harvard went the elective route, so did many others; when Harvard returns from the elective path, so will many others. The result flows from a follow-the-leader mentality. Higher education then offers a certain "sameness" which permits faculty to satisfy themselves that all is well because there is a major or concentration, there is an appropriate distribution requirement, there is a curriculum of 120 or so credits, there is a library with a certain number of books, and there is a satisfactory number of faculty who hold advanced degrees.

It is reassuring to count: set the total, reach the total, and presto!, we educate the full man. I exaggerate. But the numbers game for liberal education can be used to perpetuate three related myths:

1. that the conflict between the scientific and humanistic cultures (outlined by C. P. Snow two decades ago) is so irreconcilable that a working synthesis which leads students to appreciate what each culture means cannot be realistically managed for undergraduates;

2. that there is only *one* route to liberal learning; and
3. that students today, career oriented and ill-prepared, are hostile to liberal education.

Let us look at each. Concerning the Snow thesis, I find myself embarrassed because of defects in my own science education. Yet I believe that historian Lynn White of the University of California at Los Angeles was being more than a gadfly when, a decade ago, he shocked his colleagues with a proposal (reported in the summer 1969 issue of *Daedalus*) that there be a course on the internal-combustion engine. Said he:

> I am confident that this would be as enriching, if properly done, as a course in Shakespeare. Naturally, spines tingle when I say a thing like this, but an internal-combustion engine, properly and historically viewed, is an extraordinary manifestation of the human spirit. Nobody believes this, but people are increasingly interested in the internal-combustion engine as it becomes obsolete and an incubus on our society.

White's challenge recalls the number of brilliant scholars who themselves integrated the two cultures and whose insights can advance the liberal arts in our times—Whitehead, Wittgenstein, Chardin, to name a few.

The truth is that faculties, by and large, have given up attempts to establish the relationships of the two cultures into meaningful coherence for undergraduate education. "Let the student forage" is a widespread attitude. Writing in the February 2, 1979, issue of *Commonweal*, Bernard Murchland, philosophy professor at Ohio Wesleyan, told of one Bill Armstrong, a June graduate from a selective liberal arts college in the Midwest. Murchland had occasion to review the transcript and was struck by some rather remarkable gaps: "He had taken no history, no philosophy, no English literature, no math, no art or music, and only minimal sciences (two courses in environmental chemistry). Yet he graduated with honors." The young man may have deserved honors. His faculty did not. So liberal learning languishes when professors themselves show no enthusiasm for understanding the distinguishing characteristics of the scientific and humanistic cultures.

The second myth holds that there is one intrinsically better path to liberal learning. For science advocates one senses the appeal of Harvard's microbiologist, Edmund Wilson, who urges his colleagues to turn "to a much greater degree than has been done in the past in the social sciences and humanities to biology, and to a new and more sophisticated and enlightened form of biology." One of the great intellectual dreams since the middle of the nineteenth century was to make biology, evolutionary biology in particular, part of the foundation of the social sciences. Perhaps we have here exciting new possibilities, but the danger is that Wilson's message may spark the academic imperialists in science to downgrade the humanities.

On the other hand, humanists have never been lacking in ambition. Otto Bird, for example, has written perceptively of the humanities and has demonstrated an extraordinary knowledge of their development. Interesting to note, however, is that while Bird himself warns against academic imperialism, he concludes that one must always look for the fundamental and basic knowledge—that which is "indispensable, logically prior, and deserving more than any other to be considered the paradigm of the very idea of knowledge." Such a paradigm, in his view, is philosophy—a conclusion certain to offend nonphilosophers when philosophy itself is in an untidy state.

Perhaps the way to consider liberal education (and thus curtail self-serving interest) is to reflect on persons who, in their lives, have symbolized the "learned" man. I think, for example, of John Stuart Mill. His extraordinary father, James, shared with Bentham and the French materialists a view that man was a natural object and, therefore, should be studied by techniques common to zoology or physics. The father educated the child rigorously so that at age five John Stuart Mill knew Greek and, at nine, had reasonable mastery over algebra and Latin. There was, in the regimen, no time for religion or metaphysics or poetry. And yet the youngster himself sensed a profound lack, and when he was twelve, he concluded that while his mind was overdeveloped, his emotions were starved: he was a brilliant half-person! One day, while reading a rather pathetic story of a now forgotten French writer, he was moved to tears and realized that his emotional life, though damaged, had not atrophied. He began to read poetry madly—Wordsworth and Coleridge, Shakespeare and Shelley. Eventually he brought to his understanding much that was his father's view, but also with something new—a willingness to recognize the importance of rationality and yet allow a domain for diversity and versatility, for spontaneity and uniqueness, for intuition and emotion.

Which of the two Mills—father or son—was more liberally educated? My preference is for the son. And the choice is conditioned by my own background, training, and values. I was struck, for example, by a *Commentary* article (March 1978) by Walter Dannhauser which argued that

students were asking professors—without even knowing they are asking—
help in building their own selves; liberal education therefore must be
"concerned with the architecture of the student's soul. . . . It should
provide students not with the right answers but with the right questions,
and those questions concern three matters basically: God, love, and
death."

Dannhauser defended his position by insisting that without death or
love there can be no depth or meaning to the human experience, and
that liberal education, rooted in those common human experiences,
speaks to men throughout all ages. The argument is persuasive because
problems of death and life are all around us—in wars and famines, in
the possibility of nuclear holocaust and in the Gulag archipelago, in
Appalachia and Indonesia, in terror and in drug abuse, in assassinations
and in kidnappings.

What traditionally gave coherence to liberal education in America
was moral philosophy—clearly the most important course in the college
curriculum throughout the nineteenth century. The course, often taught
by the president, fulfilled two important functions. It unified the young
person's intellectual experiences by bringing together what the student
had studied in various courses and subjecting their premises to the test
of a higher moral law; second, moral philosophy gave to students awareness of those common values which supported the American community.
About fifteen years ago moral philosophy began to slip down—or out—of
the core curriculum. It has not regained entry.

What, if anything, can restore unity?

### The Humanities

Having warned against academic imperialism, let me take a calculated risk by arguing that the humanities can provide this function *if*
they regain their own vision. This is because any one—and all three—of
the humanities (literature, history, and philosophy) share a common concern with moral questions. But it is not whether we study this or that
discipline—or focus exclusively on one period or school of thought—that
matters. What matters is that rationality must deal with more than in-
strumental ends. In classical studies, for example, Sir Maurice Bowra
noted that their genius was to use poetry as the place where the ancients
placed "their own pondered and serious view of life, and they thought it
their duty to say what they really meant. For this reason they infused it

with the power which comes from long and intense thought." When Aeschylus constructed a tragedy, he employed the hero's action to illustrate the divine law operating through human lives; Sophocles, although keeping his own views in the background, nevertheless addressed moral issues through his characters. The characters always presented problems that troubled Sophocles himself—that vast divide between human error and divine knowledge, the difference between heroic and pedestrian standards of conduct.

Or what of history? If it is only a tale of impersonal forces and antiseptic organizations, something is lost for the student. One historian, Herbert Davis, gives a clue to what history should mean by recalling a forgotten scholar, Edward Hyde, Earl of Clarendon, who narrated the events of Charles I's reign. Clarendon, said Davis, emphasized constantly that this Stuart Monarch established a reign when authority and liberty were never more beautifully united in England's history. The tragedy of the Rebellion was not the destruction of the king's person but destruction of the king's reconciliation. Clarendon's purpose was to leave a record of the values that had been lost and, perhaps, of the way they might be regained. In his account was the clash between heroes and cowards, saints and sinners, virtues and vices. The important inference to be drawn is that, in addition to stylistic excellence, humanistic knowledge provides not prodigious formulas, but a mirror for looking at ourselves and others, and the varying ways in which truth is known and justice honored.

Prospects for this kind of history today are not so promising and several reasons explain the malaise. Historians are narrowly trained; students are antihistorical; Europe, as our cultural stimulant, is herself less vital; America's innocence, lost in Vietnam, invites cynicism toward our past. What Stanley Hoffman said of the French seems true here: "The experienced past is displaced by the past as a product of specialists, a consumer product, a subject matter for scholars, a spectacle." (*Daedalus,* Winter 1979)

This leaves philosophy. William Jones spoke of it as each person's moral common sense of what life honestly and deeply means—an individual's way of "just seeing and feeling the total pushing pressure of the cosmos. . . . It bakes no bread, but it can inspire our soul with courage; and repugnant as its manners . . . often are to common people, no one can get along without the far-flashing beams of light it sends over the world's perspectives."

But those "far-flashing beams" are presently not coming because phi-
losophers have rushed to professionalize and to fragmentize. Since ap-
prentices mirror masters, it is illuminating to note a report on the kinds
of dissertation topics appearing between 1930 and 1970 at six institutions
—Harvard, Chicago, Boston, Catholic University, Notre Dame, and St.
Louis. A significant change occurred around 1960 when all began to
stress logic and sophisticated linguistic analysis. The skill of the graduates leaned heavily toward one esoteric field, that of logic and critical
analysis. The result was a narrowing of philosophy's concerns so much
that a rather common view was expressed by Lewis Feuer when he declared (in a *New York Times Magazine* article, April 24, 1966) that
"American philosophy is dead." A distinguished British philosopher,
H. H. Price, said the same thing to his colleagues thirty years ago!

One could go on. The common points are rather easy to reduce to
syllogistic form:

> Humanities introduce students to the moral adventures of man.
> But humanists have subordinated substance to technique.
> Therefore, humanists fail their major assignment in liberal education.

What of the crude syllogism? Too tidy? Too simple? Too selective? Of
course, but also, too true. Reinvigoration of liberal education requires
not simply clearer definition but reinvigoration of the humanities themselves as well as reform of graduate education to produce teachers who
have both mastery of their specialty and broad knowledge.

### The Human Dimension

THE PRESIDENT

Top university administration is a mixed bag. One looks in vain for
the old-type leader with a commanding presence: Eliot at Harvard, Wilson at Princeton, Butler at Columbia, Gilman at Hopkins, Hutchins at
Chicago. It does not follow that these giants would be effective in today's
participatory environment. There has developed a shift in expectations
which has transformed the university president into a fund-raiser, public
relations man, pseudo-lawyer (concerned with government regulations),
rabid supporter of big-time athletics, conscientious bureaucrat, platform
performer, and alumni entertainer. A scholarly president is rare and, in

some places, actually unwelcome. Institutional size is not the determinant. One asks, therefore, whether trustees know what they want and faculty know what they need in their chief executive. Whether the typical president can be an outstanding performer in traditional academic roles and a superb "outside" man as well is difficult to answer. Something gives. When it does not, the president gives in as the abbreviated tenures of presidents demonstrate. In the present impoverished state of most institutions the primary criterion whereby a president is judged is a fund-raising ability. Heavy endowment provides some cushion—but not much; small endowments soften the job specification; tuition dependence makes cash the key. However, is cash-getting (as a measure of competence) so out of hand that administrative innovations are necessary?

## THE DEAN

Caught in contrary pulls, one of the most precious assets of an institution is a wise and courageous dean. On one hand, success depends on the confidence a dean can generate with the academic vice president and president; on the other, the faculty expects the dean to deliver salary increments, research support, secretarial back-up, and the like. Sometimes it is virtually impossible to fulfill the demands from both sides. Further, a dean must always protect legitimate student interests, and an occasional dispute between a professor and student can leave a residue of ill will that grows with each repetition of the event into conclusions that the dean is always "on the side of" the professor, or vice versa.

Often, too, the dean is expected to be a good researcher, good teacher, good administrator, good fund-raiser, and good alumni-relations advocate. The dean is a key instrument in making a good school; if many universities are in trouble, it follows that many deans simply are not doing the job.

The selection process is critical and one may ask which of the two modes currently employed is better: by presidential appointment or by faculty vote? In either case, the dean is seen as dependent more on one than the other for survival. In the present context where faculty political power is relatively high, and where hard decisions must be made, my inclination is to give the president final powers of selection and to surround the dean's office with institutional safeguards to protect the incumbent from faculty or student whiplash.

**THE FACULTY**

The single most important change in higher education has occurred within the faculty. During the late nineteenth and early twentieth century, faculty at the most prestigious institutions were recruited largely from the upper-middle class—usually a rebellious son uninterested in following his father's footsteps. But the son had such sufficient claims to wealth that he could remain disdainfully indifferent to petty squabbles over money. Not surprisingly, the salary scales at the most prestigious institutions often lagged substantially behind others. And what did the rebellious sons bring to a faculty? High culture, extensive travel, important social connections, and, generally, hostility to dominant political or economic systems. The professor was truly a reflection of the ancient ideal of the leisured man. Recruited from the elite, he taught the future elite: gentlemen taught gentlemen.

The first cracks in the social system were visible around the time of the coming of the land-grant colleges. Dedicated to such practical pursuits as mining and farming, both faculty and students in these schools showed greater interest in career preparation than in pure scholarship; since the land-grant college was an authentic expression of the basic American ideology, it was no surprise that this type of institution should grow in numbers and in influence, and should gradually extend its concerns from mining and farming to other professions and other vocations. With the new-type professor and the new-type student, subtle changes came to academe and faculties would wrestle more frequently with trying to reconcile the ideals of liberal education with those of practical education; in short, different ideas on the purpose of higher education would become more pronounced.

If the social composition of faculty started to change with the coming of land-grant colleges, the truly explosive transformation occurred after the GI Bill of Rights. Elitism was on the defensive before egalitarianism; meritocracy was challenged by the philosophy of entitlements; smallness yielded to the giants called the multiuniversities. Faculties changed even more dramatically. Sons of blue-collar workers saw the doctorate as a passport to a social system that would rank them in public esteem almost on a par with the family doctor—and above lawyers and accountants. To be called "Doctor" or "Professor" was to be given special recognition in most communities of America. The young sensed how easy was their climb up the social ladder by simple acquisition of a teaching position at a university or a college.

Because the new crop of academics was not independently wealthy, adequate salaries and retirement programs were increasingly important. Their concern for cash and job security often irritated the old-style professor. What exacerbated the irritation, however, was the fact that the new academic was often an entrepreneur who made little effort to disguise his entrepreneurial qualities and ambitions. Books and articles came to be written not to promote the frontiers of knowledge but to promote one's career. The number of scholarly and professional journals grew to accommodate faculty needs, and book publishing became a thriving business. Anything that enhanced a faculty member's visibility and, subsequently, his purse, seemed to be justifiable: a stint in Washington or at the state capital, consultancy to a major corporation, a tour of duty in a large foundation. And when the institution rearranged its incentive system to accommodate to the new breed, the older professors began to nurture strong resentments. One has heard tales of the erudite professor of medieval history or comparative literature earning a third less than a younger compatriot in the business or engineering schools or on the law or medical faculties. Magisterial scholarship and magnificent teaching were downgraded to a point where the professor realized that time spent in the classroom or with a student had relatively little payoff.

The next steps in the evolutionary process became predictable. The different disciplines and professional societies, supported by their respective accrediting association, began to disseminate salary scales and to use such as one determination of quality. For example, law deans exchanged financial data with other law deans through their professional associations. In due course, other faculties caught on—but playing the game led to greater divisiveness among faculties, to decline of collegiality, to strong assertions of participatory governance as one way to protect the economic flanks, and, again, to substantial, if not massive, indifference toward students.

If the integrity of the institution is more and more questioned, the major fault lies on faculty who play the grantsmanship game, or define scholarship by counting articles and books published. They have learned an important lesson: payoff comes in inverse proportion to the services given to the employing institution.

In addition to the changed social composition of faculty came alterations in expectations; how did the professoriate define the different obligations to the discipline, the institution, the student? In most responses, the primary commitment was to the field of study; trailing behind was the institution itself, and, at a distant third, was the student.

By way of summation, what might be said? A not unfair response would take into account the fact that the present professoriate consists of people who, recruited largely from the lower-middle class, are entrepreneurial, highly specialized, and quite political. To unionize and to bargain collectively against the university does not strike them as unprofessional or disloyal. In times of market glut and financial pressures, the professors may come to feel that union-style adversarial relationships are to be preferred to the traditional forms of collegiality. Such a preference is viewed as another manifestation of the decline in academic integrity.

Also asked is whether, compared to their predecessors, today's professors are better trained but less well educated, that is, they have better mastery over their specializations but less appreciation of the interconnectedness of knowledge. The question does not lend itself to ready answers. Surely, however, it is fair to ask whether the teacher's preparation is sufficiently broad to meet the undergraduate's educational needs. I think not. As an art form, teaching pleads for imagination, stage presence, sense of timing, and insights into the learning process; as a science, it requires certain skills for which there is precious little training in our graduate schools.

There is still another aspect to the faculty profile, and this relates to a decline in esteem for the professionals. When poorly paid, professors were held in fairly high public esteem on the premise, no doubt, that since they were not dumb, they could earn more in business but stayed in teaching. Obviously, then, to be a teacher was to be committed. So a large measure of quirkiness was tolerated; often, too, the professor compensated for lack of purse by affluence in self-esteem. If "psychic income" was to count, one of its expressions was the ego trip. Professor R. J. Kaufmann's story of a young Oxford don is apposite. During the battle of Britain, the teacher was confronted by a strong, governessy middle-aged female compatriot who seized two loose lapels of his academic gown and, with righteous indignation, demanded harshly: "Young man, why aren't you out fighting for civilization?" "Madam," he replied cooly, "I *am* civilization."

Americans have come to doubt that professors represent the best in civilization. The overall results are three-fold: the campus atmosphere is less polite, the faculty is less secure psychologically, and the public's willingness to criticize has increased.

## THE STUDENT

Today's student has been so frequently dissected that repetition of generalizations is unnecessary. So let me, quite illogically, repeat some. That he is more career-minded is supported by the evidence. In March of 1976 a "Conference on Undergraduate Education" was held at Harvard and attended by student delegates from sixteen *American liberal arts colleges.* At that meeting, Amanda Aldrich, a Radcliffe student leader, described her fellow students as being "intensely job-oriented, careful to avoid the risk of education, and seemingly unconcerned with educational breadth." The description was confirmed and reaffirmed by other delegates throughout the three-day event: "Jobs and careers, not the cherished cliches of liberal learning, are reasons why most American undergraduates are in college."

More disturbing is the steady decline in student aptitude test (SAT) scores. A wide variety of reasons has been given: the minority influx, students from broken homes or with working mothers, parental permissiveness, and the like. Care is needed in sifting such evidence. Psychologist Arthur Jensen of the University of California has insisted that the low average IQ among American blacks is attributable to genetic traits. However, studies by Thomas Sowell of UCLA and Sandra Scarr of Minnesota tell a different tale. Sowell, for example, has demonstrated that low test performances are not restricted to one group; indeed among white ethnic groups who now rank at, or above, the national IQ average, many scored poorly at earlier phases of their existence in America. For example, in 1926 the median IQ of Slavic immigrants was measured at 85.6; for Greeks, 83; for Poles, 85; for Spaniards, 78; for Portuguese, 84. Five years earlier, 83 percent of the Jewish immigrants at Ellis Island were labeled "feeble-minded." Certainly in this area we must view the data with caution. Attitudes and cultural backgrounds are far more important variables, and since attitudes can be changed by a courageous faculty, one gets the uneasy feeling that professors have discovered in low student scores a convenient excuse for their own failures.

Christopher Jencks has argued rather persuasively that the real reason for decline is a deterioration in the more complex skills and knowledges that the SATs are designed to measure: a capacity to infer and to analyze, a reasonable breadth of reading, a knowledge of the humanities and science. This slump is due, in Jencks' view, to that crisis of legitimacy which occurred during the sixties. If students have come to feel they are entitled to advancement, regardless of performance, that feeling has not been substantially altered by mediocre elementary and secondary schools; and institutions of higher learning can be faulted for not making serious efforts to help upgrade secondary education in the United States. It might indeed be argued that this indifference is not the only manifestation of irresponsibility but that the evil has been compounded by colleges who, to attract students, lower admission standards and then neglect to provide remedial programs.

### Recommendations

In light of a review which suggests (1) that universities have not faced forthrightly the need to restate their purpose, (2) that core liberal learning is not being well served, and (3) that the human element requires new care, what, then, might be done?

With possibly more courage than wisdom do I dare offer a bill of particulars—again with the reminder that neither one suggestion nor all combined provide the total answers. Rather, it is hoped that the recommendations might stimulate a soul-searching process by different schools which, in turn, will produce a few answers, some half-answers, and many frustrations. Nevertheless, had I the powers of a benevolent academic dictator I would push them vigorously as a necessary first step in restoring greater order and integrity to the academy.

While it is impossible to maintain precise demarcations among the items, the general subdivisions employed in the body of the chapter offer useful guides. Accordingly, the suggestions will be presented as they impinge primarily on (1) the university as a distinct organizational entity, (2) the liberal arts, and (3) the human factors.

#### THE UNIVERSITY

1. Each institution must make more explicit its goals and purposes and, through annual academic audits, report regularly its successes and failures as measured against the stated goals.

2. After appropriate consultation, the trustees should develop (and promulgate in official announcements) an institutional code of ethics. The mode will, among other things—

   a. provide monitoring mechanisms and disciplinary measures;

   b. make explicit the institution's expectations of behavior for trustees, administrators, faculty, staff, and students;

   c. prohibit late job offers to professors at other schools as one step toward ending the scandals of last-minute resignations; and

   d. pledge to open no off-campus satellites unless library and faculty resources equal campus arrangements.

3. Because of generally ambiguous—and sometimes blatant misrepresentations—course descriptions in catalogs should be eliminated. Course syllabuses should be available at cost.

4. To roll back the tide of multiplying specialized accreditations, universities should accept only an *institutional* visitation carried out by the regional accrediting association. The evaluation team should also consist of persons competent to judge the professional schools and departments, but only *one* report—approved by the entire visitation team—should be rendered. Such reports should, in due course, be made part of the public record.

5. In view of the proliferating kinds of education (professional, paraprofessional, continuing, etc.) and the number of organizations moving to meet these needs, the university should serve as catalyst to bring the various groups together to discuss how the public interest may be best served. In the catalytic role, universities should be concerned to bridle their own imperialistic ambitions.

6. Universities should develop policies designed to repulse claims by professional associations and their related accrediting groups over general policy and administrative matters. Examples of things to be proscribed are externally established regulations regarding tuition and fees, selection procedures for deans, promotion policies for faculty, requirements for special library or classroom buildings.

7. Recognizing the demands made for more and more trustee energy and time, universities should—

   a. limit a trustee to no more than two university boards—and

these on different kinds of institutions (e.g., private college or
public university, secular or church-related, technologically
oriented or humanities oriented);

b. require periodic academic audits by a trustee-chaired committee; and

c. arrange an annual trustee forum for the entire academic community.

8. Universities should prohibit recruitment for intercollegiate athletics as a necessary step to help coaches fulfill their own code of
ethics which states: "Parents turn their dearest possessions to the
coach's charge; winning is never more important than character
building."

9. To prevent faculty salaries in professional schools from running
to scandalous extremes above the salaries of teachers in arts and
science, theology, performing arts, etc., universities should establish policies which restrict average differentials to a level acceptable
to the University Senate.

10. Retain tenure, but tighten policies and allow for a comprehensive
peer review of teaching performance and research productivity of
tenured faculty before a sabbatical is approved. Give to the dean—

a. the right to stipulate certain undertakings if serious short-
comings are revealed, and

b. the right to review work done during sabbatical when the professor returns.

LIBERAL ARTS

11. Restore the integrity of the master's degree by a three-term program in the major or concentration.

12. Eliminate the major in liberal arts at the baccalaureate level and
reduce the time required for the degree to three years.

13. Drop freshman English composition and require, instead, the
passing of a competency examination. Remedial noncredit courses
may be offered.

14. Recognizing that each institution will define liberal arts according to its lights, encourage, nevertheless, certain steps which may

lead to nation-wide improvements in competency of teaching and performance by students. These steps could include—

a. structured efforts to explore, through freshman tutorials, the meaning of liberal education, where new students would read some of the classic statements on liberal education (Plato, Aquinas, Newman, Whitehead, Trilling, *et al.*). Use the reading as preparation for comparative analyses of liberal arts programs at other—and different type—institutions. The final requirement would have the freshman outline, in writing, how he or she proposes to carry out such learning. Before graduation the student would review the statement with his or her faculty/mentor to assess progress in intellectual growth. Students would also be asked to comment on institutional strengths and weaknesses, and these comments would be sent to the dean and president;

b. required oral examinations (because ours is a "conversation" society) by two or three professors before spring break at both the second and third years and recommendations given to the student by the examiners to correct identified difficiencies;

c. written comprehensive as a requirement for graduation—and add two important innovations:

(1) have an extern review the examinations and report to the faculty impressions of the quality of the tests and the level of student performance, and

(2) use as a portion of the comprehensive (counting no more than 25 percent of the final grade) a standardized unit prepared under the supervision of distinguished scholars. Faculty and students would compare the results on the locally-prepared exams with those of the nationally-prepared examinations; and

d. assuming a normal five-course load, allowing the student to take one course each term on a pass/fail basis.

15. Require a comprehensive review of the general education program at four-year intervals by a small faculty committee. Presumption for change will be given to the committee and the faculty shall provide reasons for holding the status quo.

16. Since faculty are responsible for curriculum and since each insti-

tution's faculty presumably has distinguishing qualities of outlook, background, and preparation, require the faculty to prepare
its own first-year core courses—including selection of original readings, preparation of introductory essays for the readings, development of visual aids (with emphasis on original preparation),
writing original narrative and/or case material, etc. Such efforts
would not only minimize use of the textbook "crutches" in the
introductory core, but would add vitality and imagination by
*putting the institution's original stamp on the curriculum.*

17. Place on faculty full responsibility for determining students to be
    admitted and insist on adequate academic counseling by faculty.

18. Given the contemporary world situation, require students to take
    one course in the literature, history, or social science of another
    culture, with course readings in the language of that culture or
    nation. (When necessary, preparation in the language will be pro-
    vided on a noncredit basis.)

19. To provide for continual update of curricula—

    a. require each member of the faculty to prepare a brief essay on
       a book which, in his or her judgment, has enlarged the indi-
       vidual's understanding of liberal education or deepened under-
       standing of the discipline and use the best essays for periodic
       faculty discussions; and

    b. when essays lend themselves to public discussion or debate,
       schedule open forums for faculty *and* students. (The intellec-
       tual listlessness of faculty toward students, students toward
       faculty, and faculty toward faculty would soon be dissipated
       by such fora.)

20. Provide undergraduates with an organized way to share in lively
    *intellectual* debates that have occurred throughout history so that
    they may see how first-rate minds have wrestled with difficult in-
    tellectual matters. The range of debate (and debaters) is infinite
    but would be determined by faculty interests and expertise. Ex-
    amples: William Sumner and Lester Ward's debate over Social
    Darwinism, Lon Fuller and Hans Kelsen on the nature of law,
    B. F. Skinner and Noam Chomsky on language and meaning,
    Rawls and Nozick on justice, Aquinas and Bonaventure on the-
    ology, John Locke and Thomas Hobbes on government, etc.

21. Accept fully the role of the creative and performing arts in liberal education.

22. To assure full opportunities for liberal learning, protect undergraduates from exploitation—whether such exploitation occurs in intercollegiate athletes, the performing arts, student journalism, or in any other activity.

### THE HUMAN COMPONENT: ADMINISTRATION

23. Because of enormously changing demands on presidents, universities should add to the president's office another top-level position for a chancellor. The president would be responsible for the academic vitality of the institution and would represent it before appropriate learned societies. The chancellor would supervise all fund-raising efforts, manage and oversee the budgets, and represent the institution before nonacademic external groups. Both would be appointed by the trustees, and both would be members of the board.

24. Formal job-performance appraisals for both president and chancellor should be carried out by a trustee committee.

25. Guarantee to the president and chancellor the right, after appropriate consultation, to hire and fire their respective top administrative aides.

26. Universities should (a) provide sabbaticals for top administrative officers on the same basis as faculty, and (b) develop career paths, including appropriate training, for junior administrators.

### THE HUMAN COMPONENT: FACULTY

27. Faculty should recommend for trustee approval a faculty code of ethics. Among other things the code should—

    a. require disclosure to the president of money earned through royalties, honoraria, consultancies, and the kind of work followed;

    b. require fulfillment of attendance obligations at faculty and departmental meetings, formal university convocations, and commencement exercises; and

   c. require counseling to students as an important element in the institution's expectations;

   d. incorporate monitoring procedures through a faculty oversight committee and provide disciplinary mechanisms for serious infractions of the code.

28. Endowed chairs should be held on a term basis—possibly five years and renewable no more than twice.

29. To fulfill obligations to future members of the teaching profession, faculty should overhaul present doctoral programs to include—

   a. show-cause reports to dean and president when a full-time doctoral student does not complete all requirements within a five-year period (the Association of Graduate Deans could monitor the process);

   b. when all requirements for the doctorate have been met, withhold awarding the degree until the student who plans a teaching career spends a full academic year as a paid guest of the institution. During this year the student will be (1) exposed to classroom teaching experience, (2) sent (at the institution's cost) to at least one professional meeting, and (3) required to do extensive readings in fields *outside* the major research and teaching interests.

   NOTE: To assist in the foregoing work, use "The Elders," that is, professors emereti, who themselves have been recognized for breadth of knowledge and superb teaching.

30. Because faculty will carry added burdens—

   a. establish mechanisms to revitalize the faculty itself. (One promising proposal made at Columbia University called for the formation of a group of senior and junior teachers, selected on the basis of distinction and scholarship, and giving the group a special designation—such as "University Fellows." Each year the group itself would designate replacement for half of its members, direct itself to a special educational problem, and involve an advanced graduate student to work as a coteacher with senior scholars in other fields. The senior scholar must select his coteachers from a different department or school.)

The thought behind this proposal is excellent: to provide apprenticeship in pedagogy which allows a senior professor an opportunity to exchange views with a still maturing graduate who is himself sensitized to his own generation; and

b. launch a massive and coordinated drive with foundations and corporations for greater financial support, with emphasis on salary improvements.

In occasional lapses into elfland I dream the impossible dream—an exciting surge forward. After all, there are success stories in education, as Jonathan Kozol (writing in the August 1978 *Harvard Educational Review*) demonstrated for Castro's Cuba when, in 1960, a million illiterate adult Cubans were taught to read and write within a year. If more success stories for higher education are needed, so, too, are more successful efforts to make institutions of higher learning what the American people expect of them—enclaves of intellectual and moral integrity.

# Index

Accreditation:
  institutional, 70, 71-77
  specialized, 70, 77-84
Ada Comstock Scholars, 175
*Adams v. Califano* (1970), 59
Administration and governance, 90-117, 145
  budget, 101, 109-11
  economic problems (*see* Economic problems)
  faculty and, 91-97, 138-40, 141
  goal setting, 107-8
  internal management, 111-13
  president (*see* President)
  strategic planning, 115-17
  students and, 6, 146-48, 161-64
  trustees (*see* Trustees)
Admissions, 158-60
  open, 6, 8-9
Aeschylus, 191
Affirmative action, 56, 70, 123
Aldrich, Amanda, 197
American Association of Collegiate Registrars and Admissions Officers, 74
American Association of University Professors, 137
American Bar Association, 82, 83
*American College President, The* (Cohen and March), 90
American Council on Education, 6, 117
American Institute for Foreign Trade, 122
Amherst College, 180-81
Anderson, Richard E., 17-39
Antioch College, 4
Apprenticeship, 15
Aptitude tests, 158
Aquinas, St. Thomas, 202
Association of American Law Schools, 82
Association of American Medical Colleges, 61
Astin, Alexander, 35
Athletic programs, 148-49

Atomic bomb, 4, 8
Attendance rates (*see* Enrollments)
Authority structure of faculty, 139
Auxiliary income, 21, 23, 27

*Bakke* case, 59
Ben-David, Joseph, 3, 132
Bentham, Jeremy, 183, 189
Biology, 188-89
Bird, Otto, 189
Black studies, 6
Blaug, 34
Bloch, Ernest, 121, 122
Bolman, Frederick deW., 1-16
Bologna University, 3
Bonaventure, St., 202
Boston University, 192
Bowen, 24, 34
Bowra, Sir Maurice, 190
Brigham Young University, 30-31
Brown, Norman, 186
Bryn Mawr College, 169
Budget, 101, 109-11, 162
Bunting, Mary, 175
Business, 70, 84-86
Butler, Nicholas Murray, 192

California, University of, at Los Angeles, 171
California State Colleges and Universities (CSCU) System, 50
Career education, 82
Carnegie Commission on Higher Education, 14, 22, 23, 28
Carnegie Foundation, 187
Catholic University of America, 169, 171, 192
Chairman:
  functions of, 104-5
  selection of, 99
Chesterton, Gilbert, 183-84
Chicago, University of, 171, 185, 192

# The American Assembly

## COLUMBIA UNIVERSITY

### About The American Assembly

The American Assembly was established by Dwight D. Eisenhower at Columbia University in 1950. It holds nonpartisan meetings and publishes authoritative books to illuminate issues of United States policy.

An affiliate of Columbia, with offices in the Graduate School of Business, the Assembly is a national educational institution incorporated in the State of New York.

The Assembly seeks to provide information, stimulate discussion, and evoke independent conclusions in matters of vital public interest.

AMERICAN ASSEMBLY SESSIONS

At least two national programs are initiated each year. Authorities are retained to write background papers presenting essential data and defining the main issues in each subject.

A group of men and women representing a broad range of experience, competence, and American leadership meet for several days to discuss the Assembly topic and consider alternatives for national policy.

All Assemblies follow the same procedure. The background papers are sent to participants in advance of the Assembly. The Assembly meets in small groups for four or five lengthy periods. All groups use the same agenda. At the close of these informal sessions, participants adopt in plenary sessions a final report of findings and recommendations.

Regional, state, and local Assemblies are held following the national session at Arden House. Assemblies have also been held in England, Switzerland, Malaysia, Canada, the Caribbean, South America, Central America, the Philippines, and Japan. Over one hundred thirty institutions have co-sponsored one or more Assemblies.

ARDEN HOUSE

Home of the American Assembly and scene of the national sessions is Arden House, which was given to Columbia University in 1950 by W. Averell Harriman. E. Roland Harriman joined his brother in contributing toward adaptation of the property for conference purposes. The buildings and surrounding land, known as the Harriman Campus of Columbia University, are 50 miles north of New York City.

Arden House is a distinguished conference center. It is self-supporting and operates throughout the year for use by organizations with educational objectives.

The background papers for each Assembly are published in cloth and paperbound editions for use by individuals, libraries, businesses, public agencies, nongovernmental organizations, educational institutions, discussion and service groups. In this way the deliberations of Assembly sessions are continued and extended.

The subject of Assembly programs to date are:

1951___United States-Western Europe Relationships
1952___Inflation
1953___Economic Security for Americans
1954___The United States' Stake in the United Nations
___The Federal Government Service
1955___United States Agriculture
___The Forty-Eight States
1956___The Representation of the United States Abroad
___The United States and the Far East
1957___International Stability and Progress
___Atoms for Power
1958___The United States and Africa
___United States Monetary Policy
1959___Wages, Prices, Profits, and Productivity
___The United States and Latin America
1960___The Federal Government and Higher Education
___The Secretary of State
___Goals for Americans
1961___Arms Control: Issues for the Public
___Outer Space: Prospects for Man and Society
1962___Automation and Technological Change
___Cultural Affairs and Foreign Relations
1963___The Population Dilemma
___The United States and the Middle East
1964___The United States and Canada
___The Congress and America's Future
1965___The Courts, the Public, and the Law Explosion
___The United States and Japan
1966___State Legislatures in American Politics
___A World of Nuclear Powers?
___The United States and the Philippines
___Challenges to Collective Bargaining
1967___The United States and Eastern Europe

# DATE DUE

| | |
|---|---|
| 3. 20. '81 | |
| 12. 02 '82 | |
| 10. 20. '83 | |
| | |
| | |
| | |
| | |
| | |
| | |
| | |
| | |
| | |
| | |
| | |
| | |
| | |
| | |
| | |
| | |

BRODARi, INC.　　　　　　　　　　　　　　　Cat. No. 23-221